SOCIAL WORK AND RURAL DEVELOPMENT

SOCIAL WORK AND RURAL DEVELOPMENT

P.R. Gautam
R.S. Singh

CENTRUM PRESS
NEW DELHI-110002 (INDIA)

CENTRUM PRESS

H.O.: 4360/4, Ansari Road, Daryaganj,
New Delhi-110002 (India)
Tel: 23278000, 23261597, 23255577, 23286875

B.O.: No. 1015, Ist Main Road, BSK IIIrd Stage,
IIIrd Phase, IIIrd Block, Bangalore-560085 (INDIA)
Tel: 080-41723429

Email: centrumpress@gmail.com
Visit us at: www.centrumpress.com

Social Work and Rural Development

First Edition, 2011

ISBN 978-93-80836-04-1

PRINTED IN INDIA

Printed at Balaji Offset, Delhi.

Contents

Contents

Preface

Rural development in general is used to denote the actions and initiatives taken to improve the standard of living in non-Urban neighbourhoods, countryside, and remote villages. These communities can be exemplified with a low ratio of inhabitants to open space. Agricultural activities may be prominent in this case whereas economic activities would relate to the primary sector, production of foodstuffs and raw materials. Rural development actions mostly aim at the social and economic development of the areas. These programs are usually top-down from the local or regional authorities, regional development agencies, NGOs, national governments or international development organizations. But then, local populations can also bring about endogenous initiatives for development. The term is not limited to the issues for developing countries. In fact many of the developed countries have very active rural development programs. The main aim of the rural government policy is to develop the undeveloped villages. To develop a country not only industrialization is sufficient but also the every common man has to survive.

The Government mission is to examine and analyse the factors contributing to the improvement of economic and social well-being of people in rural areas on a sustainable basis with focus on the rural poor and the other disadvantaged groups through research, action research and consultancy efforts. And to

facilitate the rural development efforts with particular emphasis and focus on the rural poor by improving the knowledge, skills and attitudes of rural development officials and non-officials through organising training, workshops and seminars.

Gandhi focused on rural development for last 30 years of his life. He felt intuitively that future of India is in decentralized rural development. His concept of dream village was based on local rural production and consumption. Taluka strategy as a step towards fulfilling his dream. Evolution of decentralized systems can be helped by biomimicry-based solutions. Gandhiji's philosophy.

The book endeavours to provide all requirements of students, teachers, social workers, social work institutions to enable them to achieve success in social work and related activities.

—Authors

1

Rural Community Development

Development Actions

Rural development actions mostly aim at the social and economic development of the areas. These programs are usually top-down from the local or regional authorities, regional development agencies, NGOs, national governments or international development organizations. But then, local populations can also bring about endogenous initiatives for development. The term is not limited to the issues for developing countries. In fact many of the developed countries have very active rural development programs. The main aim of the rural government policy is to develop the undeveloped villages. To develop a country not only industrialization is sufficient but also the every common man has to survive.

Rural community development encompasses a range of approaches and activities that aim to improve the welfare and livelihoods of people living in rural areas. As a branch of community development, these approaches pay attention to social issues particularly community organizing. This is in contrast to other forms of rural development that focus on public works (e.g. rural roads and electrification) and technology (e.g. tools and techniques for improving agricultural production).

Rural community development is important in developing countries where a large part of the population is engaged in farming. Consequently, a range of community development methods have been created and used by organisations involved in international development. Most of these efforts to promote rural community development are led by 'experts' from outside the community such as government officials, staff of Non-governmental organizations and foreign advisers. This has led to a long debate about the issue of participation, in which questions have been raised about the sustainability of these efforts and the extent to which rural people are-or are not – being empowered to make decisions for themselves.

Rural Community Development in the United Kingdom

In the UK rural community development is seen as very important. Rural areas are often some of the most deprived in the country. Rural Community Councils around the country support local rural communities in securing sustainable futures. The local rural communities are supported by experienced community development workers.

Rural Community Development in the United States

. In the United States, rural community development is an essential tool in keeping rural areas economically viable in a competitive global arena. Under the United States Department of Agriculture, this is addressed through the Rural Development mission area, comprising the Rural Housing Service, Rural Utilities Service, and Rural Business-Cooperative Service. Research and data sources for rural areas of the United States is also addressed by the United States Department of Agriculture through the Economic Research Service and the National Agricultural Library's Rural Information Centre.

Part of the United States Department of Commerce, the Economic Development Administration (EDA) is tasked within it's mission "to generate jobs, help retain existing jobs, and stimulate industrial and commercial growth in economically distressed areas of the United States. EDA assistance is available to rural and urban areas of the Nation experiencing high unemployment, low income, or other severe economic distress."

There are four Regional Rural Development Centres in the United States that coordinate "rural development research and extension (education) programs cooperatively with the land-grant institutions regionally and nationally. The Centres support and strengthen individual state efforts in rural areas by developing networks of university research and extension faculty from a variety of disciplines to address rural issues."

Community Development in India: An Overview

As India has the largest population of poor people, community development has assumed high priority. The initial programme aimed at upliftment of the rural poor, covered agriculture, animal husbandry, roads, health, education, housing, employment, social and cultural activities. However, food security being the main cause of concern, agriculture received significant attention.

In 1957, a three-tier-system of rural local Government, called.Panchayati Raj. (Rule by Local Councils) was established. These were Gram Panchayat (Village level), Panchayat Samiti (Block level) and Zilla Parishad (District level). The aim was to decentralise the process of decision making and encourage peoples participation. As the programme could not fulfil the expectations of the rural poor, the Integrated Rural Development Programme (IRDP) was introduced in 1979, with specific focus on the weaker sections of the society. By mid eighties, the Government was able to meet the minimum needs of the poor, which included elementary education, health, water supply, roads, electrification, housing and nutrition.

In 1987, the Planning Commission decided to consider block as the basic unit for development planning. The task of planning at the district level was entrusted to the District Planning and Development Council which had wider representation of the society. Panchayati Raj reforms were introduced through the 73rd Constitutional Amendment to facilitate planning at the micro-level and to strengthen the Gram Sabha (village assembly).

The Government of India has also been encouraging voluntary action to mobilise the rural people. Several initiatives of the non-government organisations in the last two decades have had significant impact on the development. NGOs such as BAIF Development Research Foundation are promoting sustainable livelihood through dairy husbandry, water resource management, wastelands development and various income generation activities in several states.

Farmers in several states have established cooperatives for processing sugarcane, oil-seeds, milk, fruits and vegetables. With professional management and application of modern technologies, these organisations have brought economic stability and eliminated exploitation by intermediary traders. To strengthen peoples organisations, Self Help Groups (SHGs), comprising of poor families have been promoted under the Ninth Five Year Plan (1997-2002). It is only the peoples initiatives and involvement which can sustain the development. The government and political power have the will to support peoples movement and this should promote sustainable rural development in India.

Background

After 63 years of independence and a population of over one billion, India is the largest democracy in the world. To sustain this democracy and freedom, it is necessary to ensure economic empowerment and better quality of life for all the citizens. Unfortunately, the annual per capita Gross National Product of USD 370 in India is one of the lowest as compared to USD 860 in China, USD 2450 in Asia, USD 5170 in the world and over USD 20,000 in the developed countries. Despite significant advancement in industrial development, Indian economy is dependent on agrobased activities. Over 65% of the population living in rural areas are primarily dependent on agriculture for their livelihood. A majority of these families spend over 90% of their earnings on basic needs such as food, fuel and health care. Over 35% of the rural families being poor, tackling their problems is the national priority to ensure social justice and better quality of life.

Problems of the Poor

Poverty in India is judged by the income generated by the family. A family of 4-5 members need at least Rs. 11,000 (USD 275) per annum, to meet their minimum basic needs. Those who cannot earn this income are classified as poor. Unemployment and underemployment are the major causes of rural poverty. The other factors are small land holdings, harsh agro-climatic conditions, poor infrastructure and limited opportunities for rural industrial development, poor health care, illiteracy, social suppression, addiction to alcohol and exploitation by vested interests.

Land is the major resource in India, which provides livelihood to the rural population. According to a survey conducted in 1991-92, about 11.25% of the rural families are landless and among the land holders, over 69.35% own less than 1 ha (marginal farmers) and 21.25% own between 1 and 2 ha (small farmers). Water is another critical resource required to enhance the agricultural production. Out of the total arable area of 169 million ha, only 28% area is under irrigation and the rest is dependent on rains, where hardly one crop can be grown in a year. About 40% of the cropping area is located in low rainfall regions where the employment opportunity is hardly for 40 to 50 days in a year and crops generally fail twice in five years. Decline in many traditional occupations and poor institutional infrastructures have further reduced job opportunities.

Thus about 90% of the rural population, who are deprived of adequate land holding have to look for other means of livelihood for their survival. Livestock is another important natural resource owned by the poor. Generally the rural families keep 1-2 cows or buffaloes for milk, a pair of bullocks for farming and a few sheep, goats and poultry for supplementary income. Although fodder is in scarcity, most of the poor families maintain large herds and let them graze on common lands. Dairy husbandry has good scope, as there is good demand for milk.

However, most of the important breeds of cattle and buffaloes are genetically eroded and about 80-85% of the livestock are unproductive and cause undue pressure on forest resources while the rural poor are unable to take advantage of these animals. It is feasible to make sustainable use of these natural resources through application of appropriate technologies and use of idle labour.

Apart from inadequate earning for livelihood, the rural people also suffer from poor health arising from starvation, lack of immunisation, hygiene and sanitation. Over 25% villages do not have year-round supply of drinking water and about 75% of the potable water sources are polluted. Consumption of polluted water is the main source of illness particularly during the rainy season.

Most of the villages have no drainage and sanitation and less than 10% of the rural people use latrines. Medical and immunisation services do not reach remote villages. Illiteracy in rural areas is high particularly among women, varying from 55% to 75%. This has a direct bearing on the population growth, child health and education. With the annual birth rate of 28 per 1000, as compared to 23 in Asia, the family size has been growing without any addition to the income.

Unable to meet the growing needs, the rural poor have to depend on money lenders, to meet their emergencies and fall into the debt trap. They often try to forget their problems by consuming alcohol.

While some migrate to cities, others live in chronic poverty. They lose confidence in others as well in their ability to live a decent life. This is a vicious cycle.

Community Development Programme

The concept of community development in India was initiated well before independence. Even during the struggle for independence, under the leadership of Mahatma Gandhi-the Father of the Nation, considerable attention was given to rural upliftment and reconstruction. He emphasized on a nineteen point constructive programme for complete independence by truthful and non-violent means.

He often warned the leaders that true independence could be enjoyed only when the rural economy was strengthened and poverty eradicated. He advocated communal harmony, economic equity, social equality, deaddiction from alcohol and narcotics, promotion of khadi (hand spun and hand woven cloth) and village industries, sanitation, health care, education and empowerment of women. The aim was to generate gainful employment in rural areas and to improve the quality of life.

The Government of India Act, 1935 under the British Rule, while confirming autonomy on the provinces, included rural development as an important programme to be initiated for the welfare of the people. With the outbreak of World War II and Bengal Famine of 1943, food supply was a critical problem in most parts of the country. Emphasis on food production was provided through. Grow More Food Campaign which included the supply of free seeds, subsidies for construction of wells and embankments, supply of manure, fixing a minimum price for grain, etc. However, there was limited scope under the Zamindari system where a small number of rich farmers owned the agriculture lands and the rest of the villagers worked as labourers.

After the independence of India in 1947, community development assumed high priority. In 1948, a pilot community development project was launched through the Etawah Project.

Later in 1952, the Government of India launched 55 Community Development Projects, each covering about 300 villages or a population of 30,000. This programme was multidimensional but the major emphasis was placed on agricultural production, as the areas selected for launching the project were located in irrigated areas or where the rainfall was assured. In 1953, the National Extension Service Project was launched with similar objectives to cover larger areas, including the dry regions.

This project of three-year duration, demarcated the blocks of 150-300 villages as manageable units for initiating community development programmes. The objectives and activities of the Project were modified from time to time and continued as a permanent multi-function extension agency in each block. These community development blocks were treated as normal administrative units for planning and development with regular budgetary allocations.

By the end of the First Five Year Plan (1952), 1114 blocks covering 163,000 villages were in operation and by sixties, the community development programme covered the entire country. The programme was characterised by the following features: comprehensive in content; economic progress as the core objective; flexible programmes and posting of a multipurpose worker at the village level.

The plan defined the central objective of planning as creation of conditions in which living standards are reasonably high and the citizens have full and equal opportunity for growth and justice (Sachidananda, 1988). The programme aimed at upliftment of the rural poor, covered agriculture, animal husbandry, roads, health, education, housing, employment, social and cultural activities. While aiming at economic development through agriculture and cottage industries, efforts were made to improve literacy, health, sanitation, housing, transport and communication.

To implement the multifacet programme, an extension organisation, headed by a Block Development Officer (BDO) was established at each block or the revenue tehsil, with a team of subject specialists and village level workers (VLW). Each VLW covered a population of 5000-6000, spread over 5-10 villages to implement various development programmes launched by different departments. The VLWs were expected to meet the farmers and persuade them to take part in various development schemes.

The BDO was assisted by eight Extension Officers, one each for agriculture, animal husbandry, panchayat, cooperation rural industries, rural engineering, social education and women and child welfare. In addition, a medical officer with support staff was posted in each block to provide medical assistance.

The extension officers reported primarily to the BDO and to their senior as well, in the respective department, based at the district headquarters. The BDOs reported to the District Collector, who is the administrator of the district. The Development Commissioner, at the state level was responsible for coordinating community development through the District Collectors. At the National level, the administration of the community development programme was entrusted to the Planning Commission During the initial phase of community development, the government officials prepared the plan under the guidance of the Planning Commission.

There was no opportunity for the community to demand any facilities to solve their problems. As the intention was to ensure peoples participation, advisory committees were subsequently established at various levels. A state level consultative committee consisting of state legislators was constituted for advising on community development. District development or planning committee consisting of officials and non-officials was formed under the chairmanship of the collector. A block level advisory committee was constituted with block level officers and non-officials, member of the parliament and state legislators, heads of educational institutions, progressive agriculturists and representatives of voluntary organisations. As the nonofficials were generally interested in matters of personal concern, they did not look at their roles in the proper perspective. Furthermore, as the development programmes approved at the central and state level were rigid, the consultation process remained merely an academic exercise (Maheshwari, 1985).

From 1950s till mid 1970s, there was no significant achievement and poverty was on the verge of increasing. The Indian economy had become slower compared to those in the East and South East Asia over the post independence period. The levels of living were unacceptably low for a large section of the population. The Land

Reforms Act of 1956 did remove vestiges of the feudal-colonial rule from the scene, but the enactment of the laws did not help the poor and landless to gain control over the land, particularly in North India.

There were fluctuations in the poverty status but the most prominent increase in poverty was observed in the late sixties and early seventies (55%-69%), when rainfall levels were less than normal and monsoon failures prolonged beyond a year. Even the core programme of agricultural development failed to enhance food production. In early seventies, India was compelled to import food grains. Trickling benefits of development were wiped out by the growing population. Improvement in agricultural productivity improvement in the absence of education and infrastructural development was not sustainable. The resources allotted for community development during 1952-67 were also so low that it worked out to hardly Rs.10 per head over this period.

Panchayati Raj Institutions

In 1957, five years after launching the community development programme, the Government appointed the Balvantrai Mehta Committee to suggest measures to remove obstacles in implementing the programme. The Committee recommended the formation of a three-tier-system of rural local Government, to be called Panchayati Raj. (Rule by Local Councils). These were Gram Panchayat (Village level), Panchayat Samiti (Block level) and Zilla Parishad (District level). The aim was to decentralise the process of decision making and to shift the decision making centre closer to the people, encourage their participation and place the bureaucracy under the local peoples control.

However, the Panchayati Raj was not able to fulfil all the expectations of the people and planners. A major reason was the domination of socially and economically privileged sections of the local community, who ignored the welfare of the weaker sections. The other reasons were lack of harmony among the elected members due to political fractions and prevalence of corruption and inefficiency (Maheshwari, 1985).

In mid sixties, the national priority was shifted to agricultural production and a distinct technological orientation was given to agriculture. Under the Fourth and Fifth Five Year Plans (1969-74 and 1974), the central government introduced independent administrative hierarchies to carry out special programmes, bypassing the Panchayati Raj institutions. Special programmes like Small Farmers. Development Agency (SFDA), Intensive Agricultural Areas Programme (IAAP), Intensive Agricultural District Programme (IADP), Tribal Development Agency (TDA), Marginal, Small Farmers and Agricultural Labourers Development Agency (MFAL) and area development agencies such as Command Area Development, Drought Prone Area and Hill area Development Programmes were financed and operated directly by the Central Government.

Integrated Rural Development Programme

The special programmes to boost the agricultural production in late sixties certainly helped to raise the food production but the benefits were largely reaped by those who had necessary resources. Small and marginal farmers trailed behind, as they were not directly benefited by the Green Revolution. On the contrary, their economic position worsened as the rich farmers declined to offer their lands for shared cropping.

Thus to tackle the problems of the rural poor, the Integrated Rural Development Programme (IRDP) was introduced in 1979, with specific focus on the weaker sections of the society, particularly those living in poverty and to involve them in programme implementation. While the earlier programmes emphasized on the delivery systems which suppressed self-reliance, there was good scope for peoples initiatives to build up their economy with dignity. Heeding to the criticism, further changes were made in the programme during the Seventh and Eighth Plans.

These included the linkage between infrastructure and employment schemes, designing of the programme as a credit based self-employment activity, rather than a subsidy distribution and decentralisation of programme implementation through District Rural Development Agency and block authorities. Several sub-schemes such as Development of Women and Children in Rural Areas (DWCRA), Training of Rural Youth for Self-employment (TRYSEM), National Rural Employment Programme (NREP), Jawahar Rojgar Yojana (JRY) were also launched to target the weaker section of the society.

By mid eighties, the Government was able to meet the minimum needs of the poor, which included elementary education, health, water supply, roads, electrification, housing and nutrition. In 1993-94, about 32.37% of the population in India was poor. The percentage of population living in poverty was high by about 17-22% among the Scheduled Castes and Scheduled Tribes, compared to general categories. This was mainly due to small land holdings, landlessness or illiteracy.

Decentralised Planning for Rural Development

Based on the Sivaraman Committee report, the Planning Commission issued guidelines to all the State Governments in 1987 to consider the block as the unit for planning. The task of planning at the district level was entrusted to the District Planning and Development Council or District Planning Board which had wider representation of the society. This body consisted of elected as well as nominated representatives headed by a Minister or District Collector or a non-official. It was responsible for setting up policy guidelines apart from coordination, monitoring, review, finalization of annual plans and Five Year Plans and collection of data. At the block level, the officers of different departments prepared the plan as per the guidelines received from their district heads. This process needed further articulation to prepare the plans in consultation with the Gram Panchayats for implementing the development programmes more effectively and economically. Planning at the village level can be very effective as it can address the problems directly and facilitate development at the grass root level.

Emphasis on Peoples Participation

In spite of many drawbacks in launching community development programmes, the Panchayati Raj has made significant contribution to the development of the country by creating awareness among the public and by developing political leadership. The system has also helped in reducing the gap between the bureaucracy and the people. Centralisation of power and non-involvement of people in the process of development have been the major concerns ever since the introduction of Panchayati Raj.

Although, it was widely acknowledged as the only hope for activating peoples participation which is the soul of a democratic system, the system had generated tension and factions. This necessitated Panchayati Raj reforms through the 73rd Constitutional Amendment in 1992, which empowered the PR institutions to shoulder the responsibility of development and decentralized planning. Till then, all the functions were carried out by the government machinery and there was no scope for participation by the villagers. This had created a dependency syndrome and enabled the government officials to dictate terms to the people (Thapliyal, 1995).

Under this constitutional amendment, 29 items of development were transferred to PRIs. These can be grouped under the following sectors: Agriculture; Forestry and Environment; Industries; Infrastructure, minimum needs; Social welfare; Poverty Alleviation and Maintenance of community assets. Considering the weak status of the Gram Panchayats to facilitate village level micro-planning for development, the District Planning Committee has been strengthened with members representing various government and non-government organisations.

To facilitate the planning at micro-level, it is proposed to strengthen the Gram Sabha (village assembly). The Gram Panchayat can use the Gram Sabha as a forum for discussion and finalization of annual plans. Such a forum can also set the priority for implementing various development programmes. Simultaneously, a suitable mechanism should be developed to sustain the interest of the villagers in Gram Sabha activities. In the absence of adequate participation, vested interests may influence the proceedings for their own benefits. Initiatives from farmers. organisations, self help groups, educational institutions and other voluntary organisations to nominate their representatives on the Gram Sabha can ensure their participation in the proceedings and safeguard the interest of the common people.

Presently, through the democratic process, over 3.3 million elected leaders have assumed positions at different levels of the Panchayati Raj administration covering 227,678 village Panchayats, 5906 Panchayat Samitis and 474 Zilla Parishads. The mandatory provision of 33% reservation for women and SC/STs have resulted in active participation of these groups. The women could place some priority issues like safe drinking water, girls education and basic health services on the Panchayati Raj agenda (NIRD, 1999).

Role of Non-Government Organisations

The major factor influencing the successful implementation of rural development in India is motivation of the poor families to ensure their active participation. Development of suitable peoples organisations is also necessary to avail the benefits of various schemes, particularly by the illiterate poor. To ensure peoples involvement in the development process and to take them into confidence, they should be involved in the programme, right from the stage of planning. Several innovative programmes implemented on a pilot scale have shown that many rational suggestions made by even the poor people can be easily implemented to produce good results. Such an approach demands flexibility in the programme. The target families should be motivated to assume the responsibility of implementing the programme, while the implementing agencies should play the role of a catalyst. In this task of integrated rural development, voluntary agencies can play an important role (Sachidananda, 1988).

The voluntary organisations or non-government organisations (NGOs) in general focus their voluntary action and service to tackle the problems of the common people or to help them face their challenges. The main characteristic of voluntary agencies is human-touch. Organisations with strong voluntarism and professionalism can implement the programme efficiently. Dedication of the volunteers and staff, their relationship with the community, flexibility in the programme, innovative approaches to solve the problems can result in greater success. Agencies having deep roots in rural areas can serve the community more effectively (Paul Choudhary, 1990).

It was only during the seventies that the government recognised the role of voluntary agencies in supplementing governments effort in rural development. Prior to this, the NGOs formed by religious institutions and enlightened public were involved in operating hospitals and educational institutions. With assistance from international donor agencies, the Ministry of Agriculture formed an independent organisation called Freedom from Hunger Campaign to support the voluntary organisations involved in rural development. This Organisation was reorganised and renamed as. Peoples Action for Development-India (PAD-I). PAD-I was merged with Council for Advancement of Rural Technology in 1986 and renamed as Council for Advancement of People's Action and Rural Technology (CAPART). Since then, CAPART has been providing financial assistance to voluntary agencies engaged in rural development. In the last two decades, several initiatives of the non-government organisations have had significant impact on the development. Widespread success of these initiatives have now encouraged many state governments to launch schemes to promote peoples participation and several centrally sponsored schemes have stipulated the development of community based organisations to plan and implement the programme.

With better opportunities for promoting self-employment through investment in agriculture and micro-enterprise, facilities were created for availing soft loans from banks and other financial institutions. The Reserve Bank of India issued guidelines to all the bankers not to insist on collateral security up to Rs.25,000 drawn by the poor for investment in development activities. As a result, over Rs.250 billion was distributed as rural credit in 1995-96, of which 50% amount was from the cooperatives and the rest from other banking institutions. Nevertheless, as the formal banking operations were not convenient for many villagers because of their rigidity, distance and high cost of operation, several innovative banking institutions have been established by the NGOs.

BAIF-A Leading NGO Committed to Rural Development

BAIF Development Research Foundation is a voluntary organisation established by Dr. Manibhai Desai, a disciple of Mahatma Gandhi at Urulikanchan, a village near Pune in 1967, with the objective of providing gainful self employment to the rural poor. BAIF has been promoting integrated rural development through sustainable management of degraded natural resources such as land, livestock, water and vegetation, using the idle time of the local people. The programmes also address the problems of health, illiteracy, empowerment of women and environmental pollution to ensure quality of life. BAIF has been focussing on weaker sections of the society through a family based approach and has demonstrated that a family maintaining three high yielding cows or a hectare of degraded land under horti-forestry can earn an annual income of Rs.20,000.25,000 (US 500) per year. The gestation period to eradicate poverty through these programmes is only 5-6 years.

BAIF has been promoting peoples participation through formation of Self Help Groups and Local Planning Committees who discuss their problems and find out suitable solutions. The members of these groups are trained in various agro-based skills to develop them into local resource persons. The training emphasizes on selection of appropriate technologies, optimum use of resources and management aspects of project implementation.

The Cattle Development Programme operated through 725 centres covering 10,000 villages in seven states is providing breeding services to cattle and buffaloes, at the doorsteps of the farmers. The programme has helped over one million farmers to upgrade their livestock and to increase their income through milk production. Dairy husbandry has been providing an excellent opportunity for women and small farmers to earn a sustainable livelihood, while promoting ecofriendly practices such as organic farming, bio-gas production and stall feeding.

Development of wastelands through tree based farming and water resource management is being implemented in about 1000 villages by providing technical guidance and critical inputs to convert 0.5 to 1.0 ha degraded lands owned by poor families into productive orchards. They are encouraged to plant multipurpose tree species on the bunds and borders of the orchard to serve as wind break and a source of green manure, herbal medicine, fodder, fuel and timber. The interspace used for growing cereals and vegetables has been generating regular income while ensuring food security. A tribal development programme covering these components in Dharampur block of Valsad district in Gujarat has rehabilitated over 16,000 families in the recent past.

This programme is being widely replicated in other parts of India with necessary modifications to address the local problems. Community health, an integral part of the overall development strategy, focuses on improved health status of the families through promotion of safe drinking water sources, hygiene and sanitation facilities, nutritious diet, immunisation, mother and child health care, nutrition gardens and health education. Use of traditional health practices with a wide range of home grown herbs and alternate methods of garbage disposal are also being popularised. BAIF has been emphasizing on the formation of peoples organisations in all its development programmes for ensuring sustainable development.

Peoples Initiatives for Progress

Farmers in several states have established cooperatives for processing sugarcane, oil-seeds, milk, fruits and vegetables. With professional management and application of modern technologies, these organisations have brought economic stability and eliminated exploitation by intermediary traders.

Encouragement is being given to strengthen such organisations throughout the country. Under a nationwide programme for water resource development, involvement of NGOs as facilitators and formation of water users organisations have been encouraged to prepare the microlevel plan and implement the project directly. This programme has made a significant impact on the supply of drinking water and greater awareness is being created on the need to conserve water and energy resources. There is scope for promoting such peoples organisations in other fields as well to develop necessary infrastructure required to enhance economic prosperity.

Considering the need for promoting peoples initiatives and local organisations, Self Help Groups, comprising of poor families have been promoted under the Ninth Five Year Plan (1997-2002), through the Swarnajayanti Gram Swarojgar Yojana (SGSY) in 1999. SHGs consisting of 10-20 members belonging to backward socioeconomic status encourage the participants to meet regularly to collect their savings and disburse it as loan to needy members. During this process, they also discuss their problems and find suitable solutions. Finally, it is the peoples initiative which can sustain the development. The government has the will to support peoples movement and this is the only ray of hope for sustainable development of the rural poor in India.

2

Effects of Globalization on Rural Population

Economies: The Case of India

Although various aspects of *globalization* are intentional and reflexive, many globalising forces are impersonal and beyond the control and intentions of any individual or group of individuals. In response to the contemporary globalization process, economic liberalisation has been taking place in India— a labour surplus dualistic economy— over the past two decades. In the current chapter, the author would like to focus on the change, if any, of the degree of socioeconomic dualism in India that has adopted a comprehensive economic reform in July 1991. Many argue that the liberalisation policy has been, in many ways, erratic, hasty, and unplanned.

According to the critics, it has eroded the role of the planning process and aggravated the social problems of unemployment and poverty, and also increased the external vulnerability. In order to test validity or otherwise of these arguments made, let us first mention that India has a *structural dualism* at the very aggregate level. This means that India has two different socio-economic-technological environments— the *organised* (or modern) segment (predominantly *capitalistic*) and the *unorganised* (or traditional) segment (predominantly *pre-capitalistic*)— co-exist within its geographical boundary.

The *organised* segment includes all establishments in the Public Sector irrespective of size of employment and non-agricultural establishments in the Private Sector employing 10 or more persons.

The *unorganised* (or traditional) segment is usually defined to be the segment that is not recorded under any factory legislation. This segment is mostly comprised of self-employed households and casual labour with no steady employment and, therefore, no secure or sustainable incomes, and above all with no access to the benefits of social security. Although the share of the organised segment in Net Domestic Product (NDP) (at factor cost) has increased from 30% during 1980-81 to 39.1% during 1998-99, but that in employment has steadily declined from only 7.49% of total workers in 1981 to only 6.38% in 1999. As a result, the unorganised segment continues to contain over 93% of India's labour force, in spite of the decline in its share in net domestic product from 70.0% in 1980-81 to 60.9% in 1998-99.

In his address to the nation on the eve of the Golden Jubilee of the Indian Republic in 2000, the then President, Shri K. R. Narayan takes pride in India's achievements of being the world's largest democracy and one of the 10 fastest growing economies in the world. He also reminds us that, over the past fifty years, in our sovereign democratic Republic 'Justice— social, economic and political— remains an unrealised dream for millions of our fellow citizens.' He himself describes different facets of the unrealised dream saying:

Voluntary Action

A voluntary action is one that is produced because of conscious choice of the organism. The organism, would in turn also be aware of the action while it is executed. This is the opposite of involuntary action, which occurs without the free will of the organism. When this involuntary action occurs in response to a specific stimulus that may arise outside the body (e.g., sudden glare that would result in closing of the pupil) or inside the body (e.g., or widening of the pupil that might occur with excitement or anxiety). Thus, an involuntary action need not be a reflex if it is not a direct response to a stimulus, e.g., alternate contraction and relaxation of skeletal muscles during a "fit" (seizure). Another distinction is that reflexes tend to have a protective value for the organism, and are seen in all members of a species, but involuntary movements may not be.

Some responses are involuntary, but may be also generated by free will, like blinking of the eyelids and respiratory movements.

Cultural Heritage, Cultural Empowerment and Development

All over the world a sentiment and a concern for sustainable development is growing. Increasing numbers of individuals and organisations are becoming aware of the growing ecological and environmental crisis produced by the culture of hedonism and self-gratification built into present-day industrial, scientific and technological civilisation wedded to the pursuit of profit as an end in itself.

Thinking people are getting perturbed by the manner in which a sense of history, tradition and purposive long-term action are being given up as of no use by those who occupy the citadels of global power and material riches. A longing for self-reliant, communitarian and spontaneous cultural development is being expressed by diverse sections of the world population.

In the words of Saul Bellow, the old forms of existence have worn out, so to speak, and the new ones have not yet appeared and people are prospecting, as it were, in the desert for new forms. And yet it would be worthwhile to acknowledge at the outset how difficult and complex a task it is to work out cohesive and practical policies and models to achieve holistic creative development. In the arena of culture and creativity in particular, the reasons do no lie so deep as to seem unfathomable.

In spite of very high GNPs, individuals in post-modern societies have come to realise that in everyday life, the bonds that build fellowship and reciprocity in family, work-place and community are getting attenuated. People do not feel confident that they can live in tune either with time or with place. This feeling has been caught well by a contemporary observer of the Western scene. Invoking the perceptions of modernity entertained by Marx, Nietzsche and Baudelaire, he says:

They can illuminate the contradictory forces and needs that inspire and torment us. Our desire to be rooted in a stable and coherent personal and social past, and our unstable desire for growth — not merely for economic growth but for growth in experience, in pleasure, in knowledge in sensibility — growth that destroys both the physical and social landscapes of our past, and our emotional links with those lost worlds; our desperate allegiances to ethnic, national, class and sexual groups which we hope will give us a firm 'identity', and the internationalization of everyday life — of our clothes and household goods, our books and music, our ideas and fantasies — that spreads all our identities all over the map; our desire for clear and solid values to live by, and our desire to embrace the limitless possibilities of modern life and experience that obliterate all values.... Experiences like these unite us with the nineteenth century modern world: a world where, as Marx said, 'every thing is pregnant with its contrary' and 'all that is solid melts into air'; a world where as Nietzsche said, 'there is danger, the mother of morality — a great danger... displaced onto the individual, onto the nearest and dearest, onto the street, onto one's own child, one's own heart, one's own innermost secret recesses of wish and will'.

But we begin to experience a sense of resignation and remoteness when we consult the metropolitan thinkers for solutions. In relating culture to whatever is named as modernisation or late capitalism or post-industrial society, or in relating culture to the social relations of production, power, and class, these thinkers get themselves polarised, although not for accidental reasons, into two warring camps. Contemporary German social theory, for example, represents the first camp.

The erosion of the distinction between high culture and so-called mass or popular culture in today's consumer society disturbs it. It therefore produces massive critiques of the culture of industry and consumerism in the age of late capitalism and culminates in the theory of communicative action. And yet these massive works fail to provide any practical and political guide for action. As Rick Roderick puts it:

The lessons the critical theorists drew from the history of marxism was that an inattention to philosophical and methodological questions had disastrous theoretical and practical effects. In this context, they argued for the relative autonomy of theory.... With the exception of Marcuse at certain points in his career and the early Horkheimer, the critical theorists rejected any direct links between the elaboration of theory and participation in political struggles.

Working in the hoary tradition set by Aristotle and refashioned by Kant, which associates melancholy and sympathy with moral freedom and sensitivity, critical theory in effect defends nostalgia. It is no wonder, then, that in spite of their stout defence of the philosophical discourses of modernity celebrating emancipatory reason, order, coherence, unity, and universality, both Marcuse and Habermas exclude Third World concerns from the ambit of their analyses and disown any responsibility towards it.

The new French social theory represents the other camp. In terms of its critical theory antagonists, it represents an emotional current of our time which has penetrated spheres of intellectual life. It has put on the agenda theories of postenlightenment, postmodernity, and even of posthistory.

Emphasising the new forms of technology and information, the computerisation of society, the increasing role of simulations and models, the superabundance of cultural goods, the effacement of the boundary between art and everyday life and so on, current French theory talks about the post-industrial age, the erasure of the distinction between the real and the appearance, and even the end of the social.

To face this novel world, it wants to shape a matching radical stance which would go beyond the philosophers of modernity and Marx in particular And yet the new French social theory culminates in the politics and aesthetics of desire, sensation and immediacy. In its practical effects it appears to be primarily negative. Catherine Zuckert has provided a good demonstration of this point while discussing the politics of Derridean deconstruction. She states:

In arguing that there is no stable system of meaning or order — natural, logical, or historical — Derrida may free his readers from the spectre of 'totalization', but by virtue of the same argument, he deprives them of the capacity to think, much less to act on their own behalf. If all opposites are fundamentally and inseparably linked, as Derrida maintains, there are no alternatives, no 'either-or's between which to choose. We may be freed *from* complete domination, but we are not free *to do* much. Difference continues to operate whether we will it or no....As Derrida himself observes, 'it is not certain that such thinking can bring together a community or found an institution in the traditional sense of these words'. According to Derrida, we do not completely and simply share anything with anyone — ourselves, much less our nation or species. There may be a good deal of historical overlap in language and customs, but there is no common room or ground. There are only and always differences and hence, opposition, division and strife. Thus the new French social theory's endeavours to keep alive 'historicity' in the face of a teleological history end in varieties of messianic messages which on examination are found unfortunately to be full of passivity. Its political and cultural implications are 'parochial, if not provincial'.

The current spectrum of theoretical dissent in the United States is also quite big. It spreads, say, from Frederic Jameson on the one hand to Richard Rorty on the other. But in reality these dissenting voices get totally smothered by the voices raising the cries of the end of history and so on, the triple-angled domination in the spheres of polity, economy and culture is so complete and so elemental.

Our voyage of discovery in the realm of current cultural discourses in the post-modern societies in search of guidelines for practical, transformative models for facing the desert-like cultural reality within our own country has thus been proved practically futile. Yet such journeys will be both unavoidable and desirable for the present and also for a long time to come for the following reasons.

Let us first note the compulsive element or elements. In the first instance, globalization as it operates today is bound to threaten the plurality and diversity of all cultures. In the words of Panikkar:

Today culture is an important component of domination, both of and within developing societies. The ideological apparatuses of state and of multinational agencies brought into being by [the] technological revolution have ushered in this possibility. During the last couple of decades, [the] culture industry in the capitalist west has undergone transformation beyond recognition. A very large volume of capital has gone into this industry... and that cultural capitalism has displaced manufacturing as a source of wealth and influence.

Panikkar also Reminds us that

what is happening, however, is not such an innocent process of acculturation, permitting the acceptance or rejection of cultural elements based on freedom of choice. On the contrary, the power differential inherent in economic relations determines cultural interaction.... The exogenous cultural presence is not only unsettling the indigenous but also trying to hegemonise it for legitimising a concept of social development modelled on the advanced capitalist societies.

In the Second Instance, as M.P. Rege Puts it so Well

The concept of science as the only rational form of knowledge and that of civil society as the only rational form of society came to us as gifts of a colonial rule which disrupted the traditional forms of life in India. This certainly complicates our situation. But even if they had been presented to us in an altogether peaceful manner they would have posed a serious challenge, indeed a threat. For diverse, and more often competing and even contradictory reasons, diverse sections of our society from the top to the bottom want to realise these two concepts in accordance with their requirements. We therefore are bound to follow the post-modern societies in the future as well.

In the third instance, we may have very cogent and legitimate reasons to question the extrapolation of these Western culture-bound rationalizations to encompass Third World situations. And yet we find ourselves in a situation in which the question is not 'how to maintain and express their autonomy in the sphere of cognition but how to reclaim it'.

But there do exist superior and more dignified reasons for watching the advanced societies to better know how to link our own cognitive and cultural heritages for strategies for sustainable development.

Paulo Freire and Edward Said have identified one such factor well in understanding the relationship between home and homelessness, exile and critic, or another self and one's own identity. Border-crossing not only helps to break taken-for-granted barriers of thought and experience, but more importantly, saves intellectuals from the risk of being too remote in their work as intellectuals from the most real, most concrete experiences, and of being sometimes lost, and even somewhat contended, because they are lost in a game of words... 'specializing in the ballet of concepts'.

Paul Ricoeur has put this relationship still better. According to him, recognition of the error in identifying science and technology with 'the relationship of truth which we can have with all things' induces us 'to discover what, in the cultures of the past, is more than merely pre-scientific'. For the same reasons, receptiveness to other cultures prepares us 'to apply to ourselves the distinctive significance of a particular tradition'.

Mahatma Gandhi had taught these insights with a far sharper sense of reality and a clearer vision moulded by the various traditions within our country. Making a distinction between imitation and assimilation, he wanted us 'to build a new culture based on the traditions of the past, enriched with the experience of later times'. This was for the simple reason that his religion, 'whatever it may be called', demanded the fulfilment of all cultures.

The detour taken in the third section was necessary for a simple reason. Culture-wise, India nowadays is as much part of the kingdom of darkness as of the so-called post-modern world. Now if any flicker of hope and enlightenment is available, our refusal to accept it would offer another demonstration of the sunken state of our civilisation and culture by laying open our misplaced pride and smugness. But the problem is that as we have seen, even the most advanced consciousness and thought in the advanced capitalist world have nothing to offer in terms of a fresh utopia and praxis to their own and to the rest of the world. In the given situation, we are led to listen to the voices of our own tradition, and they are not that inaccessible if we care to follow them. Moreover, some of these voices possess a rare virtue — a practical ability to link stark realities with utopian norms and vision.

Listen to Ananda K. Coomarswamy, for instance. His following statements reveal a courage to grasp reality as it is: We have gone so far as to divorce work from culture and to think of culture as something to be acquired in hours of leisure; but there can be only a hothouse and unreal culture where work itself is not its means; if culture does not show itself in all we make we are not cultured.

Culture Originates in Work and Not in Play

The artist is not a special kind of man, but every man who is not an artist in some field, every man without a vocation is an idler..... No man has a right to any social status who is not an artist.

To 'enjoy' what does not correspond to any vital needs of our own and what we have not verified in our life can only be described as an indulgence. The ideal of voluntary poverty, which rejects utilities, can be readily understood. It is easy to see that an indefinite multiplication of utilities, the means of life, may end in an identification of culture with comfort, and the substitution of means for ends.

It was not indeed 'taste' that brought us to the use of homespun, nor, on the other hand, was this merely an outwardly imposed privation;... for the present we are assured that to be arrayed in glorious garments is not merely bad economy, but also bad taste.

Mahatma Gandhi Urged us to Think about the Following Issues

Self-expression and self-government are not things which may be either taken from us by anybody or which can be given us by anybody. It is quite true that if those who happen to hold our destinies, or seem to hold our destinies in their hands, are favourably disposed, are sympathetic, understand our aspirations, no doubt it is easier for us to expand. But after all self-government depends entirely on our own internal strength, upon our ability to fight against [the] heaviest odds. Indeed, self-government which does not require that continuous striving to attain it and to sustain it is not worth the name (Gandhi 1927). The duty of renunciation differentiates mankind from the beast.

Some object that life thus understood becomes dull and devoid of art, and leaves no room for the householder. But renunciation here does not mean abandoning the world and retiring into the forest.... Joy has no independent existence. It depends upon our attitude to life.... Joy, therefore, is a matter of individual and national education.

Our (basic) system of education... leads to the development of the mind, body and soul. The ordinary system cared only for the mind.... The function of Nai Talim is not merely to teach an occupation, but through it to develop the whole man. Sankho Chaudhuri offered the following insights to us. While discussing a cultural policy for folk and tribal art he stated:

It would be wrong to label their art with a capital 'A' in the contemporary sense of conscious self-expression. What they do is only an extension of their daily existence.

We tend to associate the word 'encouragement' with the development of any form of art. This presupposes a lack of utility for the object, but if the latter is essential in a people's life it does not need this encouragement. In fact, if by encouragement we mean creating a large market, it is doubtful whether the creation of a market disproportionate to production capacity is at all beneficial.

We have seen how this exaggerated demand at times completely debases taste and demoralises the artisans. I think that the above insights provide practical guidelines for linking cultural heritage with strategies for sustainable development. In fact, there can be no better framework for policy in particular in a country where the majority of the people still suffer from poverty, want, malnutrition, dreariness and illiteracy. A set of such policies alone would nourish the self-confidence and creativity of the citizens, autonomy and experimentation of the community and a utopian and not creative memory of tradition).

The price which we have paid for deviating from the creative and critical tradition within our country is too well-known to demand repetition. The Government of India announcement of 7 May 1990 captures the depth of our failure so well. It says,

Despite efforts at social and economic development since [the] attainment of independence, a majority of our people continue to remain deprived of education. It is also a matter of grave concern that our people comprise 50 per cent of the world's illiterate, and large sections of children have to go without [an] acceptable level of primary education (Ramamurthi Committee:

Given this kind of performance of our elites, and, more pertinently, the poverty of ideas from which I suffer, I am offering the following proposals for your consideration. Though they may appear very mundane and perhaps somewhat removed from the thrust of my argument so far, I believe that somehow they do have a subterranean relation with what I have said earlier.

An Action Plan for Developing the Public Library Service

Until we develop an effective public library service for the first-generation literates who constitute the majority of our educated citizens, we will not be able to meet the real hunger of these citizens for more and better information and knowledge. Our formal educational system manufactures at the most practically semi-literate persons. We find time and again that they suffer from a lack of easy and cheap access to library facilities.

I Endorse the Observations Made by Subhag C. Biswas in this Connection

Had the public library service developed properly, alongside our educational programme, our *socioeconomic condition* would have been more encouraging that what it is. The public library network requires heavy capital investment and the returns are only indirect. State Governments are reluctant to invest large amounts from their limited resources as they feel other priority areas can provide better results for economic growth. Lack of political will prevents us from a developing a nation-wide public library service on *modern* concepts [emphases mine.

Please note that this is *not* a demand for a national library facility with huge libraries necessary for the higher echelons of the intelligentsia or policy-makers but a plea for a national library network based on community-centred, community-managed medium-sized, good but non-elitist and yet modern library centres.

A Museum System for Cultural Empowerment

If we give up traditional concepts of a museum, we will be able to dismantle the cultural barriers that prevent the participation of communities and the people as a whole in museum activity. In their new role museums can play 'an important part in shaping cultural perceptions within their communities, as people everywhere become more aware of themselves and their surroundings'.

The premise of the new museum theory coming up in the post-modern world tells us that the past is something that belongs to all, irrespective of the circumstances of their birth and upbringing. Consequently everyone should have the right to gain access to their own history, even if they choose not to avail themselves of this opportunity. Museums and similar organisations are one of the principal means by which people can gain access to the past, and everyone should thus have the opportunity to visit them and feel at home in them.

The irony is that Coomarswamy would have accepted this position, although for very different reasons. In a well-known argument concerning the exhibition of works of art he had opposed their display on grounds of 'our fashion' or 'aesthetic motives'. Treating the museum as 'the sworn enemy of the methods of instruction currently in our Schools of Art', he wanted the museum exhibition to return to the 'savage levels of culture' where objects were custom made and made for use and not for profits or novelty. The idea was to use the museum to oppose the present world based upon greed, commercialisation, and elitism.

We can therefore understand the lament of Sankho Chaudhuri about the transfer of the Museum of Tribal Art from Chhindwara to Bhopal at an earlier seminar on cultural policy held by the Indian Institute of Advanced Study, Shimla. He had made a call 'to make small museums, not for the urbanite's amusement but to be used for reference and inspiration by young tribesmen'.

The well-known artist K.G. Subramanyam offers us a similar insight in his very recent and contemporary comment. Acknowledging Ananda Coomarswamy's still compelling impact on thinking 'made more than 50 years ago' he feels disturbed by the implications of the country's new economic objectives on 'a variety of art practice, both professional and non-professional' within our country. Subramanyam is still a sober realist. He knows that we cannot keep tradition 'forcibly alive', that 'we cannot stem social change', and that 'no society exists today in isolation'. And yet knowing that 'what concerns them (the government and the trading community) most are export earnings, not human refinement', he states:

> In these circumstances the least we can do is to visually record the whole heritage, collect object specimens of the best kind, document methods of fabrication and use and house these objects and data in museums and archives region to region, speciality to speciality. These can recreate for the interested a picture of various art forms and educate them to value them. And provide, if an art form disappears, the wherewithal with which to recall it. This may motivate some to cultivate them in the new circumstances and use them for the new purposes. Even sow the seeds of tradition in a non-traditional world. And teach the future planners to be more sensitive and circumspect.

Sustainable development demands an urgent building up of such museums and archives for the future-oriented persistence of our culture and heritage in the world of post-modern technologies and capitalism.

Handing back People's own Ancient Sites and Monuments to Local Communities

Given the current state of our polity and the mood of the country, I am not sure whether it would be prudent to offer the third proposal. Its rationale and scope as well as the manner and the timing of its application demand serious consideration. The proposal is about community participation in the preservation of ancient sites and monuments.

The Unesco Document Entitled *Cultural Policy: A Preliminary Study* States:

The aim in all countries is no longer merely to preserve ancient monuments and sites but, above all, to present them to the best advantage and give them place once more in the economic and social life of the community. They are no longer merely places to be studied by archaeologists and art historians, but *means of cultural action* which can be used to awaken people and make them appreciative of the culture and of the cultural heritage of mankind as a whole. The great archaeological treasures of some countries have led to the development of excavation sites as open-air museums, tourist attractions as well as relics of the past with much to teach.... Sites and monuments are also becoming a link in the cultural action chain [emphasis mine].

The same document points out that preservation is now looked upon 'as a means of defence against an anonymous technological civilisation and of safeguarding folk values. It has, therefore, become a part of social and cultural development'. We know how due to lack of funds, trained manpower, and the lack of a truly post-colonial, people-oriented national policy on such matters, most of our pre-colonial sites and monuments, barring of course some well-known exceptions, are suffering from neglect, lack of immediate, living and creative contact with the surrounding community, and excessively narrow legalistic jealousies entertained by the government departments concerned. They appear so forlorn, so lifeless and so subject to the vagaries of nature and vandals.

Handing over these sites and monuments would no doubt demand some initial guidance and control for the sake of achieving authentic, form-faithful preservation and also the protection of the law of the land. But it is high time that we return this heritage of the people to their own custody. Let us free ourselves from the clutches of colonial and commercial concerns in such matters.

Need for a National Policy for Securing Beautiful and Useful Public Buildings

This final proposal does not involve a need for additional funds, manpower or big bureaucracy but only imagination and determination. We have spent crores of rupees on public buildings since Independence. Barring some rather rare exceptions, they do not serve the expectations of beauty and use in a fused manner or even separately or partially. They do not show a stamp or a style of any kind including even the bastard styles.

They are as soulless, graceless and inelegant as most of our post-Independence development. Spending public funds for raising structures in tune with nature and the cultural heritage is as much a part of alternative development philosophy as anything else. Anything which falls short of these norms must be deemed from now onwards as a serious failure of public responsibilities and duties.

Voluntary Action and Alternative Development in Tribal Areas

After attaining independence most Third World countries embarked on the path of modernisation to catch up with Western countries in the shortest possible time. The national elites in these countries bent their energy to accomplish this task. The experience gained during the first two development decades amply showed that the two concepts of modernisation and development were most inadequate to solve the problems facing the people in these countries. Although some economic growth was registered, the process brought in its train greater dependence on Western countries and widened the gulf between rich and poor in different countries. At some places this led to the emergence of powerful social movements. This invited a backlash from vested interests tending to promote parochial and obscurantist values which militated against the goals of modernity.

The development experience among the tribal communities is not very different from that of general society in India. In certain cases, tribals have been hurt rather than helped on account of the development effort. In most cases it resulted in development for the few and destitution for many. The experience of the pains of development is very poignant. Some of these are quite visible while others can be discovered after a deep probe into the social fabric.

In India the bulk of the tribal community is spread over middle India from Gujarat to West Bengal and in the north-east. The tribals in the northeastern states form a majority there. The tribals in middle India live interspersed with the dominant population. It is there that their deprivation and exploitation are the worst. Tribal policies in India suffer from a hangover of the colonial past. The British system of administration tended to impair their social solidarity and weakened the authority of their social heads and *pancayats*. Until recently, when rules against alienation of ancestral land were promulgated by the government, the ancient tribal customs against such alienation were disregarded.

After Independence efforts were made to integrate the tribals into the mainstream of the Indian polity through elimination of exploitation and positive measures for raising their levels of living. But even forty years after Independence they are being deprived of command over the resources which they enjoyed in their respective areas. The opening up of inaccessible tribal areas has aided this process. The tribal people along the arteries of communication are being squeezed out of their land. The new enclaves of affluence in tribal areas have no place for tribals. They are losers on all counts and are victims of a system in which those responsible for policy-making suffer no embarrassment and qualms of conscience.

The problems of tribals coming under the sway of large industrial, mining and irrigation projects are most acute. It is a pity that the difficulties of the tribals were not perceived earlier. The issues are not just alternative use of resources or cost-benefit analysis of projects. They are deeper and involve human rights, civilisation's values and national obligations. The tribal people are faced with rapid change, which tends to create a crisis in their life. Displacement spells disorganisation and destitution. They lack skills for an alternative way of life. It is at this stage that the concept of sustainable development or alternative development has to be thought of. Unfortunately not much thinking in this regard has come from the government. It is on account of this that the role of voluntary agencies in this field becomes important.

The experiment in alternative development which is the theme of this paper has been carried out in the Santhal Parganas by the Badlao Foundation during the past ten years. The Santhal Parganas is the northeastern extension of the Deccan plateau. The region is bounded on the west and south by a number of districts of Bihar and to the east by some districts of West Bengal. Ethnologically, it is the abode of two important tribes, the Santal and the Paharia. The activities of the Badlao Foundation are spread mainly among these tribes in the districts of Deoghar, Godda and Dumka.

The Santal are the largest tribe of eastern India. In Bihar alone they number more than two millions. The traditions of the Santal represent them as a group wandering from one land to another until they found their present home in Chhota Nagpur and the adjacent districts. On the basis of their traditions, several theories have been put forward to account for their origin. About the middle of the 18th century Chhota Nagpur was the chief habitat of the Santal. At the end of the century, as the jungles were being cleared and the pressure of population was keenly felt, they moved up towards the virgin forests in and around the Rajmahal hills.

The Permanent Settlement of 1793 forced the landlords to pay more attention to land improvement and reclamation, for which the Santal were increasingly used. In 1832 the government set apart a large area in the Santhal Parganas for the settlement of the Santal. This region was known as Damin-i-Koh. The population in this tract increased from 3,000 in 1838 to 82,795 in 1851. Thus from the middle of the last century Damin-i-Koh became the main concentration of the Santal.

In reclaiming land and clearing jungle the Santal have few equals in India. They live in villages consisting of a long street with a single row of dwellings on either side. Santal houses are built of mud but roofed with country-made tiles. The houses are kept very neat and clean and the outside walls are painted with exquisite designs. The Santal are settled agriculturalists and use simple agricultural implements. However, they derive a part of their sustenance from the forest, since their agricultural field are monocropped. The Santal produce rice, maize, millets, beans, and vegetables. About 82 varieties of wild plants, 70 varieties of fruits,

7 varieties of resins, 31 varieties of mushrooms and several varieties of jungle millets are gathered at one time or other. Wild foods are collected by women who work together in groups. Santal men go on hunting expeditions.

The Santal live in nuclear families and are patrilineal in descent. Several kinds of marriage are prevalent, but the most prestigious one is that in which bride-price has been paid. A daughter does not have a share in her father's property but she can hold moveable property like money, goods and cattle. Women's status in society is high and in most cases they run the households. However, they do not have political or religious rights.

They are not members of the village *pancayat*, although Santal society is highly democratic. Women work with men in fields, farms and forests. They go to the market and strike bargains for the surplus produce of the family. Santal society is marked by a spirit of cooperation and it is manifested not only on the occasion of festivals but also in all kinds of social and economic activities. Friends share wedding expenses with each other, help each other in cultivation, lend each other plough cattle and rally to each other's help at birth, sickness, or death and assist each other with loans that are free of interest. Santal religion is a potent force in strengthening the social solidarity of the people.

The Santal concept of righteousness is bound up with its social or tribal consciousness. They have an excellent and well-ordered village organisation with a hierarchy of village officers and courts for dispensing their unwritten law. The unique form of punishment called *bitlaha* is used to bring to book persons guilty of transgressing the social code regarding sexual relations inside the clan and outside the tribe.

The Sauria Paharia, the largest Paharia group, accounted for 65,000 persons in 1988. The Sauria Paharia are basically shifting cultivators and live on mountain spurs in very small villages. They have a feeling of animosity toward the Santal who live largely on the plateau and use more sophisticated tools for agriculture. They speak a language which belongs to the intermediate Dravidian group so widely different from the Austric speech of the Santal.

Sauria Paharia settlements comprise ten to fifty houses. The houses are very small and rickety compared to Santal houses. Their main occupation is slash-and-burn cultivation, known locally as *kurwa*. They move from field to field after a few years. They use only the digging stick for putting in the seeds. They grow maize, millets, beans and pulses. Some of these tribesmen have picked up settled cultivation if they have some plain land.

The Paharia as compared to Santal are more dependent on the forest. Earlier they used to make some money by cultivating *sabai* grass. But now they do not do so in a big way as its market has shrunk. The cutting down of forests and the restrictions placed on their exploitation led to a reduction of their resource base. Although the Sauria Paharia have cherished a healthy relationship between nature, man and the spirits for a long time, they are extremely frustrated as their gods have failed to protect them from the ravages of time. Abject poverty and disease have made them panic. The steps taken by government for their welfare have largely bypassed them, and they remain one of the most backward tribal groups in the state. It is in this background that the Badlao Foundation is concentrating its effort. In recent years, voluntary initiatives have raised debates on new issues and concerns which have emerged from our development programme over the past four decades. The issues of deforestation, air and water pollution, ecology, rights of women and rural labour, rights of construction workers, occupational health and safety, land degradation and alienation, housing rights, right to information and work, adult literacy and education of women, etc., have been articulated by individuals and organisations involved in voluntary action. Although even earlier the role of voluntary agencies in bringing about development was recognised, it was only in the Seventh Plan document that the role of voluntary organisations was clearly set out.

Voluntary agencies were not only to supplement government efforts but also to offer the rural poor choices and alternatives. Thus the voluntary agencies could experiment and innovate new schemes and programmes to bring development to the rural poor. Since they had close links with the grassroots, they were expected to elicit people's participation in a much larger measure than otherwise.

The development package could differ from area to area and even from village to village. The voluntary agencies were not expected to supplant government efforts and replace dependence on the government by dependence on themselves, but in helping people help themselves. People have to be made aware of their own problems. They have to work out the priorities themselves in view of the limitation of resources.

The Badlao Foundation was established by certain activists who were inspired by the J.P. movement which took place in the mid-1970s. In the early 1980s there was no voluntary organisation in the pockets in which work was started.

The area chosen was about eight kilometres from Mihijam on the Bihar-Bengal border. Long economic deprivation and the excesses perpetrated on them by the moneylenders had put the tribal population in a state of despondency. In such a situation an all-round effort had to be made to generate income for them through fresh schemes, i.e. sericulture, livestock, milch cattle, cottage industry, small trades, social forestry, spinning, weaving, etc. In addition to this, there was urgent need for educational and health programmes for the people.

The Foundation set before Itself the Following Tasks

1. To develop skills and self-reliance in social, economic, cultural and political fields through raising social consciousness and sense of civic responsibility among the tribal and poor population for bringing about their socioeconomic transformation
2. To initiate small economic programmes for women through the creation of Mahila Sabhas
3. To mobilise different segments of the society, particularly the youth
4. To organise discussions, meetings, environmental festivals, exhibitions, cultural programmes, and to conduct tours for tribal people to acquaint them with successful development efforts
5. To conduct training in ecology and environment.

The fast depletion of forest cover in the region affected the life of tribals very adversely. They depended for their livelihood, in large measure, on the forest. They took advantage of various kinds of timber and non-timber produce. In the lean months of the year, they could subsist on products like *mahua* and jackfruit. The cutting of forests was accelerated by the local contractors in collusion with the lower functionaries of the Forest Department. They cut more forest than they were permitted to.

The Forest Department held that the illegal cutting was the work of tribals, and a large number of Santal and Paharia were sent to jail on this ground. The depletion of forest resources led to the disappearance of a large number of medicinal plants which were used for curing human and animal diseases. It also led to the disappearance of a large number of animal species. Valuable pasture land was also lost and it has become a problem for the grazing of domestic animals. In some areas where certain communities were dependent on pastoral activities, their source of income disappeared.

The cottage industries in the village, which provided sustenance for certain communities, decayed in course of time due to lack of availability of raw materials which were derived from the forest. Prominent among them was the production of cotton, *taser* silk, the lac industry and the growing of *sabai* grass, which was used for the production of paper.

To add to this environmental degradation, the proliferation of stone quarries and stone crushers brought untold misery to the people. After the quarries were exhausted the entire landscape was marked by pits and nothing could be produced there. On account of strong winds stone dust coming from the stone crushing machines spread along the nearby fields and reduced their fertility. Not only this, the health of the people working in the quarries and living in nearby areas was also affected.

They began to suffer from lung diseases such as silicosis and asthma. They also complained about skin diseases and deafness. Protests made by local people against the opening of stone crushers went unheeded on account of the influence of capitalist interests. Another impact of the depletion of forests was the drying up of rivers and other sources of water. Many rivers which were earlier perennial changed their character and water was available in them only in the rainy season. The amount of precipitation was also reduced, resulting in scarcity of water. As a result, people have to drink stale and contaminated water. This has led to the appearance of many diseases.

The landscape changed a great deal on account of large-scale soil erosion. In many areas land was rendered uncultivable due to sand and the formation of gullies. All this led to reduction in the cultivable area. The process of desertification has set in and more and more land is turning barren.

Faced with this ecological problem the Badlao Foundation took steps to restore the ecological balance by arresting further degradation and conserving and regeneration of the existing natural resources. The steps taken were threefold: adoption of sericulture as a supplement to agriculture in a big way, ecological cultivation and afforestation.

All this needed building of awareness about environmental degradation among the people by pointing out how it was affecting their life adversely and how it was going to affect future generations. Since the women suffered most on account of environmental degradation by way of loss of food resources, employment opportunities, and migration of the menfolk in search of employment away from home, an effort was made to carry on the awareness programmes most vigorously among them through village Mahila Sabhas.

It was seen that the area was ideally suited for the plantation of *arjun, asan* and mulberry trees on which silkworms could be reared. The Foundation started a training programme to impart knowledge to a group of women about the complete process of sericulture, from silkworm rearing to silk production. The men were left undisturbed to carry on their own activities. The training was divided into phases. Once the training in worm rearing was completed, the women were trained in reeling and spinning. Later on they were also trained in weaving on looms. Nowhere in these parts do we find women engaged in weaving, but here women have eagerly taken up this activity. Engagement in such activity gives them supplementary income. This was augmented by other income generation schemes like goat rearing, raising of fruit and vegetable seedlings, horticulture, etc. A number of case studies of women showed that family income went up with these activities. The example set by some of the beneficiaries were ample demonstration to their neighbours to follow suit.

The second activity of the Foundation to restore the ecological balance was ecological cultivation. On account of the decline in the productivity of land, government effort was directed towards the use of more and more chemical fertilisers. However, it was found that the excessive use of chemical fertilisers was extremely harmful to the land in the long run. It has been observed that a balanced integration between plants, animals and insects is essential for sustainable development. The tribals had a strong tradition of using green manure for better produce. The Paharia engaged in shifting cultivation, which was an appropriate technology designed to regenerate forest and restore soil fertility.

The burning of the undergrowth provided ample fertiliser for the shifting cultivation plot. After a few years, the plot was left fallow, the forest regenerated and thus the shifting cultivation cycle was maintained. In the shifting cultivation field there has been a tradition of mixed cropping. If one crop fails, the other crop helps the people to tide over the crisis and there is never a total famine in such areas.

However, with the conversion of many of these plots into settled cultivation fields, the regeneration process has stopped. Studies made by scientists have made it clear that this pattern of ecological degradation is marked in this area after it changed from a collectional economy to settled agriculture. Almost all the farmers of the region are small and marginal farmers with uneconomic holdings. They are now looking for opportunities other than agriculture to make a living. Large numbers of them have become daily wage earners and migrate to neighbouring areas in search of seasonal employment. The Badlao Foundation targeted this group for experimenting in ecological cultivation.

To start with, the Foundation introduced ecological cultivation in ten villages of Madhupur Block of Deoghar district in 1989 with the following objectives:

1. To raise awareness and knowledge about ecological cultivation among individuals and peasant groups
2. To train and mobilise peasants in the operational area for reducing the use of chemical fertilisers in order to retain and enhance the productive capacity of the land
3. To train the farmers about the need to preserve and increase environmental capital for future generations
4. To discuss with the beneficiaries some of the aspects of the traditional cultivation system in relation to ecological constraints

5. To increase among beneficiaries knowledge of the environment
6. To safeguard the environment for the present and achieve full harmony with nature.

Thus the spectrum of ecological cultivation has four components:

(a) awareness,

(b) analysis of the situation,

(c) conservation and

(d) sustainable development.

Awareness includes making individual farmers conscious of the physical, social and economic aspects of the environment.

The experiment in ecological cultivation started with four farmers, two using the present system and two the innovative method. Before launching the programme, comprehensive soil testing and crop-wise doses of green manuring required in the fields were done by the Foundation. When the final accounting was done, it was evident that ecological cultivation is a viable proposition. In the present system 35 per cent of the operational cost is incurred on chemical fertilisers and pesticides. In the experimental area green manuring and compost accounted for only 23.5 per cent of the cost. In addition to economy, ecological cultivation ensured the retention of soil fertility over a longer period of time.

Later on the area of ecological cultivation was extended. Training was provided for this purpose to farmers in a number of villages. The popularity of green manure has gradually increased. Many farmers are now retaining *dhaicha* seed for use year after year. The main reason for the adoption of ecological cultivation is reduction in the cost of inputs. This is accompanied by water harvesting, which has reduced the cost of irrigation. The environmental programme of the Foundation was also devoted to the regeneration of forests. In some areas where large chunks of land were available, the Foundation began afforestation work by planting trees yielding fruit, fodder and fuel. In some villages in the Jarmundi Block such plantations was done over 177 acres. Both grafted and local trees of different species were planted. Mango, guava, lemon, *amla* and coconut trees were most popular. The plantations were done in four villages. A total of 3,900 fruit trees wee planted, fodder and fuel species numbering more than 16,000. Irrigation was provided for the new plants. Grafts, seedlings, manure and agricultural implements were given to the farmers in these villages. In about three years the barren fields have turned green. Some of the quick-growing fuel and fodder trees are being used by the village people. The fruit trees will begin to give yields in a couple of years.

The village people have realised the importance of these plantations. They take care of the plants and protect them from being destroyed by animals. They also look after the nurseries with loving care.

In all its activities the Foundation has involved the beneficiaries in the different programmes so that they do not regard the innovations as impositions from above. Participation of the people is coming in large measure because the Foundation is interested in their integrated or total development.

The educational and health programmes have endeared this voluntary organisation to the people. Increasing awareness has made them conscious of their own ability to contribute to their well-being. They now take full advantage of governmental schemes and the credit facilities being extended by banks. Their concern for conservation of the environment is evident in their efforts to minimise the felling of existing forests and saving them from the depredations of unscrupulous elements. The apathy to their environment and development is no more evident in the operational area of the Foundation. With alternative avenues of income from agriculture, sericulture and other activities, both men and women are keen to improve their quality of life.

Their aspirations have gone up. Thus the Badlao Foundation has shown ways in which the tribals in the area and other people can help themselves. It has also set an example for other voluntary organisations to work for sustainable development in tribal areas.

3

Social Work Among Tribe Population

Malnutrition

Malnutrition is the insufficient, excessive or imbalanced consumption of nutrients. A number of different nutrition disorders may arise, depending on which nutrients are under or overabundant in the diet.

The World Health Organization cites malnutrition as the gravest single threat to the world's public health. Improving nutrition is widely regarded as the most effective form of aid. Emergency measures include providing deficient micronutrients through fortified sachet powders, such as peanut butter, or directly through supplements. The famine relief model increasing used by aid groups calls for giving cash or cash vouchers to the hungry to pay local farmers instead of buying food from donor countries, often required by law, as it wastes money on transport costs. Long term measures include investing in modern agriculture in places that lack them, such as fertilizers and irrigation, which largely eradicated hunger in the developed world. However, World Bank strictures restrict government subsidies for farmers and the spread of fertilizer use is hampered by some environmental groups.

Causes

Agricultural Productivity

Food shortages are mostly caused by the lack of technology needed for the higher yields found in modern agriculture, such as nitrogen fertilizers, pesticides and irrigation. Reasons for the unavailability include moves to stop supplying fertilizer on environmental grounds, cited as the obstacle to feeding Africa by the Green revolution pioneer Norman Borlaug. As a result of widespread poverty, farmers cannot afford or governments cannot provide the technology. The World Bank and some wealthy donor countries also press nations that depend on aid to cut or eliminate subsidized agricultural inputs such as fertilizer, in the name of free market policies even as the United States and Europe extensively subsidized their own farmers. Many, if not most, farmers cannot afford fertilizer at market prices, leading to low agricultural production and wages and high, unaffordable food prices.

With 95% of all malnourished peoples living in the relatively stable climate region of the sub-tropics and tropics, climate change is of great importance to food security in these regions. According to the latest IPCC reports, temperature increases in these regions are "very likely." Even small changes in temperatures can lead to increased frequency of extreme weather conditions. Many of these have great impact on agricultural production and hence nutrition. For example, the 1998-2001 central Asian drought brought about an 80% livestock loss and 50% reduction in wheat and barley crops in Iran. An increase in extreme weather such as drought in regions such as Sub-Saharan would have even greater consequences in terms of malnutrition. Even without an increase of extreme weather events, a simple increase in temperature reduces the productiveness of many crop species, also decreasing food security in these regions.

Thomas Malthus noted overpopulation will outgrow food production as increases in food production occur along a slow arithmetic progression while population growth follows much faster geometric progressions causing food shortages. This argument has long since been refuted on several grounds but has nonetheless served as a backdrop for understanding of the causes of malnutrition. Food supplies can also be disrupted by impacts of natural disasters, from the results of conflict and war, as an impact of the HIV/AIDS pandemic as a consequence of other health issues such as diarrheal disease or chronic illness from lack of education regarding proper nutrition, or from countless other potential factors. The use of biofuels as a replacement for traditional fuels may leave less supply of food for nutrition and raises the price of food. The UN special rapporteur on the right to food, Jean Ziegler proposes that agricultural waste, such as corn cobs and banana leaves, rather than crops themselves be used as fuel.

Colony collapse disorder is a phenomenon where bees are dying in large numbers. Since many agricultural crops worldwide are pollinated by bees, this represents a serious threat to the supply of food. An epidemic of stem rust on wheat caused by race Ug99 is currently spreading across Africa and into Asia and, it is feared, could wipe out more than 80% of the world's wheat crops.

Poverty and Food Prices

As much as food shortages may be a contributing factor to malnutrition in countries with lack of technology, the FAO (food and agriculture Organization)has estimated that eighty percent of malnourished children living countries in the developing world produce food surpluses. The economist Amartya Sen observed that, in recent decades, famine has always a problem of food distribution and/or poverty, as there has been sufficient food to feed the whole population of the world. He states that malnutrition and famine were more related to problems of food distribution and purchasing power.

It is argued that commodity speculators are increasing the cost of food. As the real estate bubble in the United States was collapsing, it is said that trillions of dollars moved to invest in food and primary commodities, causing the 2007-2008 food price crisis.

Dietary Practices

The lack of breast-feeding leads to malnutrition in infants and children. Possible reasons for the lack in the developing world may be that the average family thinks bottle feeding is better. The WHO says mothers abandon it because they do not know how to get their baby to latch on properly or suffer pain and discomfort.

Many tend to think malnutrition only in terms of hunger, however, overeating is also a contributing factor as well. Many parts of the world have access to a surplus of non-nutritious food, in addition to increased sedentary lifestyles. In turn, this has created a universal epidemic of obesity. Yale psychologist Kelly Brownell calls this a "toxic food environment" where fat and sugar laden foods have taken precedent over healthy nutritious foods. Not only does obesity occur in developed countries, problems are also occurring in developing countries in areas where income is on the rise.

Effects

Mortality: According to Jean Ziegler (the United Nations Special Rapporteur on the Right to Food for 2000 to March 2008), mortality due to malnutrition accounted for 58% of the total mortality in 2006: "In the world, approximately 62 million people, all causes of death combined, die each year. One in twelve people worldwide is malnourished. In 2006, more than 36 millions died of hunger or diseases due to deficiencies in micronutrients".

According to the World Health Organization, malnutrition is by far the biggest contributor to child mortality, present in half of all cases. Underweight births and inter-uterine growth restrictions cause 2.2 million child deaths a year. Poor or non-existent breast-feeding causes another 1.4 million. Other deficiencies, such as lack of vitamin A or zinc, for example, account for 1 million. According to The Lancet, malnutrition in the first two years is irreversible. Malnourished children grow up with worse health and lower educational achievements. Their own children also tend to be smaller. Malnutrition was previously seen as something that exacerbates the problems of diseases such as measles, pneumonia and diarrhea. But malnutrition actually causes diseases as well, and can be fatal in its own right.

Psychological: According to the Lancet, Malnutrition, in the form of iodine deficiency, is "the most common preventable cause of mental impairment worldwide." Even moderate iodine deficiency, especially in pregnant women and infants, lowers intelligence by 10 to 15 I.Q. points, shaving incalculable potential off a nation's development. The most visible and severe effects—disabling goiters, cretinism and dwarfism — affect a tiny minority, usually in mountain villages. But 16 percent of the world's people have at least mild goiter, a swollen thyroid gland in the neck.

Research indicates that improving the awareness of nutritious meal choices and establishing long-term habits of healthy eating has a positive effect on a cognitive and spatial memory capacity, potentially increasing a student's potential to process and retain academic information. Some organizations have begun working with teachers, policymakers, and managed foodservice contractors to mandate improved nutritional content and increased nutritional resources in school cafeterias from primary to university level institutions. Health and nutrition have been proven to have close links with overall educational success. Currently less than 10% of American college students report that they eat the recommended five servings of fruit and vegetables daily. Better nutrition has been shown to have an impact on both cognitive and spatial memory performance; a study showed those with higher blood sugar levels performed better on certain memory tests. In another study, those who consumed yogurt performed better on thinking tasks when compared to those who consumed caffeine free diet soda or confections. Nutritional deficiencies have been shown to have a negative effect on learning behaviour in mice as far back as 1951.

"Better learning performance is associated with diet induced effects on learning and memory ability". The "nutrition-learning nexus" demonstrates the correlation between diet and learning and has application in a higher education setting.

"We find that better nourished children perform significantly better in school, partly because they enter school earlier and thus have more time to learn but mostly because of greater learning productivity per year of schooling."

91% of college students feel that they are in good health while only 7% eat their recommended daily allowance of fruits and vegetables.

Nutritional education is an effective and workable model in a higher education setting.

More "engaged" learning models that encompass nutrition is an idea that is picking up steam at all levels of the learning cycle. There is limited research available that directly links a student's Grade Point Average (G.P.A.) to their overall nutritional health. Additional substantive data is needed to prove that overall intellectual health is closely linked to a person's diet, rather than just another correlation fallacy.

Nutritional supplement treatment may be appropriate for major depression, bipolar disorder, schizophrenia, and obsessive compulsive disorder, the four most common mental disorders in developed countries. Supplements that have been studied most for mood elevation and stabilization include eicosapentaenoic acid and docosahexaenoic acid (each of which are an omega-3 fatty acid contained in fish oil, but not in flaxseed oil), vitamin B12, folic acid, and inositol.

Cancer: Cancer is now common in developing countries. According a study by the International Agency for Research on Cancer, "In the developing world, cancers of the liver, stomach and esophagus were more common, often linked to consumption of carcinogenic preserved foods, such as smoked or salted food, and parasitic infections that attack organs." Lung cancer rates are rising rapidly in poorer nations because of increased use of tobacco. Developed countries "tended to have cancers linked to affluence or a 'Western lifestyle' — cancers of the colon, rectum, breast and prostate — that can be caused by obesity, lack of exercise, diet and age."

Metabolic Syndrome

Several lines of evidence indicate lifestyle-induced hyperinsulinemia and reduced insulin function (i.e. insulin resistance) as a decisive factor in many disease states. For example, hyperinsulinemia and insulin resistance are strongly linked to chronic inflammation, which in turn is strongly linked to a variety of adverse developments such as arterial microinjuries and clot formation (i.e. heart disease) and exaggerated cell division (i.e. cancer). Hyperinsulinemia and insulin resistance (the so-called metabolic syndrome) are characterized by a combination of abdominal obesity, elevated blood sugar, elevated blood pressure, elevated blood triglycerides, and reduced HDL cholesterol. The negative impact of hyperinsulinemia on prostaglandin PGE1/PGE2 balance may be significant.

The state of obesity clearly contributes to insulin resistance, which in turn can cause type 2 diabetes. Virtually all obese and most type 2 diabetic individuals have marked insulin resistance. Although the association between overweight and insulin resistance is clear, the exact (likely multifarious) causes of insulin resistance remain less clear. Importantly, it has been demonstrated that appropriate exercise, more regular food intake and reducing glycemic load all can reverse insulin resistance in overweight individuals (and thereby lower blood sugar levels in those who have type 2 diabetes).

Obesity can unfavourably alter hormonal and metabolic status via resistance to the hormone leptin, and a vicious cycle may occur in which insulin/leptin resistance and obesity aggravate one another. The vicious cycle is putatively fuelled by continuously high insulin/leptin stimulation and fat storage, as a result of high intake of strongly insulin/leptin stimulating foods and energy. Both insulin and leptin normally function as satiety signals to the hypothalamus in the brain; however, insulin/leptin resistance may reduce this signal and therefore allow continued overfeeding despite large body fat stores. In addition, reduced leptin signalling to the brain may reduce leptin's normal effect to maintain an appropriately high metabolic rate.

There is a debate about how and to what extent different dietary factors— such as intake of processed carbohydrates, total protein, fat, and carbohydrate intake, intake of saturated and trans fatty acids, and low intake of vitamins/minerals—contribute to the development of insulin and leptin resistance. In any case, analogous to the way modern man-made pollution may potentially overwhelm the environment's ability to maintain homeostasis, the recent explosive introduction of high glycemic index and processed foods into the human diet may potentially overwhelm the body's ability to maintain homeostasis and health (as evidenced by the metabolic syndrome epidemic).

Hyponatremia

Excess water intake, without replenishment of sodium and potassium salts, leads to hyponatremia, which can further lead to water intoxication at more dangerous levels. A well-publicized case occurred in 2007, when Jennifer Strange died while participating in a water-drinking contest. More usually, the condition occurs in long-distance endurance events (such as marathon or triathlon competition and training) and causes gradual mental dulling, headache, drowsiness, weakness, and confusion; extreme cases may result in coma, convulsions, and death. The primary damage comes from swelling of the brain, caused by increased osmosis as blood salinity decreases. Effective fluid replacement techniques include Water aid stations during running/cycling races, trainers providing water during team games such as Soccer and devices such as Camel Baks which can provide water for a person without making it too hard to drink the water.

Fighting Malnutrition

Fighting malnutrition, mostly through fortifying foods with micronutrients (vitamins and minerals), improves lives at a lower cost and shorter time than other forms of aid, according to the World Bank. The Copenhagen Consensus, which look at a variety of development proposals, ranked micronutrient supplements as number one. However, roughly $300m of aid goes to basic nutrition each year, less than $2 for each child below two in the 20 worst affected countries. In contrast, HIV/AIDS, which causes fewer deaths than child malnutrition, received $2.2 billion—$67 per person with HIV in all countries.

Emergency Measures

Micronutrients can be obtained through fortifying foods. Fortifying foods such as peanut butter sachets and Spirulina have revolutionized emergency feeding in humanitarian emergencies because they can be eaten directly from the packet, do not require refrigeration or mixing with scarce clean water, can be stored for years and,vitally, can be absorbed by extremely ill children. The United Nations World Food Conference of 1974 declared Spirulina as 'the best food for the future' and its ready harvest every 24 hours make it a potent tool to eradicate malnutrition. Additionally, supplements, such as Vitamin A capsules or Zinc tablets to cure diarrhea in children, are used.

There is a growing realization among aid groups that giving cash or cash vouchers instead of food is a cheaper, faster, and more efficient way to deliver help to the hungry, particularly in areas where food is available but unaffordable. The UN's World Food Program, the biggest non-governmental distributor of food, announced that it will begin distributing cash and vouchers instead of food in some areas, which Josette Sheeran, the WFP's executive director, described as a "revolution" in food aid. The aid agency Concern Worldwide is piloting an method through a mobile phone operator, Safaricom, which runs a money transfer program that allows cash to be sent from one part of the country to another.

However, for people in a drought living a long way from and with limited access to markets, delivering food may be the most appropriate way to help. Fred Cuny stated that "the chances of saving lives at the outset of a relief operation are greatly reduced when food is imported. By the time it arrives in the country and gets to people, many will have died." US Law, which requires buying food at home rather than where the hungry live, is inefficient because approximately half of what is spent goes for transport. Fred Cuny further pointed out "studies of every recent famine have shown that food was available in-country — though not always in the immediate food deficit area" and "even though by local standards the prices are too high for the poor to purchase it, it would usually be cheaper for a donor to buy the hoarded food at the inflated price than to import it from abroad." Ethiopia has been pioneering a program that has now become part of the World Bank's prescribed recipe for coping with a food crisis and had been seen by aid organizations as a model of how to best help hungry nations. Through the country's main food assistance program, the Productive Safety Net Program, Ethiopia has been giving rural residents who are chronically short of food, a chance to work for food or cash. Foreign aid organizations like the World Food Program were then able to buy food locally from surplus areas to distribute in areas with a shortage of food.. Not only has Ethiopia been pioneering a program but Brazil has also established a recycling program for organic waste that benefits farmers, urban poor, and the city in general. City residents separate organic waste from their garbage, bag it, and then exchange it for fresh fruit and vegetables from local farmers. As a result, this reduces its countries waste and the urban poor get a steady supply of nutritious food..

Long Term Measures

The effort to bring modern agricultural techniques found in the West, such as nitrogen fertilizers and pesticides, to Asia, called the Green revolution, resulted in decreases in malnutrition similar to those seen earlier in Western nations. This was possible because of existing infrastructure and institutions that are in short supply in Africa, such as a system of roads or public seed companies that made seeds available. Investments in agriculture, such as subsidized fertilizers and seeds, increases food harvest and reduces food prices. For example, in the case of Malawi, almost five million of its 13 million people used to need emergency food aid. However, after the government changed policy and subsidies for fertilizer and seed were introduced against World Bank strictures, farmers produced record-breaking corn harvests as production leaped to

3.4 million in 2007 from 1.2 million in 2005, making Malawi a major food exporter. This lowered food prices and increased wages for farm workers. Proponents for investing in agriculture include Jeffrey Sachs, who has championed the idea that wealthy countries should invest in fertilizer and seed for Africa's farmers.

Breast-feeding education helps. Breast-feeding in the first two years and exclusive breast-feeding in the first six months could save 1.3 million children's lives. In the longer term, firms are trying to fortify everyday foods with micronutrients that can be sold to consumers such as wheat flour for Beladi bread in Egypt or fish sauce in Vietnam and the iodization of salt.

Restricting population size is a proposed solution. Thomas Malthus argued that population growth could be controlled by natural disasters and voluntary limits through "moral restraint." Robert Chapman suggests that an intervention through government policies is a necessary ingredient of curtailing global population growth. Garret Hardin takes an anti-immigration, isolationist approach arguing that "...all sovereign states must accept the responsibility of solving their population problems in their own territories" and that immigration acts as a sort of pressure release valve which allows countries to continue to ignore solving their population problems.

For Amaryta Sen, "no matter how a famine is caused, methods of breaking it call for a large supply of food in the public distribution system. This applies not only to organizing rationing and control, but also to undertaking work programmes and other methods of increasing purchasing power for those hit by shifts in exchange entitlements in a general inflationary situation." One suggested policy framework to resolve access issues is termed food sovereignty, the right of peoples to define their own food, agriculture, livestock, and fisheries systems in contrast to having food largely subjected to international market forces. Food First is one of the primary think tanks working to build support for food sovereignty. Neoliberals advocate for an increasing role of the free market. The World Bank itself claims to be part of the solution to malnutrition, asserting that the best way for countries to succeed in breaking the cycle of poverty and malnutrition is to build export-led economies that will give them the financial means to buy foodstuffs on the world market.

When aiming to prevent rather than treat overeating, which is also a form of malnutrition, starting in the school environment would be the perfect place as this is where the education children receive today will help them choose healthier foods during childhood, as well as into adulthood. As seen in Singapore, if we increase nutrition in school lunch programs and physical activity for children and teachers, obesity can be reduced by almost 30-50%.

Some initiatives have been done to reduce malnutrition, especially hunger. A great example has been done by Muhammad Yunus called The Grameen Bank to combat hunger. It provides small loans to help very poor women generate income and those loans can lift women out of poverty, and yet yield nutritional benefits. Some studies show when a woman is provided with an income, she will spend nearly all of it on household needs, especially food. Therefore, by focusing on women empowerment, poverty can be reduced, and also malnutrition, especially hunger can be fought.

Micro-credit initiatives focus predominantly on women because hunger disproportionately affects females more so than males. By targeting women, micro-credit initiatives strive to reduce malnutrition by promoting both employment and educational opportunities. If women are able to receive employment, they can then earn enough money to feed themselves and their families. Furthermore, if we allow girls the chance to become educated they can hopefully achieve a more equal status with men, and therefore, reduce a gender bias that men require more food than women. Ultimately, with the presence of micro-credit initiatives we can hopefully reduce the number of women who are malnourished throughout the world.

Middle East

Malnutrition rates in Iraq had risen from 19% before the US-led invasion to a national average of 28% four years later.

South Asia

According to the Global Hunger Index, South Asia has the highest child malnutrition rate of world's regions. India contributes to about 5.6 million child deaths every year, more than half the world's total. The 2006 report mentioned that "the low status of women in South Asian countries and their lack of nutritional knowledge are important determinants of high prevalence of underweight children in the region" and was concerned that South Asia has "inadequate feeding and caring practices for young children".

Half of children in India are underweight, one of the highest rates in the world and nearly double the rate of Sub-Saharan Africa.

Research on overcoming persistent under-nutrition published by the Institute of Development Studies, argues that the co-existence of India as an 'economic powerhouse' and home to one-third of the world's under-nourished children reflects a failure of the governance of nutrition: "A poor capacity to deliver the right services at the right time to the right populations, an inability to respond to citizens' needs and weak accountability are all features of weak nutrition governance."

The research suggests that to make under-nutrition history in India the governance of nutrition needs to be strengthened and new research needs to focus on the politics and governance of nutrition. At the current rate of progress the MDG1 target for nutrition will only be reached in 2043 with severe consequences for human wellbeing and economic growth.

United States

Childhood malnutrition is generally thought of as being limited to developing countries, but although most malnutrition occurs there, it is also an ongoing presence in developed nations. For example, in the United States of America, one out of every six children is at risk of hunger. A study, based on 2005-2007 data from the U.S. Census Bureau and the Agriculture Department, shows that an estimated 3.5 million children under the age of five are at risk of hunger in the United States. In developed countries, this persistent hunger problem is not due to lack of food or food programs, but is largely due to an underutilization of existing programs designed to address the issue, such as food stamps or school meals. Many citizens of rich countries such as the United States of America attach stigmas to food programs or otherwise discourage their use. In the USA, only 60% of those eligible for the food stamp program actually receive benefits. The U.S.

Department of Agriculture reported that in 2003, only 1 out of 200 U.S. households with children became so severely food insecure that any of the children went hungry even once during the year. A substantially larger proportion of these same households (3.8 percent) had adult members who were hungry at least one day during the year because of their households' inability to afford enough food.

Overeating vs. Hunger

Although a lot of the focus regarding malnutrition centres around undernourishment, overeating is also a form of malnutrition. Overeating is a lot more common in the United States, where for the majority of people, access to food is not an issue. The issue in these developed countries is choosing the right kind of food. Americans are consuming too much fast food. The reason for this mass consumption of food is the affordability and accessibility. Oftentimes the fast food, low in cost and nutrition, are high in calories and heavily promoted. That is why when these eating habits are combined with increasingly urbanized, automated, and more sedentary lifestyles, it becomes clear why gaining weight is difficult to avoid.. However, overeating is also a problem in countries where hunger and poverty persist. In China consumption of high-fat food have increased while consumption of rice and other goods have decreased.. Overeating and hunger are equally serious issues depending on what part of the world you live in. Overeating leads to many diseases such as, heart disease and diabetes, that result in death. To aid in fixing this issue of overeating, health care could recognize obesity as a disease and cover weight-loss and other nutritional interventions. An encouraging first step in this direction is Mutual of Omaha's decision to cover intensive dietary and lifestyle modification program of patients with heart disease, an initiative they hope will eliminate costly prescriptions and prevent surgeries months or years down the road. A logical next step for the industry might be to cover regular nutrition checkups, akin to dental check-ups, as part of a basic insurance coverage.

Starvation

Starvation is a severe reduction in vitamin, nutrient, and energy intake. It is the most extreme form of malnutrition. In humans, prolonged starvation can cause permanent organ damage, and eventually death. The term *inanition* refers to the symptoms and effects of starvation. According to the World Health Organization, hunger is the gravest single threat to the world's public health. The WHO also states that malnutrition is by far the biggest contributor to child mortality, present in half of all cases. According to the FAO, starvation currently affects more than one billion people or 1 in 6 people.

Common Causes

The basic cause of starvation is an imbalance between energy intake and energy expenditure. In other words: the body expends more energy than it takes in as food. This imbalance can arise from one or more medical conditions and/or circumstantial situations, which can include:

Medical Causes

- Anorexia nervosa
- Bulimia nervosa
- Coma
- Depression
- Diabetes mellitus
- Digestive disease.

Circumstantial Causes

- Famine for any reason, including overpopulation and war.
- Fasting, when done without proper medical supervision and lasting more than a month.
- Poverty
- Deprivation.

Signs and Symptoms

Individuals experiencing starvation lose substantial fat (adipose) and muscle mass as the body breaks down these tissues for energy. *Catabolysis* is the process of a body breaking down its own muscles and other tissues in order to keep vital systems such as the nervous system and heart muscle (myocardium) functioning. Vitamin deficiency is a common result of starvation, often leading to anemia, beriberi, pellagra, and scurvy. These diseases collectively can also cause diarrhoea, skin rashes, edema, and heart failure.

Individuals are often irritable and lethargic as a result. Atrophy (wasting away) of the stomach weakens the perception of hunger, since the perception is controlled by the percentage of the stomach that is empty. Victims of starvation are often too weak to sense thirst, and therefore become dehydrated.

All movements become painful due to atrophy of the muscles, and due to dry, cracked skin caused by severe dehydration. With a weakened body, diseases are commonplace. Fungi, for example, often grow under the esophagus, making swallowing unbearably painful.

The energy deficiency inherent in starvation causes fatigue and renders the victim more apathetic over time. As the starving person becomes too weak to move or even eat, his or her interaction with the surroundings diminishes.

Biochemistry

When food intake ceases, the body's glycogen stores are used up in about 24 hours. The level of insulin in circulation is low and the level of glucagon is very high. The main means of energy production is lipolysis.

Gluconeogenesis converts glycerol into glucose and the Cori cycle converts lactate into usable glucose. Two systems of energy enter the gluconeogenesis, proteolysis provides alanine and lactate produced from pyruvate. Acetyl CoA produces dissolved nutrients (Ketone bodies), which can be detected in urine and are used by the brain as a source of energy. In terms of insulin resistance, starvation conditions makes more glucose available to the brain.

Efforts

Treatment: Starving patients can be treated, but this must be done cautiously to avoid refeeding syndrome.

Prevention: For the individual, prevention obviously consists of ensuring they eat plenty of food, varied enough to provide a nutritionally complete diet. Short of sitting in front of a potentially starving person and offering him or her food, to address societal mechanisms by which people are denied access to food is a slightly more complicated matter. Supporting farmers in areas of food insecurity through such measures as free or subsidized fertilizers and seeds increases food harvest and reduces food prices.

Example of Successful Response in Malawi

For example, in Malawi, almost 5 million of its 13 million people needed emergency food aid. Then, however, deep fertilizer subsidies and lesser ones for seed, abetted by good rains, helped farmers produce record-breaking corn harvests in 2006 and 2007, according to government crop estimates.

The government reported that corn production rose from 1.2 million metric tons (mmt) in 2005, to 2.7 mmt in 2006 and 3.4 mmt in 2007. The harvest also helped the poor by lowering food prices and increasing wages for farm workers. Malawi became a major food exporter, selling more corn to the World Food Program and the United Nations than any other country in Southern Africa.

Over the 20 years prior to this change in policy, some rich nations that Malawi depended on for aid had periodically pressed it to cut back or eliminate fertilizer subsidies, in the name of free market policies.

This is despite the fact that the United States and Europe extensively subsidized their own farmers. However, many, if not most, of its farmers are too poor to afford fertilizer at market prices. Proponents for helping the farmers includes the economist Jeffrey Sachs, who has championed the idea that wealthy countries should invest in fertilizer and seed for Africa's farmers. He also conceived the Millennium Villages Project (MVP), which provides seeds and fertilizers, as well as training, to qualifying farmers. In one Kenyan village, application of this policy resulted in a tripling of its corn harvest, even though the village had previously experienced a cycle of hunger.

Many organizations have been highly effective at reducing starvation in different regions. Aid agencies give direct assistance to individuals, while political organizations pressure political leaders to enact more macro-scale policies that will reduce famine and provide aid.

Hunger Mortality Statistics

- On the average, 1 person dies every second as a result, either directly or indirectly, of hunger-4000 every hour-100 000 each day-36 million each year-58 % of all deaths (2001-2004 estimates).

- On the average, 1 child dies every 5 seconds as a result, either directly or indirectly, of hunger-700 every hour-16 000 each day-6 million each year-60% of all child deaths (2002-2008 estimates).

As Capital Punishment

Historically, starvation has been used as a death sentence. From the beginning of civilization to the Middle Ages, people were immured, or walled in, and would die for want of food.

In ancient Greco-Roman societies, starvation was sometimes used to dispose of guilty upper class citizens, especially erring female members of patrician families.

For instance, in the year 31, Livilla, the niece and daughter-in-law of Tiberius, was discreetly starved to death by her mother for her adulterous relationship with Sejanus and for her complicity in the murder of her own husband, Drusus the Younger.

Another daughter-in-law of Tiberius, named Agrippina the Elder (a granddaughter of Augustus and the mother of Caligula), also died of starvation, in 33 AD. (However, it is not clear whether her starvation was self inflicted.)

A son and daughter of Agrippina were also executed by starvation for political reasons; Drusus Caesar, her second son, was put in prison in 33 AD, and starved to death by orders of Tiberius (he managed to stay alive for nine days by chewing the stuffing of his bed); Agrippina's youngest daughter, Julia Livilla, was exiled on an island in 41 by her uncle, Emperor Claudius, and not much later, her death by starvation was arranged by the empress Messalina.

It is also possible that Vestal Virgins were starved when found guilty of breaking their vows of celibacy.

Maximilian Kolbe, a Polish friar, offered his life to save another inmate sentenced to death in the Auschwitz concentration camp. He was starved, along with another nine inmates. After two weeks of starvation, only Kolbe and three other inmates were still alive, and were executed with phenol injection.

Ugolino della Gherardesca, his sons and other members of his family were immured in the Muda, a tower of Pisa, and starved to death in the thirteenth century. Dante, his contemporary, wrote about Gherardesca in his masterpiece *The Divine Comedy*.

In Sweden in 1317, King Birger of Sweden imprisoned his two brothers for a coup they had staged several years earlier (Nyköping Banquet). A few weeks later, they died of starvation.

In Cornwall in 1671, John Trehenban from St Columb Major was condemned to be starved to death in a cage at Castle An Dinas for the murder of two girls.

Infant and young child malnutrition has profound negative consequences on the health and development of a child and thus of society. In India, a whopping 2.42 million children under the age of five die annually. There are 60 million underweight children under the age of five.

Most of these deaths are associated with infant and young child malnutrition. Worse, the survivors are not able to develop to their full potential. Malnutrition deaths in Maharashtra, astonishingly highlighted by the media, are no exception. Child malnutrition contributes to more deaths than any other health condition, globally accounting for or contributing to about six million of the 10.9 million deaths of under five children each year [*Lancet* 2003a].

We should also know that malnutrition among children occurs almost entirely during first two years of life and is virtually irreversible after that. Obviously, it tremendously impacts development outcomes, as more than 90 per cent of the brain actually develops during first two years. It impairs cognitive development, intelligence, strength, energy and productivity.

The loss of social capital is tremendous, even amongst the survivors. The negative impact it has on programmes like polio eradication makes it more serious.

In spite of these costs to the nation, workable solutions to this problem are yet to be found.

These solutions include increased spending on infant and young child nutrition during the first 24 months when malnutrition is frequent and disturbs the very foundation of life and development. Thus, evidence based and proven solutions do exist. They emerge from a clearer distinction between 'hunger' and 'malnutrition' and the knowledge that child malnutrition is directly associated with inappropriate feeding practices. This requires a shift in thinking from 'food-based' approaches towards 'family-based' feeding behaviour change. Decisions on how much to invest on infant and young child nutrition and development must now be taken. The basis of this was laid down at Copenhagen, in May 2004, when eight of the world's distinguished economists (three of them Nobel laureates) gathered to set priorities among a series of proposals to confront 10 global challenges. The experts were to address the challenges and answer the question, 'What would be the best ways of advancing global welfare, and particularly the welfare of developing countries, supposing that an additional $50 billion of resources were at governments' disposal?' These challenges included hunger and malnutrition, particularly child malnutrition. The experts examined 30 proposals and then ranked them in descending order of desirability, creating what is now known as the "Copenhagen Consensus 2004". The highest priority was given to HIV/AIDS and policies to attack hunger and malnutrition followed close behind. Additional spending on infant and child nutrition, and reducing the prevalence of low birth-weight, were among the top 17 projects accepted by the expert group.

Towards a Clearer Distinction

Hunger and malnutrition are both scandalous problems that demand solutions. Malnutrition is more often due to the lack of care or poor health rather than the lack of food. Providing food to hungry people is important but is unlikely to reduce the worst forms of child malnutrition. The main source of confusion is that while a lack of food can cause both hunger and malnutrition, malnutrition can be and is often caused by other things as well. At the Copenhagen Consensus, the expert paper on hunger and malnutrition noted though low income poverty is a significant determinant of child undernutrition, almost half of the cross country variation in the prevalence of child stunting is not explained by differences in per capita income. In Jamaica, for example, only 4.4 per cent of children are stunted, while 25-30 per cent are stunted in Albania, Peru, and the Philippines; countries in the same per capita income bracket. While there are no easy solutions, in light of the current evidence, we need to take a fresh look at the problem and find innovative answers other than the old hackneyed economic formula: 'just eliminate poverty'! The simplistic view that economic growth will automatically eliminate or reduce malnutrition has long been discredited. Rather, the view that nutrition is critical to economic growth and development, including human development, is now gaining ground. Addressing 'food security' should thus include children right from birth to two years.

Unfortunately, very few of our policy and programme managers understand infant and young child malnutrition. The media carries the same confusion. Hunger, according to its traditional Oxford dictionary definition is 'an uneasy sensation, exhausted condition, caused by want of food'. But mostly hunger is used as an alternative, even a proxy, for malnutrition and undernutrition.

This confusion is avoidable but needs careful understanding. When the term hunger is used instead of malnutrition, it sometimes leads to an emphasis on actions that are largely food and agriculture based. Yet malnutrition in young children is frequently not a problem of food availability and access to food. It is often due to the lack of optimal breast-feeding during the first two years, particularly the lack of exclusive breast-feeding during the first six months. Frequent childhood illnesses such as diarrhoea and respiratory infections, chronic diseases such as helminth infections, inadequate caring practices, and poor appetite contribute to malnutrition significantly.

Recent malnutrition deaths in Maharashtra caught attention both in print and electronic media. This made it abundantly clear how well the media and others who are responsible understand malnutrition. As one of the officers in Maharashtra, waiting to receive Arjun Singh, said on NDTV on July 15, "We will ask for allocation of higher than Re 1 for supplementary food for each child and more buildings for anganwadi centres".

The health director of the state Salunke said, "We have brought down the mortality rate from 70 per 1,000 in 1971 to 45. The root cause of malnutrition has to be tackled by other departments, like food and civil supplies."

Programmes aimed at food supplies, which often go to elder children, cannot be expected to solve this problem as this is like locking the stable after the horses have fled. When the nature of the problem is not fully understood, we seek solutions where they do not exist.

Understanding Child Malnutrition

It is important to know that child malnutrition is intimately related to inappropriate infant and young child feeding practices and occurs entirely during the first two years. There is a global as well national understanding on this association and its risk. The government of India's 10th Five-Year Plan [GoI 2002:337] document notes, "As a result of these faulty infant feeding habits, there is [a] steep increase in the prevalence of undernutrition from 11.9 per cent at less than six months, to 58.5 per cent in the 12-23 months age."

And this percentage does not change much after two years. Similarly the WHO and UNICEF developed the 'Global Strategy for Infant and Young Child Feeding', which has been adopted through resolution 55.25 of the 55th World Health Assembly in 2001. It clearly defines the problem as: Malnutrition has been responsible, directly or indirectly, for 60 per cent of the 10.9 million deaths annually among children under five.

Well over two-thirds of these deaths, which are often associated with inappropriate feeding practices, occur during the first year of life. Looking at India's situation, the infant mortality rate (IMR) is around 65 and underfive mortality rate (U-5MR) is around 95 per 1,000 born. Nearly 1.6 million of the 2.4 million under-five child deaths, die during the first year alone. And this happens year after year. Can this be called a silent tragedy?

The late James P Grant of UNICEF called it "Three Bhopals every day of the year" and no one seems to notice! Most of these deaths are preventable; but how?

Can we Save these Children?

In February 2003, researchers from several institutions met in Bellaagio [*Lancet* 2003b], Italy, to define what could be done to save the lives of approximately six million children who die annually from preventable causes. This expert group published its findings and recommendations a year ago, which show that at least one proven and practical intervention is available for preventing or treating each main cause of death among children younger than five years. If all these interventions were universally available, then something like 63 per cent of child deaths would be prevented. In other words, the interventions needed to achieve the UN mandated millennium development goal of reducing child mortality by two-thirds by 2015 are available, but they are not being delivered to the mothers and children who need them.

The group did an exercise to determine how many children could be saved from death if the current coverage levels of interventions were increased to universal coverage. According to the analysis, breast-feeding was identified as the single most effective preventive intervention, which could prevent 13 to 16 per cent of all childhood deaths in India. Adequate complementary feeding between 6 to 24 months could prevent an additional 6 per cent of all such deaths.

Solutions Lie in First Two Years

The commonly held assumption is that food insecurity is the sole or even primary cause of malnutrition. School feeding programmes have been going on for more than four decades; these cater to the needs of older children, who in fact suffer from malnutrition since they are young. Supplementary nutrition is distributed among younger children also.

India's famous Integrated Child Development Services (ICDS) programme has been sustained for 25 years and has been successful in many ways but has not made a significant dent in child malnutrition. It is because critical elements of care and education are missing as noted by the Tenth Plan document "child care and nutrition education of the mother is poor or non-existent" [GoI 2002:342].

Perhaps this is because these inputs require skill development of grass roots workers, and are time-intensive; you cannot just buy them! Thus, undernutrition is important in its own right and deserves special attention but should not be confused with hunger or food insecurity or micronutrient deficiencies (especially vitamin A, iodine and iron) which are highly prevalent among mothers, infants and young children, with often irreversible consequences.

Clearly, direct nutrition interventions before two years of age, including those to improve maternal nutritional status are therefore essential. These are critical to human development and so cannot be ignored. First, among proven cost-effective direct nutrition interventions are efforts to assure every child receives exclusive breast-feeding for the first six months, adequate and appropriate complementary feeding along with continued breast-feeding after six months to two years or beyond. It should be known to all concerned that only 40 per cent of babies under the age of six months are exclusively breastfed, ideally this percentage should be 90-100 per cent.

The Tenth Five-Year Plan sets state specific targets to improving optimal breast-feeding practices, and considers it most critical to reduce the prevalence of undernutrition and at the same time notes that it does not require additional spending [GoI 2002:360]. It is here that we need to take some positive and forward looking decisions; we can continue putting money into buying and distributing food, and in providing skills to frontline workers to counsel families on optimal feeding practices aiming at behaviour change.

It would be interesting to find out how much we spend each year on food and how much on skill building and education in this sector. Ensuring good breast-feeding practices contributes to poverty reduction. It has huge economic value. In 1993, it was estimated, "The net value of human milk currently being produced is about Rs 6,500 crore..." [Gupta and Rohde 1993].

Viewed from the perspective of an individual, the costs of artificial feeding are substantial Rs 450 is required each month to feed a healthy infant. Artificial feeding thus impacts an individuals daily spending and possible spending on the treatment of diseases. Thus it perpetuates poverty.

Poor mothers who must work are particularly vulnerable and employment conditions often do not allow young infants to accompany mothers. Worse yet, the public misperception that bottle-feeding is modern and better must be more aggressively countered.

Most communities need to be mobilised to understand the needs of women. Nutritionists agree that poor infant care and feeding should be at the top of the action list but much more than 'enabling conditions' are needed. Being vague and non-specific does not help to achieve the kind of behaviour change needed in communities.

If we continue to believe that malnutrition can be eliminated mainly by attention to agriculture and food availability; it might not happen or take a very long time. It is critical that all decisionmakers, policy and programme persons appreciate that while lack of food can cause hunger and malnutrition, the latter can have other causes that are vitally important and need to be addressed.

Food interventions in schools, besides providing meals for students could potentially be a place where pre-school children could receive food, or where it could be supplied for families to take home. To base nutritional interventions in schools overshadows present evidence-based strategies to reduce malnutrition, many of which currently enjoy much professional consensus. Most importantly, school feeding is highly unlikely to address infant feeding and young child malnutrition.

The emphasis on 'food supply' is understandable but unfortunately ineffective; it too often goes to older children. Although school feeding may be an effective educational intervention, evidence that it improves the health and nutritional status of school children is weak, and evidence for its impact on child underweight and nutritional status of other family members is non-existent [Allen and Gillespie 2001].

Moving Forward

School feeding and other supplementary feeding programmes may continue, but interventions that aim at a notable reduction in infant and child malnutrition should receive greater emphasis and more resources. Most agree that largely behaviour change interventions are required to improve the nutritional status of pre-school children, especially in the first two years of life.

It would be alarming if we fail to attend to such direct and cost saving actions to improve infant health and development. Benefits of such direct interventions during the first two years of life are proven, affordable and sustainable. The global strategy for infant and young child feeding, which was adopted at the World Health Assembly by consensus calls upon member states to act urgently to achieve improvement in infant and young child feeding practices. The costs of further non-action are virtually unaffordable in nation building. Spending on infant and young child nutrition especially on improving infant and young child feeding should be treated as an investment pillar for improved health and development outcomes as well as poverty reduction. According to the strategy:

Inappropriate feeding practices and their consequences are major obstacle[s] to sustainable socioeconomic development and poverty reduction. Governments will be unsuccessful in the efforts to accelerate economic development in any significant long-term sense until optimal child growth and development, especially through appropriate feeding practices, are ensured.

The focus on agricultural production, marketing and economic development in leading to a trickle down effect on poverty reduction has long been proven a failure. While the underlying determinants like poverty and poor health services will take time to show improvements and may continue to be tackled in a systematic way, children under the age of two cannot wait. Children are young saplings in the garden of life; to ignore and abandon them is worse than demolishing a temple, mosque or church. It is indeed self-destructive. Children make up nearly half of our citizenry – they are the ones who will soon vote, work and sustain our country. They deserve a decent start and a healthy future. It is high time to relook at child malnutrition; the answers are before us – let us act on them.

Key Actions

The Planning Commission is about to undertake a mid-term review and it would be ideal to find out if exclusive breast-feeding for the first six months is on the rise or fall. Recently, Punjab was declared number one state in *India Today*'s conclave, but it is ironical that 29 per cent of its children under the age of three are underweight and 40 per cent are stunted. Only 36.3 per cent of babies are exclusively breastfed during the first three months. Clearly the issue is not food or hunger here. The criteria for assessing the performance of states, apart from other indicators, should include how many babies are underweight below the age of two years and how many are exclusively breastfed during the first six months.

The Mumbai High Court had to direct the Maharashtra government to take immediate measures to combat the alleged malnutrition deaths. It seems that further decisions are being taken to enhance the 'food' component, however to ensure that the right steps are taken to increase spending on infant and young child nutrition, debates should happen at the state and at the National Advisory Council level. While the prime minister is conscious that no life should be lost because of the lack of care, and the finance minister is in the process of developing the country's poverty reduction strategy papers (PRSPs), it is imperative to address the issues outlined above.

We continue to hear that the lack of resources do not allow for adequate attention to infant and young child health and development. If this is true, both the prime minister and finance minister should find resources, without a conflict of interest for this vastly ignored area of human development. Maybe another cess for infant and young child nutrition, health and development could be considered. The challenges of taxation and price rises will continue to haunt us, but children need our attention. It is unfortunate that children's health and development is currently divided between two ministries; why can we not create one ministry to deal with this when we can have one on NRI affairs.

4

Development Problems and Traditional Cultures

Reflections on the Management of the Aged in India

Humans are one. They belong to a single species. They have a long history. Even in prehistoric times there were migrations, near and distant, all over the world. Seas, rivers, lakes, mountains, deserts and forests have not been able to deter human beings moving from one place to another.

Come to think of it, migrations of people like the Jarawa (a classic food-gathering and hunting Negrito group) to another island in Car Nicobar or of the Toda to the Nilgiris, or of the Ladakhi to the Ladakh region, speak about the immense capacities of human beings.

Some such movements might have been prompted by compelling natural, social or economic circumstances, but many were not. Being mobile at one stage and sedentary at another is a part of human nature.

It appears that human beings are restless in either state (Misra 1986). They are curious about themselves, about the things around and beyond them, and are ever eager to impose order on them. Apart from the immense capacity to endeavour, to learn, to innovate and to adapt to any ecological condition, they add to their cultural baggage by borrowing. Any attempt to characterise people in terms of indigenous and non-indigenous amounts to taking a very short perspective of history. Such categories, if anything, are basically political.

Dynamics of Culture

If culture is 'the way society formulates and deals with the basic problems of human existence' (Heesterman 1972:97), people living in different environments are likely to develop different cultures. But the very fact that human beings have been restless and have been migrating should indicate that they have not been satisfied with either the way they had formulated the problem of existence or the way they dealt with it.

Whatever may have been the reason, as a result of their migrations and through various means of communication people have been exposed to different cultures. Thus cultures have grown through a process of borrowing, retaining and inventing. The process is extremely complex, because even a thing like borrowing is not simple.

The borrowed item goes through cultural processing and is only then adopted. The process is further complicated by the fact that human beings attach meaning to cultural items and meanings may be multiple depending upon the context. Culture is also not a loose assemblage of discrete items; there is some degree of integration in them.

One can argue that perfect integration is never achieved, and if that should happen a culture would never change. But cultures do change, some change very rapidly and others slowly. It is possible to argue that change is to seek better integration in the culture. To achieve that, there has to be a scheme.

This scheme has to be experimental, otherwise there would not be any necessity for borrowing or inventing. In a culture, what is seen is just like the tip of an iceberg, a lot in terms of ideas, values and morals remain submerged but directs actions. All cultural practices, beliefs, ideas, morals, values and the attempts to integrate them would be senseless if the culture does not have goals perceived and defined by it.

There can be a debate about the goals, but to claim its non-existence would mean that each aspect of culture has its own autonomous and *ad hoc* existence. If that be so, all discourse about culture would be meaningless.

While working among the East Indian population in Trinidad, I noted that the Indians there have a separate identity of their own.

The Indians there were an uprooted population — they were taken there as indentured labourers, separated from their people and villages.

They were a subordinate people, coming as they did from a colonised country to another colonised country, and they had no voice. Their cultures, languages and religions were stigmatised. Those among them who changed their religion were the favoured lot. In spite of all these odds, they were able to reconstruct a culture of their own and establish their identity. This culture is certainly different from what they brought with them but very distinct from what the local culture is.

Analysing these developments, I had written, 'in order to do what a culture does, it may adopt several strategies. It may allow individuals and some groups within to play intervening roles of bridge or buffer between the dominant groups in a multi-ethnic situation.

Then there may be some issues which may cut across the individuals and groups. Such groups, individuals and issues to some extent are responsible for the large systems to function and at the same time allow the specific cultures to play the roles they have defined for themselves'. Culture, in the long run, seems to be indestructible unless by some catastrophe. It has the capacity to regenerate itself around some ideas, some symbols, some institutions and activities.

In the case of the Trinidad Indians I have shown that their population size, acquiring land, forming uni-ethnic villages, political actions to protect their interests, formation of the Indian association, struggling to get some of their rituals recognised, collecting contributions for the Bengal relief fund, arrival of Indian films and music, visitors from India, attempts at reviving rituals, performance of community worship, building temples and mosques, building networks through pandits and *tharia-lota*, were used to form a community of their own (*ibid*). Whatever they have constructed has to cope with external pressures and inner conflicts. It is not that culture resolves all conflicts. In fact, culture may regenerate itself, weaving its way through conflicts. In Trinidad, for example, the Indians have constructed a kind of duality of 'inner' and 'outer' lives to cope with the apparently contradictory Indian and Western values.

A couple of decades ago Singer, in his study of the Indian joint family in modern industry, made a similar observation: 'Structural change and structural persistence are not mutually exclusive phenomena, they both are occurring simultaneously' (1968:438). In a detailed study of nineteen outstanding industrial families he found that there was a clear-cut separation of work and residence. The home becomes the sphere of religion and traditional values, while office and factory become the sphere of business and modern values. He calls this separation compartmentalisation. 'Compartmentalisation is an adaptive process which permits the incorporation of innovative patterns of thought and behaviour associated with modern industry without too direct a collision with traditional modes of thought and behaviour'.

A study of development programmes initiated by the Government of India among five tribal groups in south India indicated that the response of each group was different (Misra 1982). In another study it was noted that of the two tribes inhabiting the same ecological region, one tribe totally rejected most of the development programmes while the other accepted them with some enthusiasm (Misra 1970). It was found that acceptance and rejection of specific development programmes were correlated to the social structure and values of the respective tribes. This was significant because both the groups were very poor and barely managed their existence by food gathering, some agriculture and extraction of minor forest products. Yet both the groups were very concerned about their cultures and retaining their respective identities.

Even in a situation where there were enormous existential difficulties, Thorbek, in her study of a slum in Sri Lanka, found that the slum dwellers there were more concerned with their relations with spouses, children, mothers, relatives, neighbours, performance of rituals and what was right and wrong, than with money alone, in short with their culture and values (1994).

Cultural Variety

Elsewhere too, particularly in the emergence of ethnic conflict all over the world, it has been noted that cultures cannot be changed or preserved at will. The indirect evidence of the existence of the immense varieties of cultures all over the world in spite of powerful forces unleashed by modernisation supports the above hypothesis. Culture has its own internal dynamics. Each culture, in a way, is unique. In the process of its growth it develops its own emphasis. These emphases make each culture appear different. They allow people to feel 'good' and 'satisfied'.

Thinking of the varieties of culture and their interrelations, the image that comes to mind is that of an unspoiled tropical forest where there are immense trees, plants and creepers, growing in and out of each other, together providing shelter and nourishment to innumerable varieties of creatures. The whole is a system but each element in it has its own identity and function. For obvious reasons this imagery cannot be pushed too far in understanding human societies, yet keeping it in view I would like to make the following points.

The individual culture is part of a larger system. The relevance and meaning of the individual culture can be appreciated and fully understood only in the context of the larger system. Deviation from this perspective leads to distortion in understanding, though it is true that big and strong societies have grown at the expense of small and weak ones. It is difficult to conceive of a world which has a uniform culture.

None can deny that despite pressures even the small and weak have been able to maintain their cultural identities. By this I do not mean that they have remained static. Far from it, they too have been adapting and changing, and also influencing the larger system through a complex process of inter-culturation.

The very fact that cultural variety has existed both in time and space shows that there are innumerable ways to formulate and deal with the problem of human existence. The larger system, if it is a system, has to be connected with its constituent parts – howsoever remote and thin these connections may be. This way the distinctions between endogenous and exogenous models of development, tradition and modernity, become dim. It is true that cultures cannot be kept isolated. It was not possible in the past and is much less possible now in the wake of the communications revolution.

Culture and Development

This is the era of development. The world has been divided into developed and developing. The developing are exhorted to hasten and catch up with the developed. All kinds of packages have been created so that the developing world is able to meet at least the basic needs of its people. Meanwhile, in spite of all pious thoughts and plans, the gap between developed and developing within and between states has widened.

This has increased anxiety the world over, particularly on account of the realisation that the world is an integrated system. The problems of one region, whether they are ecological, social, economic or political, are bound to affect the other regions too.

There is yet another realisation, that development without intense humanism is self-destructive — it is the Hiroshima path. The situation now is far more dangerous than it was fifty years ago. Several countries have developed perilous capacities.

Now the crucial question is whether it is possible to break or change the direction of development. One of the ways that has been suggested is to bring the required thrust of humanism into the development process. In this volume Kasai writes that tradition should continue to guide individuals and societies in their search for a just order and society, and development should supply more effective means for their search. But in Japan, he writes, tradition was exploited for just the opposite ends.

There is enough evidence from all over the world that culture has been used for economic development and hegemonic tendencies. Even Kasai, after expounding the profoundest thoughts of Japanese tradition, ends by saying that the events of the past are the reminders of the violence of the development. Why does this happen? It is seen that in practice development means material advancement. All the great thoughts about developing the finer aspects of human beings do not get translated into reality. They remain in the books.

Even if it was intended, no one would know how to go about it. Therefore a peculiar situation prevails: while human beings can boast of tremendous material development, the same cannot be said about their own quality. They remain the same while they are expected to help in establishing a just order. For the same reason the matter of establishing a just order cannot be left to culture or tradition, as the context has considerably changed. Both traditional thought and modern experience will have to be focused on human development.

Human Heritage

Right from the time human beings became cultural beings, they have been exploring the external universe and making internal arrangements of living. Over time such discoveries and arrangements have become part of the human heritage. It will be futile to argue whether fire or the innumerable varieties of food that we consume, or the various tools that we use, or the idea of counting, or the families in which we live, were found in east, west, north or south.

What was found suitable was adopted with appropriate modifications by different cultures. In the same way modern discoveries are becoming part of the cultures of big and small countries.

While such developments have apparently made life easier, they have thrown up many new, serious and urgent challenges before mankind, such as the phenomenal rise of human population, environmental pollution, demographic transition, etc. In this paper I intend to focus on the problems caused by demographic transition, resulting in the rise of the population of the aged. I argue that the management of the aged raises the issue of human development.

Demographic Transition

A significant change has been taking place in the demographic structure of various countries. Their populations have been ageing. It is a dynamic phenomenon. It means more rapid increase of the proportion of old people as compared to other age segments. Till recently it was thought to be a problem of the developed countries, but now it is becoming a problem of the developing countries also. 'In 1985, there had been 427 million elderly persons (aged 60 and above) accounting for 8.8 per cent of world population.

In relative terms, demographic aging was most advanced in the more developed countries where the elderly accounted for 16 per cent of total population as opposed to 7 per cent in the less developed countries'. An international symposium on population structure and development recognised that population ageing was taking place in the context of a rapidly increasing total world population. 'Growing from an estimated 2.5 billion in 1950, it had reached 4.8 billion in 1985 and was projected to reach 8.2 billion in 2025'. In India, the ageing process of the population is yet to set in full swing since fertility has not come down significantly; but that is no relief as in absolute terms there were more than 43 million people above the age of 60 in 1981.

The percentage of persons in the age group of 60+ in 1961 was 4.57, in 1981 it was 5.14, and in 2001 it is likely to be 7.11. That is, the population of the aged in the country is already large and is going to be larger still, which is a consequence of development. What problems and issues does this demographic change bring forth?

Problems and Issues

The rise in the number of those who are 'non-productive' and who do not generate any 'hope' immediately raises an economic problem. It is also a social problem: Who is going to provide support to them and how? Apart from food and shelter, the old need care and medicines. They also crave love and tender care. They would like to interact, be heard, be visible, and would like a bit of space of their own and have a constructive and creative role to play in society. Among the old, the problems of old women, single, divorced and widowed, are different from those of old men. In a column in a newspaper an elderly male wrote: I am 65 years old and I lost my wife about two years ago. But for the feeling of loneliness which has me in its grip every once in a while, I am happily placed in life. My children are happily married and settled. They look after me well but have their limitations.

I am beginning to feel that it will become difficult to cope with life without a partner. Much of life's charm has indeed vanished ever since the death of my wife. I feel like I have everything and yet nothing. I agree with 'Mr K.', who felt that widowers and widows could lead a happier life if they have companions to avoid loneliness. And especially at a senior age, the need for a partner to share life with intensifies greatly. In today's social context, however, elderly widows and widowers have little choice but to suffer silently.

In the same paper another old person wrote, 'I am a single senior citizen and I feel there are many facets to the problems of single elderly people in our society. It concerns widowers, widows as well as bachelors and single women in advanced age groups. Harking back to past traditions and past family systems cannot be solutions'. Apart from the problems of the reasonably healthy elderly, the problems of the disabled and senile are of a very special kind.

Ageing Marginalised

There are not many studies focusing on these problems. A quick glance at the available literature indicates that Indian society does not even realise that a serious human, social and economic problem is at hand which needs immediate specialised attention.

The Western response to the problem has been liberating the old from various kinds of filial responsibilities, making them economically as viable as possible and handing over the problems of health and care to specialised institutions. In the United States of America, apart from schemes of pension, insurance and retirement benefits, the health care of the aged is linked with the social security system. Mobile home service for the aged has been devised in order to lessen the pressure on institutions and costly nursing homes. How exactly these institutions work and what problems the old people under these schemes face are a different matter. However, it is clear that while these institutions can meet the material needs of the aged, they cannot do much when it comes to love, warmth, and the desire to be heard and to be visible.

The Indian Situation

In India the situation is far more complex. An overwhelming number of people live in rural areas but migration from rural to urban areas is substantial, which creates problems for the ageing at both ends. If children go to urban areas leaving behind the aged in the rural areas, that creates one set of problems, and if the old are taken along, it creates another set of problems.

The growth of the urban population and urban centres have been haphazard, and there are acute shortages of housing and other facilities. The health care system is woefully inadequate and there is hardly any specialised agency focusing on the old. There are no programmes available to train people taking care of the aged. In other words, the entire responsibility of taking care of the old continues to be with the traditional institution of the family.

Biswas's study of 13 villages in Giridih district of Bihar conducted at two points in time shows that an overwhelming number of the aged lived with their sons — 90.32 per cent in 1960 and 88.36 per cent in 1982. There were very few who decided to live with their daughters. Biswas writes, 'In substance, therefore, sons were the first choice for old age care, and they were often referred to as old age insurance for which property was transferred to [them] as premium'. In the same study it is pointed out that 14.29 per cent old men and 57.78 per cent old women were dissatisfied with the care and service they got.

Of those in ill health, a third of the men and more than half the women felt that they were not properly cared for. As regards the interpersonal relations of the ageing with the other members of their families, the study found that a majority of them were bound by bonds of reciprocal respect and love, irrespective of complaints about accommodation, food and care. Dissatisfaction was greater among those who were fully dependent on their supporters. It grew keener and more bitter with age. Ageing women as a rule were neglected.

The study highlights that in the rural areas the families of male children provide care and support to the aged. They are bound by traditional norms of respect and love. But now they are getting increasingly marginalised.

Ageing in Urban Areas

In urban areas the problems get further accentuated. Community support is weak and the kin network is diffused over a large area and relatively ineffective. The entire responsibility of support and care of the ageing falls on the male children with whom the ageing live.

The composition of the family in urban areas is becoming nuclear and smaller, as a result of which there are fewer people available in the house to provide care and comfort to the ageing. Those who are available are torn apart by the stresses of urban living. Women too in the urban areas are now working outside the family. They have fixed schedules of work and have other pressures on them. Children are loaded with their studies, competitive examinations and concerns for making their careers.

The authority that the ageing exercised on their children in the past as a result of greater experience has almost vanished, and the aged are now told, 'You don't know'. There are several reasons for this admonishment. First, the children of the ageing are not in the same profession. Second, the quantum of information which their children claim to have makes the ageing look almost primitive. Third, the whole techno-economic situation has now completely changed, which leaves the ageing bewildered and redundant. When paucity of accommodation, high cost of living, general stress and tensions at all levels are added to these, the problems of the aged are extremely serious.

Discussion

The ageing pose a serious human problem. Since they are considered 'non-productive' and as they also do not generate any hope, it is all the more necessary that serious attention be paid to them. They raise moral questions and direct our attention towards transcendental values. In the past, ageing was not a serious issue and societies did not give it priority. They dealt with it as a natural phenomenon. Family members were responsible for the care and management of the old. But now the situation is different. The size of the people in the ageing category is already bulging and it is growing very fast.

The problems posed by ageing are by no means accidental and isolated. They have grown as a result of the development process itself. The entire emphasis of development is on individual success, career promotion, entrepreneurship, investment, capital building and profit. In such a scheme of things, there is hardly any scope for thoughts about human development. At family, community and government levels the problems of the ageing get no or very low priority. It is taken for granted that the problem will get solved on its own or that it is a problem of individual families, with communities and governments having nothing to do with it.

The family, where the ageing are supposed to get care and comfort, is on the rocks and in any case shrinking. The members of the family are spread around in pursuit of their careers.

The old, on their part, are not getting detached either. They think that they are going to live for ever and that in any case this is not the time to quit. The ideas of *vanaprastha* and *samnyasa* are too remote and idealistic. They are bored looking after grandchildren, listening to religious discourses and devotional music, making rounds of holy places or just sitting before the small screen. They seek companionship, appropriate creative and constructive roles. Modern societies are following an ostrich-like policy in this regard. The Western solution to the problem has been old age homes, pensions, social security and health care. No doubt these are important steps, but these programmes are caught up in the conceptual groove that the old have lived their lives and at best they need some material comforts. In any case the old are marginal, backyard people and come in the category of waste. This attitude is exactly what development has to avoid. Development that does not develop the sensitivities and quality of human beings is a potential monster, a Hiroshima.

The management and care of the old illustrates this point very well. A concern for non-productive people, sparing a thought for those who have been consigned as waste, would resolve most doubts about development. Development in the last analysis should mean enhancing the capacity of people to establish a just society.

In India even systematic thinking as to what should be the policy towards the ageing has not begun. At this stage in history the country is caught up in the whirlpool of market forces and resultant consumerism. Consumerism thrives on waste and decay. Consumer as well as producer know very well that this kind of development is not sustainable. A shift from consumption to conservation, from individual to community, is bound to take place, which will be in keeping with the Indian ethos. It is possible to be modern with the emphasis on conservation and focus on the community. This point gets very well illustrated in the management of the ageing.

Taking care of the aged means highlighting the importance of conservation and humanitarianism. It will also strengthen the community, for the aged can be best taken care of within the fold of the family, bound by filial rights, duties and obligations. There is no institution that can replace the family but there is room to build into it the ideas of equality, justice and freedom. All this will not happen automatically. The focus has to be human development. That will provide new strength to the family and further support from the community. The old and infirm may find loving care.

As far as the ageing of the disabled and senile is concerned, apart from giving them specialised attention through nursing homes and mobile health units, family members will have to be trained in their care. It is to be borne in mind that care cannot be given by mere emotions and a sense of obligation. There has to be proper understanding of the problem and of the remedial measures which can be provided by modern knowledge of health and medicine. Thus a combination of modern knowledge and intense feeling for those who are non-productive can provide physical and emotional comfort to the old.

Voluntary Work-What's it all About?

The main feature of this sector is the lack of profit and the dedication to a particular cause. The voluntary sector in the UK currently has a turnover of £20 billion and continues to grow. The type of experience that can be gained is very varied. There are many opportunities ranging from working in an administrative or commercial capacity such as in marketing to practical work such as environmental field projects, campaigning, fundraising or shop-work.

Some volunteering opportunities require people to offer individual support to groups or people such as those with illnesses or disabilities.

Benefits of Volunteering

- *Learning new skills* – these can include practical skills as well as 'soft' skills such as communication, time management and problem solving.
- *Experience* – you can gain valuable experience for an area that you would like a career in, for example teaching, PR or social work. The same is true if you need experience to be considered for a vocational course. Volunteering also offers you a 'safe' environment in which to test out certain career areas to see if they are something that you wish to pursue.
- *Meeting new people*-volunteering allows you to meet people outwith your own social circle. These can be students from other degree courses and universities, people in a different age group from you and people from different backgrounds. It can be a chance to find out more about the community you live in outside of university. In these situations you will no doubt form friendships but you will also find this an opportunity for you to network now and in the future.

- *Giving something back*-for some people volunteering is entirely altruistic.
- *Learning more about a cause*-if there is a cause that you have a special affinity with, then through volunteering with a relevant organisation you can learn more about it.
- *Improving confidence and feeling of self-worth*-being an important part of a team or being highly valued by an individual you are working with can do wonders for your self-esteem.

It is important to remember that all types of employers view volunteering as just as valuable, and in some cases more valuable than, paid work.

If you are interested in making a career in the voluntary sector see the section on Charities and Voluntary Organisations and also Development Work and Emergency Planning.

Thinking about Becoming a Volunteer

What's in it for me?

- a sense of personal fulfilment?
- an opportunity to 'give something back'?
- involvement in the community?
- the chance to meet new people?
- to acquire new skills?
- the opportunity to explore new areas of work; test out suitability and commitment before making career decisions?
- necessary pre-course experience?
- enhancing your CV?

Don't be surprised if your reasons are partly altruistic and partly self-beneficial. Voluntary organisations are well aware that volunteers need to gain something for themselves from the experience.

What Can I Offer?

- *Personal qualities*-projects seeking volunteers tend to value enthusiasm, new ideas and hard work more than specific skills. People skills — cheerfulness, patience and understanding — are most important.

- *Expertise*-particular abilities will always be welcomed. Conservation projects appeal to those with practical or technical skills. Teaching, advisory and counselling activities demand high levels of communication skills. Being able to drive could be a useful asset.
- *Affinity*-support for a cause, concern for a special project or group of people or sharing the aims, objectives and values of a specific organisation could lend support to your desire to be a volunteer.
- *Time commitment*-how much time can you realistically spare? Some voluntary projects may only need you on an 'as and when available' basis. Others, particularly when working in a supporting or teaching capacity or when specific training is offered, will look for regular and sustained involvement. You may need to agree a mutual trial period with the voluntary organisation.

Possible Downsides

It is also important to think about what some people regard as the more negative side of volunteering. For some the lack of contact with the people you are helping can be dispiriting, for example if you are working in the UK office of an overseas development agency.

You also have to think about the work you will be doing and whether you will find it too emotionally distressing or stressful.

You are welcome to discuss any aspects of volunteering with a careers adviser.

Volunteering in the UK

Types of Work

- *Social care*-Typical roles include: advice worker (e.g. advising on consumer, legal and employment issues); drug user support worker; kitchen assistant for homeless people; project organiser. (N.B. Information on working in social care can be found in the careers websites section under *Social, Guidance and Community Work (B)).*
- *Environment and Animals*-Typical roles include: conservation volunteer; researcher; animal fosterer;

farming assistant; rescue worker; fundraiser. (N.B. Information on working with the environment and animals can be found in the careers websites section under *Natural Resources and the Environment (R)* and *Animal and Plant Resources (S))*.

- *Education and Youth Work*-Typical roles include: literacy/numeracy tutor; IT tutor; Girl Guides/Scout leader; youth leader; student tutor in schools. (N.B. Information on careers working in education and youth work can be found in the careers websites section under *Education (A)* and *Social, Guidance and Community Work (B))*.
- *Children and Families*-Typical roles include: befriender; childsitter; telephone counsellor; crèche worker; mentor. (N.B. Information on careers working with children and families can be found in the careers websites section under *Social, Guidance and Community Work (B))*.
- *Health*-Typical roles include: hospital "buddy" (i.e. providing friendship to people in long term care); information officer; providing therapeutic care (e.g. massages for those in hospitals, hospices and respite care); ward helpers; care worker. (N.B. Information on careers in health can be found in the careers websites section under *Health Care and Psychology (C))*.
- *Arts, Sports and Culture*-Typical roles include: music group facilitator; choir organiser; crafts group support assistant; historic house guide; lifeguard; sports coach; referee. (N.B. Information on arts, sports and culture can be found in the careers websites section under *Publishing, Media and Performing Arts (Y), Leisure, Sport and Tourism (F)* and *Information, Patents and Heritage Management (W))*.
- *Equality*-Typical roles include: web designer; committee member; administrator.
- *Community Development*-Typical roles include: community radio staff; assistant in children and women's groups; journalist (community magazines/newspapers).
- *Working with the Elderly*-Typical roles include: IT teacher; mini bus driver; café assistant; social club helper; day care assistant.

Issues to Consider

Before you get started you should be clear about how much time you can devote. If you are studying you should remember that your workload will vary throughout the year and you do not want to disappoint anyone when you are under pressure and are unable to volunteer.

If you find an opportunity that you are interested in you should find out as much as you can about it. Most projects will have a volunteer manager or coordinator and they should be able to give you a good explanation of what your role will be.

If you are keen to volunteer in a different part of the UK, there are plenty of residential placements that exist. The length of these range from a week to a year. Find out in advance as much as you can about what the placement will involve so that things like the standard of accommodation or number of hours you are requested to work don't come as a surprise when you get there!

Volunteering in the Edinburgh Area

Here are some starting points for finding out about the huge variety of opportunities that exist to volunteer in Edinburgh:

- *SAGE*-any volunteering opportunities that the Careers Service is made aware of are advertised on SAGE. SAGE is updated daily so you should check it regularly.
- *Student Volunteer Centre*-provides information and advice for University of Edinburgh students (and staff) who are considering volunteering in Edinburgh, the UK or abroad. The centre can also help student **voluntary groups.** They are based at 5/1 Bristo Square and are open for you just to drop in.
- *Volunteer Centre Edinburgh*-acts as a placement and advice service for volunteers in Edinburgh. Their website contains a searchable database of current opportunities.
- *Student Societies*-many student societies are involved in local volunteering projects.
- *LEAPS (Lothians Equal Access Programme for Schools)*-aims to increase participation in higher education amongst students from non-traditional backgrounds through a programme that includes a pre-application interview and

enquiry service, school and university-based events and an eight-week summer school for school leavers. Student volunteers are welcome and the experience is especially useful if you are thinking about going into a teaching/ social work career.

- *Power of 5*-this website is aimed at 16-25 year olds in Edinburgh who want to find out more information about volunteering. The site has case studies of current volunteers and details of how to get involved in volunteering.

Volunteering Overseas

Benefits

Volunteering overseas has all the benefits of volunteering in the UK as well as providing the opportunity to experience a new culture and country.

Many volunteering placements have the option of travelling after the placement has ended. A large number of placements take place in rural locations and provide you with the opportunity to see areas off the beaten track. By working and/or living with local people you will learn a lot about the culture of a country and, potentially, a new language.

You should bear in mind that it will take you longer to organise a volunteer placement overseas than it would in the UK so make sure that you allow yourself enough time.

Types of Work

What you could be doing overseas is very varied. The main types of volunteer work that students and graduates are involved in are:

- *Conservation*-projects include monitoring species populations and habitats on land and in the sea. Some projects also include an educational element, for example you would teach the importance of conservation to local people. (N.B. Information on careers in conservation can be found in the careers websites section under *Natural Resources and the Environment (R)).*
- *Construction*-building places that will benefit whole communities, such as schools, community centres and houses. (N.B. Information on careers in construction can

be found in the careers websites section under *Construction, Civil Engineering and Property (Q)).*

- *Teaching/Education*-this includes teaching English, sports and music to young children through to adults. Health education is also a popular area to volunteer in and can often be done in conjunction with a teaching placement. (N.B. Information on careers in education can be found in the careers websites section under *Education (A)).*
- *Youth Work*-includes working with children in orphanages, children with disabilities and street children. (N.B. Information on youth work can be found in the careers websites section under *Social, Guidance and Community Work (B)).*
- *Social and Community Work*-working in a community, sometimes with specific groups, such as women, to promote awareness of a wide range of issues. (N.B. Information on social and community work can be found in the careers websites section under *Social, Guidance and Community Work (B)).*
- *Healthcare*-using skills already gained in healthcare in projects overseas. Medical students early on in their studies can be involved in some projects. (N.B. Information on healthcare can be found in the careers websites section under *Health Care and Psychology (C)).*

Cost and Length of Placement

You will find that most overseas placements will require you to pay something towards taking part (sometimes called a 'donation'). This is usually to cover things like accommodation, food, travel within the country and insurance (n.b. flights aren't always included in the cost). Some placements can be quite pricey so it makes sense to 'shop around' and find exactly where your money would be going. How much you pay is usually dependent on how long you intend to be volunteering for.

The length of placements varies, from a week to a year. It is unusual to find placements that last longer than twelve months and those that do are usually for specialist roles such as medics and engineers. It is the policy of the Careers Service not to advertise placements on SAGE where costs seem excessive compared to other similar placements. However, we can take no responsibility for organisations, the work or the costs involved.

Research and Fund-raising

Research the organisation: Before signing up for anything it is essential that you have fully researched the organisation and what you will actually be doing once you are overseas. You should read Some Basic Questions to Ask Before Accepting an Overseas Placement.

Try to get in contact with previous volunteers and don't just rely on information in promotional literature or on websites. Some voluntary organisations hold information events where previous volunteers are on hand to talk about their experiences.

Find out how much support you will have from the organisation when you are overseas and what they do to help volunteers if there is an emergency. It is worth thinking about whether your placement will result in a local person being denied a job. Most organisations will strive to avoid this happening.

Fund-raising

The amount that you require for your placement will probably mean that you will have to do some fund-raising. Voluntary organisations should be able to help you with fund-raising by providing ideas and suggesting possible sources of funds. You may find it useful to look at our funding information. We also keep lots of helpful reference books which relate to funding. We also have the program FunderFinder on our PCs, which can help you identify suitable potential sources of financial help. The University's Scholarships and Student Finance office may also be able to help.

How you find the funds to be able to do your placement is very much part of the whole experience and you will find that you will gain a wide range of valuable skills from this exercise alone. It is essential that you allow enough time for your fund-raising.

Emergency/Relief Work

Many people are attracted to the idea of being involved in emergency/relief work overseas. While this is quite understandable it is important to bear in mind a couple of points. This type of work is usually carried out by highly qualified specialists which the country in crisis either does not have or does not have enough of. This will include professions such as firefighters, engineers and healthcare professionals. Even if there is a need for semi-skilled or unskilled workers it is preferable that these positions are filled by local people. If you are interested in this kind of work it may be useful to have a look at the RedR website. RedR is an international organisation which assists frontline organisations with finding personnel.

Non-Governmental Organization

Non-governmental organization (NGO) is a term that has become widely accepted as referring to a legally constituted, non-governmental organization created by natural or legal persons with no participation or representation of any government. In the cases in which NGOs are funded totally or partially by governments, the NGO maintains its non-governmental status and excludes government representatives from membership in the organization.

Unlike the term *intergovernmental organization*, "non-governmental organization" is a term in general use but is not a legal definition. In many jurisdictions these types of organization are defined as "civil society organizations" or referred to by other names.

The number of internationally operating NGOs is estimated at 40,000. National numbers are even higher: Russia has 277,000 NGOs. India is estimated to have between 1 million and 2 million NGOs.

History

National NGOs go back to antiquity. International non-governmental organizations have a history dating back to at least 1839. Rotary, later Rotary International, was founded in 1905. It has been estimated that by 1914 there were 1083 NGOs. International NGOs were important in the anti-slavery movement and the movement for women's suffrage, and reached a peak at the time of the World Disarmament Conference. However, the phrase "non-governmental organization" only came into popular use with the establishment of the United Nations Organization in 1945 with provisions in Article 71 of Chapter 10 of the United Nations Charter for a consultative role for organizations which are neither governments nor member states—see Consultative Status. The definition of "international NGO" (INGO) is first given in resolution 288 (X) of ECOSOC on February 27, 1950: it is defined as "any international organization that is not founded by an international treaty". The vital role of NGOs and other "major groups" in sustainable development was recognized in Chapter 27 of Agenda 21, leading to intense arrangements for a consultative relationship between the United Nations and non-governmental organizations.

Rapid development of the non-governmental sector occurred in western countries as a result of the processes of restructurization of the welfare state. Further globalization of that process occurred after the fall of the communist system and was an important part of the Washington consensus.

Globalization during the 20th century gave rise to the importance of NGOs. Many problems could not be solved within a nation. International treaties and international organizations such as the World Trade Organization were perceived as being too centred on the interests of capitalist enterprises. Some argued that in an attempt to counterbalance this trend, NGOs have developed to emphasize humanitarian issues, developmental aid and sustainable development. A prominent example of this is the World Social Forum which is a rival convention to the World Economic Forum held annually in January in Davos, Switzerland. The fifth World Social Forum in Porto Alegre, Brazil, in January 2005 was attended by representatives from more than 1,000 NGOs. Some have argued that in forums like these, NGOs take the place of what should belong to popular movements of the poor. Others argue that NGOs are often imperialist in nature, that they sometimes operate in a racialized manner in dominant countries, and that they fulfil a similar function to that of the clergy during the high colonial era. The philosopher Peter Hallward argues that they are an aristocratic form of politics. However, this philosophy would suggest that organizations of indigenous peoples are not represented, which is untrue. Whatever the case, NGO transnational networking is now extensive.

Types of NGOs

Apart from "NGO", often alternative terms are used as for example: independent sector, volunteer sector, civil society, grassroots organizations, transnational social movement organizations, private voluntary organizations, self-help organizations and non-state actors (NSA's).

Non-governmental organizations are a heterogeneous group. A long list of acronyms has developed around the term "NGO".

These Include

- *CSO:* short for civil society organization;
- *DONGO:* Donor Organized NGO;
- *ENGO:* short for environmental NGO, such as Global 2000;
- *GONGO:* are government-operated NGOs, which may have been set up by governments to look like NGOs in order to qualify for outside aid or promote the interests of the government in question;
- *INGO:* stands for international NGO; Oxfam is an international NGO
- *QUANGO:* are quasi-autonomous non-governmental organizations, such as the International Organization for Standardization (ISO).

(The ISO is actually not purely an NGO, since its membership is by nation, and each nation is represented by what the ISO Council determines to be the 'most broadly representative' standardization body of a nation. That body might itself be a nongovernmental organization; for example, the United States is represented in ISO by the American National Standards Institute, which is independent of the federal government. However, other countries can be represented by national governmental agencies; this is the trend in Europe.)

- *TANGO:* short for technical assistance NGO;
- *GSO:* Grassroots Support Organization
- *MANGO:* short for market advocacy NGO.

There are also numerous classifications of NGOs. The typology the World Bank uses divides them into Operational and Advocacy:

The primary purpose of an operational NGO is the design and implementation of development-related projects.

One frequently used categorization is the division into *relief-oriented* versus *development-oriented* organizations; they can also be classified according to whether they stress service delivery or participation; or whether they are religious or secular; and whether they are more public or private-oriented. Operational NGOs can be community-based, national or international. The primary purpose of an Advocacy NGO is to defend or promote a specific cause. As opposed to operational project management, these organizations typically try to raise awareness, acceptance and knowledge by lobbying, press work and activist events.

USAID refers to NGOs as *private voluntary organisations*. However many scholars have argued that this definition is highly problematic as many NGOs are in fact state and corporate funded and managed projects with professional staff. NGOs exist for a variety of reasons, usually to further the political or social goals of their members or funders. Examples include improving the state of the natural environment, encouraging the observance of human rights, improving the welfare of the disadvantaged, or representing a corporate agenda. However, there are a huge number of such organizations and their goals cover a broad range of political and philosophical positions. This can also easily be applied to private schools and athletic organizations.

Methods

NGOs vary in their methods. Some act primarily as lobbyists, while others primarily conduct programs and activities. For instance, an NGO such as Oxfam, concerned with poverty alleviation, might provide needy people with the equipment and skills to find food and clean drinking water, whereas an NGO like the FFDA helps through investigation and documentation of human rights violations and provides legal assistance to victims of human rights abuses. Others, such as Afghanistan Information Management Services, provide specialized technical products and services to support development activities implemented on the ground by other organizations.

Public Relations

Non-governmental organizations need healthy relationships with the public to meet their goals. Foundations and charities use sophisticated public relations campaigns to raise funds and employ standard lobbying techniques with governments. Interest groups may be of political importance because of their ability to influence social and political outcomes.

5

Rehabilitating and Preventing Aspect of Social Work with Families

The Time and the Action

The international community recently realized that certain types of emergency assistance could have negative effects on the still to come development phases. In that context, a theme has been brought under the limelight: the "emergency-development continuum", underlying the need to design the activities in time of crisis taking into account the following stages. The hypothesis presented here tries to go a few steps further: the relationship between an emergency and development starts long before the crisis erupts and lasts long after it has ended. The analysis must therefore focus on four main points:

- What preventive and/or preparatory measures should be taken in times of peace?
- Emergency action: when, why and how should it be started and how should it be phased out?
- The various aspects of rehabilitation during and after the conflict.
- What should be done when peace has finally been restored and the guns fall silent (the final phase in the progression from emergency to development)?

A Unique Organization : The ICRC

It is doubtless useful to recall briefly the unique and often little known nature of the International Committee of the Red Cross (ICRC). Although it is a non-governmental organization, the

ICRC has been entrusted with its mandates by the explicit authority of the 185 States party to the Geneva Conventions and of those States which have signed the Additional Protocols of 1977.

Furthermore, the ICRC is part of a much broader "family", the International Red Cross and Red Crescent Movement, which is composed of the ICRC, the National Red Cross and Red Crescent Societies, and their Federation. Of the members of this family, the ICRC plays a special role in the event of conflict.

This international Movement is governed by a clear and specific ethical code based on the set of Fundamental Principles it has adopted, the most important of which are humanity, neutrality, impartiality, independence and universality. For 150 years, the ICRC's raison d'être has been the protection of war victims, and relief work is one facet of this task.

Societies Disrupted by Conflict

The wars waged in today's world seek to undermine established structures and values, often attained through arduous endeavour. A few air raids or artillery attacks, a rumble of tanks, an exchange of gunfire or knifings, and nothing is left but rack and ruin.

Until the mid-1980s, things were fairly simple: there were the soldiers, and there were civilians. Since then the rules seem to have disappeared.

All kill and are killed without distinction. We seem to have reverted to the old style of warfare that prevailed before the coming of the nation state: one human being kills another simply because he is different; and the goal is destruction not victory.

Conflicts arising from political and ethnic differences, with clannish and mafia-like overtones, are starting to outnumber those waged on ideological and geopolitical grounds. Societies have become "war prone". What action can be taken in the light of these new circumstances?

Prevention and Preparatory Action before Disasters Arise

Preventing the Crisis the Risks of Ill-conceived Development

Both in the North and in the South and in the East, ailing economies are one of the main factors heightening the risk of confrontation, for they undermine the respective country's capacity for disaster prevention and disaster response. With very few exceptions, the situation has worsened nearly everywhere: the standard of living has declined, plunging ever larger segments of the population below the poverty line; demographic growth, which increases the pressure on the environment, causes conditions of production in rural areas to deteriorate still further and speeds up (often uncontrolled or virtually uncontrolled) urbanization, heightens pressure on increasingly fragile ecosystems, aggravates friction between farmers and nomads and exacerbates the risk of ethnic and political strife.

Under the influence of the World Bank, structural adjustment programmes are streamlining administrative systems. Though necessary, this process unfortunately does not go hand in hand with improved public services, on the contrary. The first cutbacks are made in social welfare, health and educational facilities... and also disaster prevention and preparedness! What comes next? Growing poverty is conducive to crime and breeds insecurity, violence and all forms of hatred. This hatred is then channelled into ultra-nationalistic, fanatical, tribal and fundamentalist movements, triggering a vicious circle of revolt and repression. The small-scale geostrategic clashes that accompanied the Cold War have been succeeded by a multiplicity of conflicts resulting from ill-conceived development. All too often, the only response to this world wide crisis is to provide "emergency ward" treatment in the form of maize as food aid and increasingly explosive combinations of "military-political-humanitarian" diplomacy.

Under these circumstances, National Red Cross and Red Crescent Societies in many countries are trying to support certain vital services by engaging in development activities, organizing community help for the disadvantaged, setting up blood banks, AIDS prevention campaigns, youth group activities, etc., and thereby helping to promote positive socioeconomic development.

Certain Development Strategies Increase Vulnerability

Certain factors inevitably reduce the available per capita resources (whether they are renewable or not). One such factor is demographic growth, which creates disparities and heightens the risk of conflict. Some development policies unfortunately have similar results and, moreover, weaken the whole system, leaving it unable to cope with crises. The ICRC has observed the often disastrous effects of such policies in the course of many conflicts and crises, as illustrated by the following examples.

1980, Upper Casamance (Senegal): Drought had struck again. The Mandingo farmers had hardly any food stocks left. They had adopted the "all cotton extension programme" advocated by the cotton company on over 70% of their land. In the same region the Toucouleur minority, who had become settled only a short time before, had been far less receptive to the enticements of the "grow cotton" campaign. They had agreed to plant a small amount of cotton, but their staple crops came first. As a result, their stores were still half full! If the current crisis in Lower Casamance were to spread to Tambacounda, the majority groups would find themselves short of food, while the ethnic minority would experience no immediate need. What consequences could such an imbalance have?

Forced Development Campaigns with Catastrophic Results

Nampula (Mozambique), early 1992/1993: The economic reforms which followed the signing of the peace accord opened the way for ever greater liberalism. Powerful trading companies reverted to methods used during colonial times: forcible planting of large areas with cash crops (more cotton), bans on felling cashew trees (cashew nuts), virtually compulsory limits on the cultivation of staple crops (cereals or legumes). The only feasible crop left was cassava with its long productive cycle (8-12 months), its ability to grow in the shade of fruit trees and its low nutritional value. In such conditions, this policy led to malnutrition, kwashiorkor and disinvestment in a rural economy already reeling from a decade of civil war, and continues to do so. How will this situation affect the stability of a country just emerging from civil war.

Ecologically Disastrous Development Policies

The case of the trans-Amazonian highways and the agricultural concessions bordering them are well known. One of the earth's "green lungs" has been consigned to the huge land owners' bulldozers and cattle herds while the indigenous peoples, the Indians, are being mown down by private militias. One day, these Indians or their offspring, if any of them survive, may themselves take up machetes or Kalashnikovs, the modern equivalent of the traditional blowpipes and poison arrows.

Development Options Resulting in Extreme Economic Dependence

The vast cotton fields in certain countries of the former Soviet Union give rise to several questions. The first relates to the environmental cost of such production units (the drying up of the Aral Sea, the spraying of often very toxic products from the air, etc.). The second challenges the viability of such setups once the centralized, planned economy which typified the Soviet Union has disappeared. Production takes place in one area, processing in a second, food supplies come from a third. What happens when a political rift or, worse yet, a front line cuts the cotton-producing region off from its markets and its sources of food?

Action During Peacetime to Change Behaviour

In these high-risk situations, humanitarian reflexes must be created which will come into play whenever a crisis breaks out. The ICRC, in conjunction with the other components of the Red Cross and Red Crescent Movement, strives to remind the various groups involved (be they regular armed forces or guerrilla groups) of their duties and responsibilities as codified in international humanitarian law.

A host of experts, equipped with an entire range of texts and instructional materials, have been deployed on the four continents currently affected by crises and hold courses for thousands of men-at-arms every year. This activity, known as "Dissemination", is essential, for it is our only means of trying to prevent the irreparable from occurring. Indeed, every possible step must be taken to prevent those acts and atrocities from being committed in times of war that would ruin any attempt at reconciliation and sabotage any effort to negotiate. The memories lingering from the hours of war may sometimes determine whether or not peace can be successfully restored.

To what avail is such work? After seeing what took place in Rwanda, Liberia or the former Yugoslavia, that is a valid question. Yet on each occasion, in the midst of horror, a few small glimmers of humanity have shown us that our efforts were not all in vain. Delegates and ambulances were able to cross front lines, the wounded were no longer summarily executed, prisoners received visits and had their names recorded, ill-treatment ceased in prisons, food was delivered in the middle of a combat zone-small gestures brought light into the darkness.

Providing Training to Cope with Crises

One of the liveliest debates today in the development forum is focused on grassroots participation at every stage of the development process, from identification to evaluation and naturally implementation. In terms of emergency action, this same approach has been much slower. How often have teams with their white uniforms and stethoscopes descended upon astonished villages and attempted to go about their work while ignoring the human and social resources already on hand? To reverse this trend, we must first decide to train men and women among the civilian population to cope with disasters. In cooperation with a number of National Societies and their Federation, the ICRC has developed a comprehensive strategy to train aid workers and emergency personnel. But much still remains to be done.

Other leading organizations are also working in the field of disaster prevention and forecasting. The activities of international institutions such as the Asian Centre for Disaster Preparedness, UNDRO and the Department of Humanitarian Affairs (DHA) working in connection with the United Nations Decade for the Prevention of Natural Disasters should be stepped up. NGOs, both in the North and in the South, have a crucial role to play in this race against the clock to stop the deadly spread of crises. The International Red Cross and Red Crescent Movement must in any case continue to concentrate on damage control by training men and women in disaster prevention and management, whether natural disasters (which are the Federation's domain) or conflict-related (the ICRC's sphere of action).

For an Operational Information Policy on Potential Crises

One of the key elements in disaster prevention and efficient intervention (preparation of the necessary means and staff) is the information available about "high-risk" situations. How many mistakes have been made for the simple reason that the people concerned "did not know".

General and specialized maps, reports, lists of stocks and ethno-sociological data should be readily available for the emergency teams. By setting up these data banks during development programmes, any necessary emergency action (which must be linked to subsequent rehabilitation) would be considerably improved. There are virtually no situations in the world today about which nothing has been written. The problem is finding this information when one has to leave in haste for an unfamiliar country with a different culture and climate. Much preparation has yet to be done to give easy access to this information, a task which fortunately is facilitated by the progress in communications and information technology.

Prompt Detection of Crises Early Warning Systems (EWS)

Those who have been fortunate enough to be involved in setting up and monitoring early warning systems are aware of their obvious benefits, but they also know their limitations. There are at present several systems operating at different levels. The global system adopted by the Food and Agriculture Organization (FAO) covers the entire world. The Famine Early Warning System (FEWS) of the United States Agency for International Development (USAID) operates on a regional scale. Others have a country-wide or sometimes only a local range. Some of these systems use data mainly provided by satellites, while others take in only climatological and agronomical data. The most effective ones are probably those based on a combination of specialized fields including the social sciences, in particular price curve analysis and economic phenomena such as abnormal sales of livestock or other exceptional activities. Some focus on one subject, especially those designed for the anti-locust (acridian) campaign. If properly operated, the large-scale FEWS or FAO system or the anti-locust networks are extremely useful in charting overall trends and signalling a shift to orange and/or red alert.

These systems, however, are rarely operational at the very local level and are often hindered by a lack of local parameters. Only specifically-designed studies can produce the database indispensable for the setting up of effective early warning systems. Furthermore, there must be adequate means available to launch such studies, the appropriate methods to put them into effect and the capacity to make use of them. A few NGOs have attempted to do so, but their efforts have yet to be evaluated.

It is relatively costly to set up and operate these national or local early warning systems, and they do not "pay off" immediately.

Only a disaster can show whether the EWS has worked well by providing a timely warning which enabled effective action to be taken so that worse consequences were avoided. Such smaller-scale early warning systems are truly a field to which development planners and donors should devote greater attention.

Besides having regular access to the above-mentioned major early warning systems, the ICRC has its own EWS. It consists of a network of regional delegations, one of whose tasks is to keep up a constant watch for incipient crises throughout the world, and is based on constantly checking which vulnerable areas (fragile economies and precarious food supplies) coincide with high-risk areas (geopolitical factors, internecine friction).

Rapid Response Strategies to Build up Emergency Reserves

Early warning systems are worthwhile only if the "early warning" actually gives rise to a "rapid response".

Food aid can be provided in several ways, ranging from imports in the course of major relief operations launched by the World Food Programme, the European Union or USAID to the transfer of buffer stocks set up by regional bodies (Club of the Sahel, Southern African Development Coordination Conference, etc.) in combination with/or by means of counterpart funding. For the time being, the establishment of regional buffer stocks is hindered by both technical (perishable foodstuffs, inadequate storage conditions) and economic problems. Storage costs are indeed high, as illustrated by the European Community's difficulties with its own surpluses. The availability of food aid is unfortunately still largely determined by political contingencies. Timely warnings have been given of countless incipient disasters, yet a tardy response came only when public opinion was stirred to action by the appalling scenes shown on television: Ethiopia in 1983-1984; Somalia in 1992, etc. In some forgotten conflicts, when political considerations or lack of interest outweighed the right to emergency food aid, there was simply no response at all.

What Action is most needed in the Midst of Horror?

The Spectre of Famine

In ever larger areas, economic progress is being reversed by tensions and conflict. War destroys the infrastructure, disrupts services, cuts off markets from their suppliers. Worse yet, crops are sometimes burnt or looted by men-at-arms or great numbers of people displaced by conflicts. The fields may not even have been tilled or sown if the area was too unsafe or military action resumed in the area during the usual farming season. Seed reserves have been destroyed or used as food in a last effort to ward off starvation. Herds have been slaughtered, die in epidemics or are cut off from their traditional grazing lands. Food from traditional alternative sources is no longer available. The slightest climatic setback then signals the end. In extreme cases, it results in famine and long columns of rural inhabitants trudging towards towns, refugee camps or food distribution sites.

The conventional, and often indispensable, response to nutritional problems is food aid paired with medical assistance. In the last 15 years, the ICRC has assembled millions of tonnes of foodstuffs and distributed them to millions of war victims: such were the large-scale operations on the Khmer-Thai border from 1979/1981; those in Ethiopia in 1985/1986; in Angola and the Sudan in 1986/1991 and again in 1993/1994; in Somalia in 1991/1993; in Mozambique in 1992/1993, in Rwanda from 1992 to 1994; not forgetting the former Yugoslavia, Liberia, the Caucasus, etc.

Food aid, however, has its limits and itself carries certain dangers also often observed by the ICRC in the field. Among the detrimental effects of food aid the following should be noted:

- the emergence of a chronic dependence on aid whenever there are large-scale and long-lasting food distributions;
- the tendency of the population to incorporate food aid, and free assistance in general, in their strategies for survival. This often leads to a drain on emergency food reserves. The farmers become used to receiving aid to offset the vagaries of climate and other crisis factors;
- the lowering of incentives to resume agricultural production owing to the fall in commodity prices induced by the massive arrival of free foodstuffs.

Programmes must be set up which enable victims to stay alive today and to survive tomorrow. The ICRC has developed a special tool to assess the needs and most suitable means of achieving this: pluridisciplinary teams composed of nurses, nutritionists, agronomists, sanitary engineers, logistics experts and delegates specialized in several fields. The specific role of the latter is to analyse the problems involved in the protection of certain categories of victims who are of particular concern to the ICRC: prisoners of war, security detainees, etc.

The approach adopted by ICRC nutritionists and agronomists is based on a simple premise: malnutrition results from lack of access to food. To wait until malnutrition can be detected by the classic anthropometric indicators (weight/height, weight/age, etc.) generally means arriving too late.

At one point, and particularly when help is slow in coming, the only option left is to set up a large-scale operation entailing generalized distributions and special centres for supplementary and therapeutic feeding. Food programmes, though useful and necessary, provide only unsatisfactory solutions to food crises.

Emergency Rehabilitation in Times of War : A glimmer of Hope

Action plans resulting from surveys by multidisciplinary teams of agronomists and nutritionists and put into effect at the height of the emergency, alongside the provision of food aid, will lay the foundations for rehabilitation. In some programmes, by enabling farmers to stay on their land, food aid becomes an integral part of the rehabilitation policy.

The ICRC will try to detect as early as possible the potential food supply problems even in the midst of battle. It must then attempt to tackle the causes of a foreseeable famine and help people start up production again despite security constraints. Relief strategy is often based on the provision of coordinated food aid ("stay alive today") combined with support in resuming production ("survive tomorrow").

Experience in Somalia, the Sudan, Mozambique, Angola, Rwanda, Liberia and Yugoslavia has shown us just how effective this approach is. The same reasoning also applies in other areas. By repairing the water conduits of encircled towns, sinking wells in areas where water sources have been destroyed by passing tanks and sending medicines to public health facilities cut off by battle lines, some hope can be restored even before the gunfire has ceased. Without this aid, the population would have no alternative but to flee or die.

Making the Wastelands of War Grow Green Again: Aims and Methods of Rehabilitation

Philosophy of Emergency Rehabilitation

The twofold approach of "food aid/emergency agricultural rehabilitation" can have a preventive effect or at least limit the damage. The aims of emergency agricultural rehabilitation are:

- to prevent or limit damage (this is the "care and maintenance" principle, applied not to individuals but to the productive capacity of rural societies);
- to hasten the return to productive capacity after a period of rapid disinvestment in rural economies hard hit by war;
- to help restore reliable food supply networks, particularly by facilitating the renewal of food reserves and of emergency seed banks;
- to restore producers' dignity, which may have suffered during the often long and humiliating wait at food distribution sites.

Since conflicts are tending to drag on more and more, the concept of "conflict-related emergency" is being or should be replaced by a different notion: support for the survival strategies of people enduring prolonged wars.

The decades of clashes in Angola and the Sudan and the years of destruction and economic paralysis in the former Yugoslavia demand more than food aid or even mere seed distribution. How, for example, can the food derived from animal husbandry be replaced in an agro-pastoral society that has lost all its livestock? There is still much to be thought up, experimented with or tested in actual conditions.

A Key Concept : Support for Survival Strategies

Most societies have developed in conditions that were precarious in every respect. Unfavourable weather conditions, haphazard food supplies, unstable relationships with other communities, etc. Ingenious mechanisms have had to be devised to reduce risks and manage crises. Societies and groups which failed to do so have perished. The ICRC's task is to bolster such mechanisms either during or at the end of the crisis. The few examples given below will illustrate this point.

The Sudan

In the rigorous conditions of the White Nile basin, the survival strategies of the Dinka and Nuer peoples are based on five traditional activities: animal husbandry, agriculture, gathering, fishing, and trading; food aid must now be added to this list. These coping mechanisms in an inhospitable environment require comprehensive management of vast sparsely inhabited areas.

The large concentrations of people at the food distribution points mean that people are sometimes cut off for long periods of time from their own lands and sources of food and their vulnerability is increased.

As early as 1988, the ICRC decided to reinforce the productive capacities of the southern Sudanese people by launching a large-scale veterinary programme. This strategy, renewed in 1993, has proved very worthwhile.

Somalia

The war has had a particular effect on the food supply of this country, with its very diversified agro-ecological systems ranging from purely nomadic herding to essentially agrarian systems and including multiple combinations of agriculture, animal husbandry and fishing.

From the outset of the conflict, the ICRC has approached the problem by recognizing this diversity. In grazing areas, it has taken measures to protect surviving herds from the major endemic diseases and boost their productivity; in the less arid south, it has distributed seed and farming implements. Finally, along the coast and rivers, the ICRC has supplied fishing villages with hooks and lines.

Mozambique

In Mozambique, we discovered the local people's lore of edible wild plants. These plants are the key to their survival in hard times but they are not inexhaustible.

They too must have the chance to grow again. Food and agricultural assistance save these forest products from depletion by overuse. They are thus conserved during the season when the areas concerned are easily accessible and remain available for use during the rainy season or if the conflict flares up anew, making aid deliveries problematic again.

Eastern Europe

While the ICRC now has considerable experience in supporting survival strategies in tropical areas, there is still much to be learnt about conflict situations in "developed" countries. Nevertheless, over the past two years, the ICRC has gained a certain expertise in the former Yugoslavia and in the countries of the former Soviet Union where lifestyles and production methods often closely resemble our own.

Programmes have been set up to assist agriculture but also to stimulate production units. In this specific instance, experience has shown that it is essential for the ICRC to continue to be perceived as neutral by all the parties concerned. The key to the success of emergency agricultural rehabilitation programmes is dictated by their specific nature.

Since they are set up under crisis conditions, they can seldom benefit by the classic support systems for agricultural extension campaigns that give ongoing advice on their implementation and familiarize the population with the methods used. From the very beginning, these programmes must therefore make use of local know-how and traditional practices, adopting varied strategies to take local diversity into adequate account.

In order to follow closely these peasant farmers' traditional strategies, with their geographical differences and adaptability to the unpredictable, a soundly based analysis of them is needed. Emergency workers and development experts should meet and share views on the appropriate methods for such an analysis.

Rising from the Ashes: Post-disaster Development

Past Crises and Future Weaknesses

The link that exists between poverty, war and vulnerability is already well known. Everyone is not equal in the face of adversity, and crises further accentuate the disparities. It is very likely that we will again see the ravages of growing inequality, of rampant poverty and the unchecked extraction of mineral resources, further devastating a natural environment already deeply scarred by conflict and its consequences (for instance, huge numbers of displaced people have totally deforested southwest Rwanda and the Goma region in Zaire).

The aftermath of crises is a time of incredible social creativity, redistributing the cards in ways that would previously have been unthinkable.

However, these exceptionally promising moments may also simply result in chaos, crime, waste and the perpetration of gross injustice-all conditions conducive to a renewed crisis. Those who wish to help these devastated areas and their traumatized peoples to get back on their feet must demonstrate unwavering vigilance and generosity.

That same period is also a crucial one for the International Red Cross and Red Crescent Movement: it is a time to forge a spirit of and capacity for humanitarian action within a community whose wounds are still open; a time to forget hate while remembering the beneficial work of Red Cross volunteers during the conflict; to rebuild a world in which the phrase "mutual aid" has a meaning, bringing to mind those who hastened beneath heavy fire to rescue the wounded from either side; a time to restore village communities and instil a spirit of solidarity by participation in projects such as those undertaken by the ICRC in the darkest hours.

For "Emergency" Personnel, Planning the Withdrawal and Training others to Take Over

A number of leading organizations, like OXFAM, have both specialized emergency departments and other departments engaged in long-term action. If funds do not dry up when the crisis ends and media attention shifts elsewhere, these institutions can make a smooth transition from the "emergency" phase to rehabilitation and development activities. The ICRC's mandate is restrictive since it applies essentially to the period of conflict. Fortunately, many conflicts have a "happy" ending, namely peace, which usually leads to a withdrawal of the "emergency" personnel. Partners must then be found to take over the emergency rehabilitation activities and transform them into development projects with their specific methods and objectives.

There are several possible scenarios:

- *The situation favoured by the ICRC:* the country's own National Society decides to take over these activities (either alone or with the help of the Federation). In this way it has been possible to adapt programmes started during the war-medical and social work, dissemination of international humanitarian law, tracing of families separated by the conflict, etc.-to development needs and ensure that they were continued.
- *A rare situation:* the national ministries decide to take over and run the programmes themselves. Since peace has returned, the ministries and their provincial representatives theoretically can travel throughout the country (which was not always possible during the conflict and had led the ICRC to assume the role of a neutral and independent intermediary).
- *The most common situation*: an NGO or occasionally a United Nations agency is interested in taking over a programme or a specific region.

Replacing the ICRC by another organization often proves difficult, for mutual trust must be established between that organization and the people before it can step in. And things do not necessarily go smoothly simply because the ICRC has been able to donate equipment for the initial months of the NGO's operation.

Experience has therefore led us to adopt the idea of a transitional "induction" period during which the National Society or NGO concerned works for a time under the guidance of the ICRC in order to get to know the situation and meet its partners. This approach has been successfully tried out in Somalia and Mozambique and the ICRC intends to continue it.

The National Red Cross and Red Crescent Societies are often the only quasi non-governmental bodies in civil society, in the absence of a true network of non governmental organizations, which is usually nonexistent or in its infancy. Their role is all the more essential in the post-conflict period. In view of the challenges, but also of the limited absorption capacity of most of the National

Societies, one could see the importance of a dynamic policy to develop these other components of the Movement. This should take place during peace time, and it is there that the role of the International Federation of Red Cross and Red Crescent Societies has a crucial role. Strategies to develop National Societies in the middle of the conflicts have still to be further elaborated. The ICRC, alongside with the other components of the Movement, should pursue its efforts in that direction.

Looking Ahead: A World at Risk

A Comprehensive Strategic Approach must be Found

It is often depressing to glance at the newspaper or watch the TV news every day. It is becoming more and more evident on this crisis-stricken planet of ours that there is a space-time continuum, starting well before the crisis breaks and lasting long after it is over. We are beginning to recognize clearly the determining factors that make it better or worse. We also have become very familiar with the catalysts of peace and the sources of conflict and know how hard it is to build peace on the ruins and hatred left by war.

The diagnostic means devised by development specialists, the insight gained into the varying forms and degrees of vulnerability resulting from emergency operations, and the peaceful tool of international humanitarian law can and must be used.

To sum up, the "emergency-development" continuum can be represented as follows, juxtaposing the working methods of institutions such as the United Nations Organization or NGOs and those of the ICRC.

The "Emergency-Development" Continuum

Phase Activities within a more General Framework (UN, NOGs) Activities of the Components of the Movement

1 Development Programmes for socioeconomic development Disaster prevention-Disaster preparedness (analysis of factors rendering systems vulnerable, preparation of databases, creation of buffer stocks) Installation of early warning systems Disseminate knowledge of IHL (in advance, in times of peace) Identify databases and prepare data summaries Develop the

capacity of National Red Cross and Red Crescent Societies to conduct these activities Prepare for emergencies (training, set up logistic infrastructures, etc.) Analyse risk factors, monitor situations via the network of regional delegations.

2 Early warning Certain indicators show red alert Sound the warning: send an evaluation team

3 Emergency Assess the situation Prepare UN Consolidated Appeals Mobilize resources Start emergency operations Start preventive action, emergency programmes and emergency rehabilitation Disseminate knowledge of IHL (with greater immediacy, in the heart of battle) Mobilize resources

4 Rehabilitation: Mobilize resources Set up rehabilitation activities Start rehabilitation Seek partners to take over programmes and transform them into "development activities".

5 Development Resume development and reconstruction projects Programmes taken over either by a National Society with help from the Federation or by an NGO and attention gradually transferred to development problems.

The Big Challenges

The ICRC has at its disposal an entire range of skills, information and impressive relay systems whose potential is doubtless not yet fully utilized. Many of the subjects raised above should be developed in greater detail, from both the theoretical and the operational points of view. There are several areas that merit joint reflection and action.

The Time Factor

Farmers in France often say: *"il faut se faire un allié du temps"* (you must make an ally of time/weather). The dual meaning of the word *"temps"* is used to say that the weather determines the time when they can or must do their work, and that both weather and time must be put to the best possible use. A large part of the "emergency and development" issue is linked to the question of time. The contrast between "doing things fast and well" or "doing things fast OR doing them well" is one such question. "Doing things in time", and therefore "being forewarned and forearmed/ prepared" is another. Lastly, there is the question of the "durability" once the emergency is over, or what is termed in English the "sustainability", of activities begun during the emergency period.

Investing in the Collection of Information

Improved knowledge means superior planning, earlier warning and more effective action. Much work remains to be done in the collection, processing, and summarizing of the necessary information on the hot spots (past, present and future) around the globe. For example, all the urban problems with humanitarian implications in the mammoth cities in the South are uncharted territory to us.

A Fourfold Approach: Presence/Dissemination/Protection/ Assistance

While the link between assistance and protection is now fully recognized, the complete formula for the aforesaid possible approach-both as a whole and its application over time, i.e. before, during and after the crises-is less clearly understood.

6

The Social Determinants of Health Inequity

Social Determinants of Health

Social determinants of health are the economic and social conditions under which people live which determine their health. Virtually all major diseases are primarily determined by a network of interacting exposures that increase or decrease the risk for the disease. This is particularly the case for cardiovascular disease and type II diabetes with these conditions the result of social, economic, and political forces.

As stated in Social Determinants of Health: The Solid Facts (WHO, 2003): "Health policy was once thought to be about little more than the provision and funding of medical care: the social determinants of health were discussed only among academics. This is now changing. While medical care can prolong survival and improve prognosis after some serious diseases, more important for the health of the population as a whole are the social and economic conditions that make people ill and in need of medical care in the first place. Nevertheless, universal access to medical care is clearly one of the social determinants of health."

Raphael (2008) reinforces this concept: "Social determinants of health are the economic and social conditions that shape the health of individuals, communities, and jurisdictions as a whole. Social determinants of health are the primary determinants of whether individuals stay healthy or become ill (a narrow definition of health). Social determinants of health also determine the extent to which a person possesses the physical, social, and personal resources to identify and achieve personal aspirations, satisfy needs, and cope with the environment (a broader definition of health). Social determinants of health are about the quantity and quality of a variety of resources that a society makes available to its members.".

Factors

Social determinants of health have been recognized by several health organizations such as the Public Health Agency of Canada and the World Health Organization to greatly influence collective and personal well-being. A list of determinants of health — only some of which are social determinants — is below:

1. Income and social status
2. Social support networks
3. Education and literacy, i.e. health literacy
4. Employment/Working conditions
5. Social environments
6. Physical environments
7. Life skills
8. Personal health practices and coping skills
9. Healthy child development
10. Biology and genetic endowment
11. Health services
12. Gender
13. Culture.

The term social determinants of health grew out of the search by researchers to identify the specific exposures by which members of different socioeconomic groups come to experience varying degrees of health and illness. While it was well documented that individuals in various socioeconomic groups experienced differing health outcomes, the specific factors and means by which these factors led to illness remained to be identified. Overviews of the concept, recent findings, and an analysis of emerging issues are available. All these formulation share a concern with factors beyond those of biomedical and behavioural risk.

The SDOH National Conference list is unique in that it specifically focuses on the public policy environment (e.g., income and its distribution) rather than characteristics associated with individuals (e.g. income and social status). These 11 social determinants of health are:

1. early life
2. education
3. employment and working conditions
4. food security
5. gender
6. health care services
7. housing
8. income and its distribution
9. social safety net
10. social exclusion
11. unemployment and employment security.

Background

The modern study of the social determinants of health can be said to have begun with the writings of Rudolph Virchow and Friedrich Engels during the mid 19th century. Virchow and Engels not only made the explicit link between living conditions and health but also explored the political and economic structures that create inequalities in the living conditions which lead to health inequalities.

Recently, international interest in the social determinants of health has led to the World Health Organization's creating a Commission on the Social Determinants of Health. Its final report *Closing the Gap in a Generation: Health Equity through Action on the Social Determinants of Health* succinctly summarizes the current state of knowledge.

"Social justice is a matter of life and death. It affects the way people live, their consequent chance of illness, and their risk of premature death. We watch in wonder as life expectancy and good health continue to increase in parts of the world and in alarm as they fail to improve in others. A girl born today can expect to live for more than 80 years if she is born in some countries – but less than 45 years if she is born in others. Within countries there are dramatic differences in health that are closely linked with degrees of social disadvantage.

These inequities in health, avoidable health inequalities, arise because of the circumstances in which people grow, live, work, and age, and the systems put in place to deal with illness. The conditions in which people live and die are, in turn, shaped by political, social, and economic forces.

Social and economic policies have a determining impact on whether a child can grow and develop to its full potential and live a flourishing life, or whether its life will be blighted. Increasingly the nature of the health problems rich and poor countries have to solve are converging. The development of a society, rich or poor, can be judged by the quality of its population's health, how fairly health is distributed across the social spectrum, and the degree of protection provided from disadvantage as a result of ill-health.

In the spirit of social justice, the Commission on Social Determinants of Health was set up by the World Health Organization (WHO) in 2005 to marshal the evidence on what can be done to promote health equity, and to foster a global movement to achieve it.

As the Commission has done its work, several countries and agencies have become partners seeking to frame policies and programmes, across the whole of society, that influence the social determinants of health and improve health equity. These countries and partners are in the forefront of a global movement.

The Commission calls on the WHO and all governments to lead global action on the social determinants of health with the aim of achieving health equity. It is essential that governments, civil society, WHO, and other global organizations now come together in taking action to improve the lives of the world's citizens. Achieving health equity within a generation is achievable, it is the right thing to do, and now is the right time to do it. "

Canada's Role

Canada has been a leader in developing social determinants of health concepts. But Canada has been rather less successful than other wealthy nations in seeing these concepts put into action. Instead, the application of these concepts in the service of health is well established in many European nations where it has been integrated into development and application of public policy. In Canada however, the approach remains subordinate to traditional medical and behavioural paradigms of health, illness, and health care.

What are Social Determinants of Health?

The term "social determinants of health" grew out of researchers' search for the specific mechanisms by which members of different socioeconomic groups come to experience varying degrees of health and illness Everywhere, individuals of different socioeconomic status show profoundly different levels of health and incidence of disease.

Another stimulus to investigating social determinants of health was the finding of national differences in population health. For example, the health status of Americans—using indicators such as life expectancy, infant mortality, and death by childhood injury rates—compares unfavourably to citizens in most industrialized wealthy nations. In contrast, the health status of Scandinavians is generally superior to that seen in most nations. It was hypothesized that perhaps the same factors that explain health differences among groups within nations could also explain differences among national populations.

A variety of approaches to the social determinants of health exist and all of these are concerned with the organization and distribution of economic and social resources among the population. The Ottawa Charter for Health Promotion identifies the prerequisites for health as peace, shelter, education, food, income, a stable ecosystem, sustainable resources, social justice, and equity. Health Canada outlines various determinants of health—most of which are social determinants—of income and social status, social support networks, education, employment and working conditions, physical and social environments, biology and genetic endowment, personal health practices and coping skills, healthy child development, gender, culture, and health services.

A British working group charged with the specific task of identifying social determinants of health named the social (class health) gradient, stress, early life, social exclusion, work, unemployment, social support, addiction, food, and transport. And the U.S. Centres for Disease Control and Prevention highlight social determinants of health of socioeconomic status, transportation, housing, access to services, discrimination by social grouping (e.g., race, gender, or class), and social or environmental stressors.

Canadian workers synthesized these formulations to identify 12 key social determinants of health: Aboriginal status, early life, education, employment and working conditions, food security, gender, health care services, housing, income and its distribution, social safety net, social exclusion, and unemployment and employment security. These determinants are especially relevant to understanding and improving the health of Canadians. Evidence indicates that the health-related effects of each and every one of these factors equals or exceeds the influence of the so-called "lifestyle" or behavioural risk factors such as tobacco and alcohol use, diet, and physical activity, a conclusion stated as early as the mid 1970s.

Evidence

Research findings that examine the importance of the social determinants of health provide insights into: (a) the general improvement in health among citizens in developed nations over the past 100 years; (b) the health inequalities observed among populations within nations; and (c) differences in overall national health among both developed (e.g., between Sweden versus Canada versus the USA) and developing nations (e.g., between Cuba versus Argentina versus Brazil).

Improving Health Status

Profound improvements in health status have occurred in industrialized nations such as Canada since 1900. It has been hypothesized that access to improved medical care is responsible for these differences, but best estimates are that only 10–15 percent of increased longevity since 1900 in wealthy industrialized nations is due to improved health care. As one illustration, the advent of vaccines and medical treatments are usually held responsible for the profound declines in mortality from infectious diseases in Canada since 1900. But by the time vaccines for diseases such as measles, influenza, and polio and treatments for scarlet fever, typhoid, and diphtheria appeared, dramatic declines in mortality had already occurred. Improvements in behaviour (e.g., reductions in tobacco use, changes in diet, increased exercise, etc.) have also been hypothesized as responsible for improved longevity, but most analysts conclude that improvements in health are due to the improving material conditions of everyday life experienced by Canadians since 1900. These improvements occurred in the areas of early childhood, education, food processing and availability, health and social services, housing, employment security and working conditions and every other social determinant of health.

Inequalities Among Canadians

Despite dramatic improvements in health in general, significant inequalities in health among Canadians persist. Access to essential medical procedures is guaranteed by Medicare in Canada. Nevertheless, access to care issues are common and this is particularly the case in regards to required prescription medicines where income is a strong determinant of such access. It is believed however that health care issues account for a relatively small proportion of health status differences that exist among Canadians. As for differences in health behaviours (e.g., tobacco and alcohol use, diet, and physical activity, etc.), studies from as early as the mid 1970s—reinforced by many more studies since then—find their impact upon health to be less important than social determinants of health such as income and other social determinants of health.

Instead, evidence indicates that health differences among Canadians result primarily from experiences of qualitatively different living conditions associated with the social determinants of health. As just one example, consider the magnitude of differences in health that are related to the social determinant of health of income. Income is especially important as it serves as a marker of different experiences with many social determinants of health. Income is a determinant of health in itself, but it is also a determinant of the quality of early life, education, employment and working conditions, and food security.

Income also is a determinant of the quality of housing, need for a social safety net, the experience of social exclusion, and the experience of unemployment and employment insecurity across the life span. Also, a key aspect of Aboriginal life and the experience of women in Canada is their greater likelihood of living under conditions of low income.

Income is a prime determinant of Canadians' premature years of life lost and premature mortality from a range of diseases. Numerous studies indicate that income levels during early childhood, adolescence, and adulthood are all independent predictors of who develops and eventually succumbs to disease.

In Canada almost a quarter of excess premature years of life lost (mortality prior to age 75) can be attributed to income differences among Canadians. These calculations are obtained by using the mortality in the wealthiest quintile of urban neighbourhoods as a baseline and considering all deaths above that level to be "excess" related to income differences. These analyses indicate that 23% of premature years of life lost to Canadians can be accounted for by differences existing between wealthy and other Canadians.

What are the diseases that differentially kill people of varying income levels? Income-related premature years of life lost can be correlated with death certificate cause of death. Among the not-wealthy, mortality by heart disease and stroke are especially related to income differences. Importantly, premature death by injuries, cancers, infectious disease, and diabetes are also all strongly related to not being wealthy in Canada. These rates are especially high among the least well-off Canadians.

In 2002, Statistics Canada examined the predictors of life expectancy, disability-free life expectancy, and the presence of fair or poor health among residents of 136 regions across Canada. The predictors included socio-demographic factors (proportion of Aboriginal population, proportion of visible minority population, unemployment rate, population size, percentage of population aged 65 or over, average income, and average number of years of schooling). Also placed into the analysis were daily smoking rate, obesity rate, infrequent exercise rate, heavy drinking rate, high stress rate, and depression rate.

Consistent with most other research, behavioural risk factors were rather weak predictors of health status as compared to socioeconomic and demographic measures of which income is a major component. For life expectancy, the socio-demographic measures predicted 56% of variation (total variation is 100%) among Canadian communities. Daily smoking rate added only 8% more predictive power, obesity rate only another 1%, and exercise rate nothing at all! For disability-free life expectancy, socio-demographics predicted 32% of variation among communities, and daily smoking rated added only another 6% predictive power, obesity rate another 5%, and exercise rate another 3%. Differences among Canadians communities in numbers of residents reporting poor or fair health were related to socio-demographics (25% predictive power) with smoking rate adding 6%, obesity rate adding 10%, and exercise rate adding 3% predictive power.

Income-related effects are seen therefore in greater incidence and mortality from just about every affliction that Canadians experience. This is especially the case for chronic diseases. Incidence of, and mortality from, heart disease and stroke, and adult-onset or type 2 diabetes are especially good examples of the importance of the social determinants of health.

While governments, medical researchers, and public health workers emphasize the importance of traditional adult risk factors (e.g., cholesterol levels, diet, physical activity, and tobacco and alcohol use), it is well established that these are relatively poor predictors of heart disease, stroke, and type 2 diabetes rates among populations. The factors making a difference are living under conditions of material deprivation as children and adults, stress associated with such conditions, and the adoption of health threatening behaviours as means of coping with these difficult circumstances. In fact, difficult living circumstances during childhood are especially good predictors of these diseases.

In addition to predicting adult incidence and death from disease, income differences – and the other social determinants of health related to income – are also related to the health of Canadian children and youth. Canadian children living in low-income families are more likely to experience greater incidence of a variety of illnesses, hospital stays, accidental injuries, mental health problems, lower school achievement and early drop-out, family violence and child abuse, among others. In fact, low-income children show higher incidences of just about any health-, social-, or education-related problem, however defined. These differences in problem incidence occur across the income range but are most concentrated among low-income children.

In one approach the focus is on so-called lifestyle choices. In the other there is a concern with the social determinants of health.

The traditional 10 Tips for Better Health :

- Don't smoke. If you can, stop. If you can't, cut down.
- Follow a balanced diet with plenty of fruit and vegetables.
- Keep physically active.
- Manage stress by, for example, talking things through and making time to relax.
- If you drink alcohol, do so in moderation.
- Cover up in the sun, and protect children from sunburn.
- Practice safer sex.
- Take up cancer-screening opportunities.
- Be safe on the roads: follow the Highway Code.
- Learn the First Aid ABCs: airways, breathing, circulation.

The social determinants 10 Tips for Better Health:

- Don't be poor. If you can, stop. If you can't, try not to be poor for long.
- Don't have poor parents.
- Own a car.
- Don't work in a stressful, low-paid manual job.
- Don't live in damp, low-quality housing.
- Be able to afford to go on a foreign holiday and sunbathe.
- Practice not losing your job and don't become unemployed.
- Take up all benefits you are entitled to, if you are unemployed, retired or sick or disabled.
- Don't live next to a busy major road or near a polluting factory.
- Learn how to fill in the complex housing benefit/asylum application forms before you become homeless and destitute.

International Health Inequities

Profound differences in overall health status exist between developed and developing nations. Much of this has to do with the lack of the basic necessities of life (food, water, sanitation, primary health care, etc.) common to developing nations. Yet among developed nations such as Canada, less profound but still highly significant differences in health status indicators such as life expectancy, infant mortality, incidence of disease, and death from injuries exist. An excellent example is comparison of health status differences and the hypothesized social determinants of these health status differences among Canada, the United States, and Sweden.

Scholarship has noted that the USA takes an especially laissez-faire approach to providing various forms of security (employment, food, income, and housing) and health and social services while Sweden's welfare state makes extraordinary efforts to provide security and services. The sources of these differences in public policy appear to be in differing commitments to citizen support informed by the political ideologies of governing parties within each nation.

Emerging scholarship is specifically focused on how national approaches to security provision to citizens influence health by shaping the quality of numerous social determinants of health. Nations such as Sweden whose policies reduce unemployment, minimize income and wealth inequality, and address numerous social determinants of health show evidence of improved population health using indicators such as infant mortality and life expectancy. At the other end, nations with minimal commitments to such efforts such as the United States show rather worse indicators of population health.

Finally, poverty is an especially important indicator of how various social determinants of health combine to influence health. Using child – that is family – poverty rates as an important social determinants of both child and eventual health, Canada does not fare well in relation to European nations.

Cultural and Structuralist Approaches

To secure attention to the social determinants of health and build support for their strengthening, it is important to understand how social determinants of health come to influence health and cause disease. The very influential UK *Black* and *The Health Divide* reports considered two primary mechanisms for understanding this process: cultural/behavioural and materialist/structuralist.

The cultural/behavioural explanation was that individuals' behavioural choices (e.g., tobacco and alcohol use, diet, physical activity, etc.) were responsible for their developing and dying from a variety of diseases. Both the Black and Health divide reports however, showed that behavioural choices are heavily structured by one's material conditions of life. And—consistent with mounting evidence—these behavioural risk factors account for a relatively small proportion of variation in the incidence and death from various diseases. The materialist/structuralist explanation emphasizes the material conditions under which people live their lives. These conditions include availability of resources to access the amenities of life, working conditions, and quality of available food and housing among others.

The author of the *Health Divide* concluded: The weight of evidence continues to point to explanations which suggest that socioeconomic circumstances play the major part in subsequent health differences. Despite this conclusion and increasing evidence in favour of this view, much of the Canadian public discourse on health and disease remains focused on "life-style" approaches to disease prevention.

These materialist/structuralist conceptualizations have been refined such that analysis is now focused upon three frameworks by which social determinants of health come to influence health. These frameworks are: (a) materialist; (b) neo-materialist; and (c) psychosocial comparison. The materialist explanation is about how living conditions – and the social determinants of health that constitute these living conditions—shape health. The neo-materialist explanation extends the materialist analysis by asking how these living conditions come about. The psychosocial comparison explanation considers whether people compare themselves to others and how these comparisons affect health and wellbeing. In this argument individuals experience varying degrees of positive and negative exposures over their lives that accumulate to produce adult health outcomes. Overall wealth of nations is a strong indicator of population health. But within nations, socioeconomic position is a powerful predictor of health as it is an indicator of material advantage or disadvantage over the lifespan. Material conditions of life determine health by influencing the quality of individual development, family life and interaction, and community environments. Material conditions of life lead to differing likelihood of physical (infections, malnutrition, chronic disease, and injuries), developmental (delayed or impaired cognitive, personality, and social development), educational (learning disabilities, poor learning, early school leaving), and social (socialization, preparation for work, and family life) problems.

Material conditions of life also lead to differences in psychosocial stress The fight-or-flight reaction—chronically elicited in response to threats such as income, housing, and food insecurity, among others—weakens the immune system, leads to increased insulin resistance, greater incidence of lipid and clotting disorders, and other biomedical insults that are precursors to adult disease.

Adoption of health-threatening behaviours is a response to material deprivation and stress. Environments determine whether individuals take up tobacco, use alcohol, experience poor diets, and have low levels of physical activity. Tobacco and excessive alcohol use, and carbohydrate-dense diets are also means of coping with difficult circumstances. Materialist arguments help us understand the sources of health inequalities among individuals and nations and the role played by the social determinants of health.

Neo-materialist Approach

Exposures to the material conditions of life are important for health, but why are these material conditions so unequally distributed among the Canadian population but less so elsewhere?. The neo-materialist approach is concerned with how nations, regions, and cities differ on how economic and other resources are distributed among the population. Some jurisdictions have more equalitarian distribution of resources such that there are fewer poor people and the gaps that exist among the population in their exposures to the social determinants of health is narrower than places where there are more poor people and the gaps among the population are greater.

In the USA, states and cities with more unequal distributions of income have more low-income people and greater income gaps between rich and poor. They invest less in public infrastructure such as education, health and social services, health insurance, supports for the unemployed and those with disabilities, and spend less on education and libraries. All of these issues contribute to the quality of the social determinants of health to which people are exposed. Such unequal jurisdictions have much poorer health profiles than more equalitarian places.

Canada has a smaller proportion of lower-income people, a smaller gap between rich and poor, and spends relatively more on public infrastructure than the U.S. Not surprisingly, Canadians enjoy better health than Americans as measured by infant mortality rates, life expectancy, and death rates from childhood injuries. Neither nation does as well as Sweden where distribution of resources is much more equalitarian, low-income rates are very low, and health indicators are among the best in the world.

The neo-materialist view therefore, directs attention to both the effects of living conditions – the social determinants of health – on individuals' health and the societal factors that determine the quality of the distribution of these social determinants of health. How a society decides to distribute resources among citizens is especially important.

Social Comparison Approach

The argument here is that the social determinants of health play their role through citizens' interpretations of their standings in the social hierarchy. There are two mechanisms by which this occurs.

At the individual level, the perception and experience of one's status in unequal societies lead to stress and poor health. Comparing their status, possessions, and other life circumstances to those better-off than themselves, individuals experience feelings of shame, worthlessness, and envy that have psychobiological effects upon health. These processes involve direct disease-producing effects upon neuro-endocrine, autonomic and metabolic, and immune systems. These comparisons can also lead to attempts to alleviate such feelings by overspending, taking on additional employment that threaten health, and adopting health-threatening coping behaviours such as overeating and using alcohol and tobacco.

At the communal level, widening and strengthening of hierarchy weakens social cohesion, a determinant of health. Individuals become more distrusting and suspicious of others with direct stress-related effects on the body. Such attitudes can also weaken support for communal structures such as public education, health, and social programs. An exaggerated desire for tax reductions on the part of the public can weaken public infrastructure.

This approach directs attention to the psychosocial effects of public policies that weaken the social determinants of health. But these effects may be secondary to how societies distribute material resources and provide security to its citizens – processes described in the materialist and neo-materialist approaches. Material aspects may be paramount and the stresses associated with deprivation simply add to the toll on individuals' bodies.

Life-course Perspective

Traditional approaches to health and disease prevention have a distinctly non-historical here-and-now emphasis. Usually adults, and increasingly adolescents and youth are urged to adopt "healthy lifestyles" as a means of preventing the development of chronic diseases such as heart disease and diabetes, among others. In contrast to these approaches, life-course approaches emphasize the accumulated effects of experience across the life span in understanding the maintenance of health and the onset of disease. It has been argued:

"The prevailing aetiological model for adult disease which emphasizes adult risk factors, particularly aspects of adult life style, has been challenged in recent years by research that has shown that poor growth and development and adverse early environmental conditions are associated with an increased risk of adult chronic disease"

More specifically, it is apparent that the economic and social conditions—the social determinants of health—under which individuals live their lives have a cumulative effect upon the probability of developing any number of diseases. This has been repeatedly demonstrated in longitudinal studies—the U.S. National Longitudinal Survey, the West of Scotland Collaborative Study, Norwegian and Finnish linked data—which follow individuals across their lives. This has been most clearly demonstrated in the case of heart disease and stroke. And most recently, studies into the childhood and adulthood antecedents of adult-onset diabetes show how adverse economic and social conditions across the life span predispose individuals to this disorder.

A recent volume brings together some of the important work concerning the importance of a life-course perspective for understanding the importance of social determinants. Adopting a life-course perspective directs attention to how social determinants of health operate at every level of development—early childhood, childhood, adolescence, and adulthood—to both immediately influence health as well as provide the basis for health or illness during later stages of the life course.

Hertzman outlines three health effects that have relevance for a life-course perspective. Latent effects are biological or developmental early life experiences that influence health later in life. Low birth weight, for instance, is a reliable predictor of incidence of cardiovascular disease and adult-onset diabetes in later life. Experience of nutritional deprivation during childhood has lasting health effects.

Pathway effects are experiences that set individuals onto trajectories that influence health, well-being, and competence over the life course. As one example, children who enter school with delayed vocabulary are set upon a path that leads to lower educational expectations, poor employment prospects, and greater likelihood of illness and disease across the lifespan. Deprivation associated with poor-quality neighbourhoods, schools, and housing sets children off on paths that are not conducive to health and well-being.

Cumulative effects are the accumulation of advantage or disadvantage over time that manifests itself in poor health. These involve the combination of latent and pathways effects. Adopting a life-course perspective directs attention to how social determinants of health operate at every level of development—early childhood, childhood, adolescence, and adulthood—to both immediately influence health and provide the basis for health or illness later in life.

Public Policy

Much social determinants of health research simply focuses on determining the relationship between a social determinant of health and health status. So a researcher may document that lower income is associated with adverse health outcomes among parents and their children. Or a researcher may demonstrate that food insecurity is related to poor health status among parents and children as is living in crowded housing, and so on. This is what is termed a depoliticized approach in that it says little about how these poor-quality social determinants of health come about.

Social determinants of health do not exist in a vacuum. Their quality and availability to the population are usually a result of public policy decisions made by governing authorities. As one example, consider the social determinant of health of early life. Early life is shaped by availability of sufficient material resources that assure adequate educational opportunities, food and housing among others. Much of this has to do with the employment security and the quality of working conditions and wages. The availability of quality, regulated childcare is an especially important policy option in support of early life. These are not issues that usually come under individual control. A policy-oriented approach places such findings within a broader policy context.

Yet it is not uncommon to see governmental and other authorities individualize these issues. Governments may choose to understand early life as being primarily about parental behaviours towards their children. They then focus upon promoting better parenting, assist in having parents read to their children, or urge schools to foster exercise among children rather than raising the amount of financial or housing resources available to families. Indeed, for every social determinant of health, an individualized manifestation of each is available. There is little evidence to suggest the efficacy of such approaches in improving the health status of those most vulnerable to illness in the absence of efforts to modify their adverse living conditions.

Politics and Political Ideology

One way to think about this is to consider the idea of the welfare state and the political ideologies that shape its form in Canada and elsewhere. The concept of the welfare state is about the extent to which governments – or the state – use their power to provide citizens with the means to live secure and satisfying lives. Every developed nation has some form of the welfare state.

Two literature's inform this analysis. The first concerns the three forms of the modern welfare state. Esping-Andersen identifies three distinct clusters of welfare regimes among wealthy developed nations: Social Democratic (e.g., Sweden, Norway, Denmark, and Finland), Liberal (USA, UK, Canada, Ireland), and Conservative (France, Germany, Netherlands, and Belgium, among others). There is high government intervention and strong welfare systems in the social democratic countries and rather less in the liberal. Conservative nations fall midway between these others in service provision and citizen supports.

Social democratic nations have very well developed welfare states that provide a wide range of universal and generous benefits. They expend more of national wealth to supports and services. They are proactive in developing labour, family-friendly, and gender equity supporting policies. Liberal nations spend rather less on supports and services. They offer modest universal transfers and modest social-insurance plans. Benefits are provided primarily through means-tested assistance whereby these benefits are only provided to the least well-off.

Navarro and colleagues provide empirical support for the hypotheses that the social determinants of health and health status outcomes are of higher quality in the social democratic rather than the liberal nations. Some of these indicators are spending on supports and services, equitable distribution of income, and wealth and availability of services in support of families and individuals. Health indicators include life expectancy and infant mortality.

Could this general approach to welfare provision shape Canadian receptivity to the concepts developed in this volume? And if so, what can be done to improve receptivity to and implementation of these concepts?

A particularly important issue that is emerging is whether any particular analysis of social determinants of health is de-politicized or not. A de-politicized approach is one that fails to take account of the fact that the quality of the social determinants of health to which citizens in a jurisdiction are exposed to is shaped by public policy created by governments. And governments of course are controlled by political parties who come to power with a set of ideological beliefs concerning the nature of society and the role of governments.

Such analyses that recognize the role played by politics outline the particular importance of having social democratic political parties in power. Nations that have had longer periods of social democratic influence such as Norway, Finland, Sweden, and Denmark have government policymaking that is remarkably consistent with social determinants of health concepts. Nations such as the USA and Canada, dominated by liberal and neo-liberal governing parties, much less so.

A wealth of evidence from Canada and other countries supports the notion that the socioeconomic circumstances of individuals and groups are equally or more important to health status than medical care and personal health behaviours, such as smoking and eating patterns.

The weight of the evidence suggests that the SDOH have a direct impact on the health of individuals and populations, are the best predictors of individual and population health, structure lifestyle choices, and interact with each other to produce health (Raphael, 2003). In terms of the health of populations, it is well known that disparities-the size of the gap or inequality in social and economic status between groups within a given population-greatly affect the health status of the whole. The larger the gap, the lower the health status of the overall population.

Why Build a Health Promotion Evidence Base about Gender?

Gender has long been recognized as an important determinant of health service usage, but gender is increasingly important in understanding how women and men experience and respond to health promotion programs and interventions and their outcomes. Gender frameworks are vital for understanding not just the differing effects of the determinants of health on either women or men (Doyal, 1995; Krieger, 2000), but also how health programs should respond in order to improve health outcomes for either women or men. Much needs to be done to improve the evidence base in health promotion with respect to gender.

Gender, as a determinant of health, refers to inter-related dimensions of biological difference, psychological difference and social experience. Biological sex differences include the better infant survival rates of females, and women's longer life expectancy. With respect to these measures, women do seem to have some biological advantages over men, but any biological advantages that contribute to women's longer life expectancy are cancelled out by their social disadvantages (Doyal, 1995). Psychological gender differences include things like health practices, coping skills and self-concept. While these differences are often understood to be at the heart of gender experience, it is social experiences that primarily create gender difference, through social, economic, cultural and political inequities. Gender is embodied in inequities of health (Krieger, 2000) and these inequities are largely socially determined.

Inequity refers to those inequalities in health that are deemed to be unfair or that stem from some form of injustice (Kawachi et al., 2002), so in this way, health inequities cut across health inequalities. The concept of inequity involves relations of equal and unequal power (political, social and economic), and of justice and injustice. Inequity, perhaps more than inequality, is a concept that asserts the need for public policy-driven solutions. Health, as a state of well-being and opportunity, is determined by inequities and injustices related to social and economic structures more than anything else. Gender is a relational determinant of health because it alters the way we consider any of the social determinants of health, but the effectiveness of gender as a framework is dependent on how we understand it. Rather than seeing gender used as a political code for maintaining a focus on women, gender can be seen as being used selectively or comprehensively. A selective understanding of gendered health sees that it is a concept that represents analysis of men's and women's health, and of the differences between women's and men's health, in the patterns of use of general practitioners, in the uptake of health messages and personal health practices. The more comprehensive understanding of gendered health incorporates analysis of discrimination and its impact, and of the embodiment of inequities of health whereby differences are largely social determined. Mainstreaming or assimilation of women's health into generalist policies and services facilitates a selective approach to gender, rendering the political dimensions of inequity invisible.

It is when we discuss gender and inequities as social experiences that key issues for health promotion arise; these are particularly issues for women's health. There is a responsibility for anyone, whether decision-makers or advocates, when talking about gender, not to use it selectively, i.e. to only mean biological or psychological differences, but to use it comprehensively—to recognize and take responsibility for the stereotypes, societal expectations, discriminations, power relationships and social and sexual norms that shape so much of women's experience, and the social, cultural and economic environment that shapes women's opportunities. Women's particular health issues, their social position, reduced income and long-term financial security, and their vulnerability to stereotypical attitudes and assumptions about their roles in society, are different to those of men, and are frequently disempowering. Indeed, the 1997 UNDP report states that no society treats its women as well as its men. Key areas where inequities persist include women's financial security, reproductive and sexual health, emotional and mental health, violence, and caring.

Gender particularly interacts with socioeconomic circumstances (Whitehead and Diderichsen, 1997) that are manifest in women's lower levels of income across the lifespan, and in relatively subordinate positions of power and lower levels of decision-making, whether in political arenas, workplaces or within families. It is because of the evidence provided by these dimensions of gendered experience that we must continue to create a gendered health promotion agenda. Yet we must, as Lesley Doyal (Doyal, 1995) points out, reject crude universalism because gender is only one determinant of health and there are very great differences between and among women and men. The health of many different groups of women and men is differentiated by the inter-relationships between determinants of health, including the social gradient, work, violence, disability and rights.

Consideration of gender is necessary to ensure that health promotion policy implementation does not have a disproportionate and adverse impact on women. Women have sought the rethinking of policy approaches, research and program development from a gender perspective to ensure that they are gender aware and address gender equity issues. For example, gender has been shown to be critical to the organization and delivery of drug and alcohol programs, smoking interventions, and programs against violence and sexual assault.

The determinants of health are increasingly prominent in opening up new, critical approaches to strategic planning to achieve better health. All sectors need not only to understand the determinants of health and illness, but how, in particular, the vulnerable and most disadvantaged people of any society are affected by exposure to adverse determinants. Investment in women's health should be focused on seeking sustainable changes to social and health systems in order to overcome inequities that affect all women, but particularly those populations of women who are most vulnerable.

Upstream health promotion work, using models of health care delivery that are empowering, encourages participation and advocacy. Approaches that are directed at social change and policy are needed to ensure gender is not rendered an invisible determinant. Upstream strategies are much more likely to bring about sustainable change than a continual reliance on midstream and downstream strategies. It is in the field of upstream strategies that women's health services and programs have their authentic place, to ensure that research, policy and practice address the economic, social and cultural obstacles that prevent women from fulfilling their potential. Health promotion's agenda is so much more than merely the 'absence of disease', because is it about opportunities and capacities. But in developing the capacity to tackle inequities, work must be targeted more if it is to be effective. Inequity itself is a concept about unfairness and forms of injustice, and gender is a concept that embodies inequity. Therefore, gender is a concept that should be used visibly, responsibly and comprehensively, to recognize and actively tackle gendered health and social inequities. Our advocacy base must ensure that there is the capacity in governments to address gender, to enable targeting gender in public policy solutions, to improve the effectiveness of interventions and to aim to improve the evidence base about gender in health promotion interventions.

Emerging Problems, Social Change and Children of India

Children and *childhood* across the world, have broadly been construed in terms of a 'golden age' that is synonymous with innocence, freedom, joy, play and the like. It is the time when, spared the rigours of adult life, one hardly shoulders any kind of responsibility or obligations. But, then, it is also true that children are vulnerable, especially when very young. The fact that children are vulnerable, they need to be cared for and protected from 'the harshness of the world outside' and around (Holt, 1975: 22). This being so, the adult-child relation, parents in particular, is said to provide 'care and protection' – serving thereby the 'best interests of the child' and meeting their day-to-day 'needs of survival and development'. The adult is presumed to be the guardian and in that respect expected to take the responsibility of child's welfare and development. Whether or not, the premise underlying this is correct or not, the childhood 'reality' on the whole is questionable, demanding critical evaluation. Accordingly, idealistic notions and representations associated with children and childhood have been challenged, especially in relation to poverty, disease, exploitation and abuse rife across the globe. Many also believe that childhood is that period during which children are subject to a set of rules and regulations unique to them, and one that does not apply to members of other social categories. It is indeed a period in a person's life during which she/he is neither expected nor allowed to fully participate in various domains of social life. It is thus not a world of freedom and opportunity but one of confinement and limitation in which children are 'wholly subservient and dependent'. This being so, childhood is nothing short of a world of isolation, sadness, exploitation, oppression, cruelty and abuse.

To dichotomize and juxtapose these theoretical models of the child-adult relation reveals fundamentally different ways of seeing and understanding the very essence of childhood and children. In this sense, childhood is not a static, objective and universal fact of human nature, but a social construction which is both culturally and historically determined. The history of Hebrews, Greeks and Romans, whose cultures had a great impact upon the Western society, bears testimony to the fact that children, by and large, were taken for granted by their parents and the patriarchal society at large. The resultant effect of all this was that they were treated as objects of intervention rather than as legal subjects in their own right. Many labelled them as a 'problem population' whereas others reduced them to being seen as property and thus treated them as non-entities. The Roman law, for instance, provided for the *patriae potestas* whereby the father was endowed with absolute power and authority over his family. It included *just vitae necisque,* the power of life and death, and *a fortiori*, of uncontrolled corporal chastisement over wife, children and other family members. Ancient Greeks left girls and children born with disabilities on the wild hillsides, where exposure or animals were sure to kill them, and the practice was continued routinely in Rome until Christianity became the State religion. The killing of unwanted children may have become less common in the centuries since then, but it never completely disappeared. In the given adult-child power relation, the usual cliché of childhood being a 'golden age' not only seemed to be a myth but a distant dream for majority of these children.

The French historian, Philippe Ariès, in his landmark book *Centuries of Childhood,* also claimed that 'the idea of childhood did not exist at all in earlier times', as once the 'child' moved from the biological dependence of 'infancy' it 'belonged to adult society'. According to his analysis, children were 'miniature adults' as they dressed, behaved and conversed similarly, and were engaged in the same social activities and work. And that the concept of childhood as a discrete life stage emerged in Europe between the fifteenth and eighteenth centuries as part of a process driven by two primary imperatives. First, there was an affective or 'codlling' dimension 'in which the child, on account of his (sic) sweetness, simplicity and drollery, became a source of amusement and relaxation for the adult'. Second, there was an educational dimension inspired by 'churchmen or gentlemen of the robe ... moralists and pedagogues'. This secured control over children's innate 'depravity' and was developed through the influence of the Reformation, with its emphasis on discipline and knowledge of theology, humanities and sciences. It was consolidated during the period of European Enlightenment with the ascendancy of 'rationality'. Initially restricted to the domain of upper-class childhood, Ariès contended that the affective and educational dimensions eventually diffused across society and childhood became institutionalised.

The work of Ariès, however, has not been without criticism. It has been argued that his thesis underestimated the nature of childhood within changing household structures and family forms. Further, his account negated the historical constancy of the parent-child relation characterised by love and affection and above all his evidence was over-simplistic. Our intention here is not to scrutinise and evaluate the details of Ariès work but to acknowledge the profound significance of his contribution in presenting childhood as a social, cultural and historical construction that challenged populist and intellectual orthodoxy.

Lloyd de Mause, another historian, in *The History of Childhood* painted a very negative image of childhood and family life in the past. In fact, he went to the extent of saying that 'the history of childhood is a nightmare from which we have only recently begun to awaken'. He further contended that 'the further back in history one goes, the lower the level of child care, and the more likely children are to be killed, abandoned, beaten, terrorised and sexually abused'. According to him, childhood was not discovered in the way that Ariès suggested. On the contrary, it was a human universal that gradually evolved itself from one stage to the other. These stages were: (i) Infanticidal (Antiquity to 4th century A.D.); (ii) Abandonment (4th – 13th centuries); (iii) Ambivalent (14th– 17th centuries); (iv) Intrusive (18th century); (v) Socialisation (19th – mid-20th century); and (vi) Helping (mid-20th century onwards). Today, of course, we view abandonment of children in fairly tales and in legends, as if it were all fantasy. Early Western historians writing about children and their childhood were of the view that till the Middle Ages, abandonment, harsh punishment and the use of fear and other life-inhibiting measures were all part of the era's social history, economics and pattern of families. No doubt, the era of Middle Ages was rightly referred to as the Dark Ages. Perhaps, an important step in the definition of rights came in 1215, in England. After a period of Civil War, the English nobility forced King John to limit his power, which had been absolute and virtually unchecked, through the *Magna Carta*. Among other things, the Magna Carta guaranteed that no free man should be deprived of life, liberty, or property without the due process of law. This in a way provided for the system of *parens patriae* meaning thereby that the sovereign was authorised to act as the 'supreme parent of the child'. The superior 'protective' authority and role of the sovereign provided a basis for interfering with the idea of family privacy and the control of the male head of the household over other members of the family. In other words, the need to protect children's interests gradually began to surface. In a similar development, courts in Roman-Dutch law jurisdiction began to exercise the State's responsibilities as *parens patriae* and came to be considered as the 'upper' or superior guardian of minor children.

While tracing the position of children and childhood in the Western society, it would be crucial to go through the writings of Michael Freeman too. In his book '*The Moral Status of Children*'

(1997), which is a second edition to '*The Rights and Wrongs of Children*' (1983), Freeman's contention is that with thè passage of time childhood may have changed and perhaps would continue to do so. But those who toll the knell of its passing, often interpreting, what they consider to be, its demise to moral decadence, oversimplify, exaggerate and, in making the link with children's rights movement, dangerously distort the true facts. According to Freeman, then, the supposed 'disappearance of childhood', as propounded by Neil Postman (1982), at a time when there was a growing institutional recognition that children have rights, was 'facile'. His contention is that 'Childhood has not disappeared and it will not do so. A childhood in which children are granted a moral status, in which their rights are taken seriously, will be a better childhood, not a worse one'.

At this juncture, it would be worthwhile to pause and look at the overall status of children in India, especially with regard to the overall treatment meted out to them by their parents and the society at large. Historically, we all know that the major caretaker of a child was the mother, the immediate family or, at best, the joint family and secondarily *jati* (caste) relationships. Sudhir Kakar, who hasmade a detailed analysis of Indian childhood and society in his book *The Inner World— A Psycho-Analytic Study of Childhood and Society in India*, has dwelled at length on mother-child relationship and how this profoundly influences the 'quality' and 'dynamics' of social relations throughout one's life. Consistent with the belief that life begins with conception rather than at birth, five stages of childhood were identified in the Indian tradition. These were: (i) *Garbha*, or the foetal period; (ii) *Ksheerda* (0-6 months), when the infant lives entirely on milk; (iii) *Ksheerannada* (6 months-2 years), the period of early childhood in which weaning takes place; (iv) *Bala* (2-5 years); and (v) *Kumara* (5-16 years). Each of these divisions of childhood were associated with major rites and rituals, which marked its transition from one period to another. Many of these childhood *samskaras* — like *namakarana* (naming ceremony), *mundan* (tonsure ceremony) *and upanayana* (initiation into religion and wider community) are being performed even today with fanfare by the people of India. These *samskaras*, in a way, emphasised the critical period both in biological as well as social development thus paving the way for the gradual integration of the child into society. Ironically, girls and children belonging to the lower castes were largely excluded from these *samskaras*. For instance, the *sohras*– joyous songs of celebration sung at the birth of a child in the Hindispeakingbelt– are almost never sung for newborn daughters. In fact, many *sohras* express the relief of mother's over the fact that she has been blessed with a son and not a daughter. The preference for a son when a child is born, thus, seems to be as old as the Indian society itself.

Our two great epics, the *Ramayana* and the *Mahabharata* also eulogise the Indian view of childhood whereby there is an intense parental longing for children, and their upbringing is characterised by affectionate indulgence. This 'childcenteredness', however, was found to be limited to boys only. The Indian tradition all along has been indifferent, if not overtly hostile, to the developmental fate of girls. Secondly, the Indian tradition subscribed to an ideology that downgraded the role of the environment and nurture in the development of a child, and instead emphasised upon a deterministic conception of mystical heredity. This mystical heredity in the *Mahabharata* was reduced to the *karmas* of the previous life and the attributes of the father (especially his caste) transmitted through his 'seed' (Kakar, 1981: 199-200). These epics also displayed as to how young children, especially boys, were placed under the tutorship and guidance of respected gurus wherein moral precepts enjoined in the *shastras* were taught on a one-to-one basis. But, this too, was confined to the boys of the ruling upper-castes.

Likewise, in ancient Indian law, especially in the *Laws of Manu*, the child though located very near the bottom of a social pyramid was bestowed society's protection. And, this protective indulgence was best reflected in matters which concerned the children most – namely, their chastisement. Children were only to be beaten with a rope or bamboo stick split at the end. The split bamboo, as we may remember from circus clowns' mock fights, makes a loud noise but does not inflict much pain. Moreover, even this punishment was to be carried out only on the back and never on the head or the chest. All those who hold progressive views on child discipline, the beating of children may hardly seem like 'protective indulgence'. Nonetheless, the extent of this indulgence becomes strikingly clear when we compare Manu's *Laws* with legal texts of other ancient societies where brutal forms of child abuse and maltreatment existed. As already mentioned in the beginning, there is evidence in the law codes and digests of ancient Rome to suggest that brutal forms of child abuse were common mistreatment, which the more enlightened emperors attempted to mitigate. And, that it was only as late as 374 A.D. that infanticide was declared a capital offence in the Roman world. In short, though Manu's *Laws* by modern standards have been severely condemned as a repository of inequity, their attitude towards children – one of protective nurturance– is unexceptionable, at least within the premises of the patriarchal society which gave the *Laws* their birth. Surprisingly, Manu also expressed that kindness be shown to the daughter as she is 'physically more tender and her emotions are more delicate'.

Interestingly, though historical and sociological documentation of early Indian civilisation points out towards the pervasive biases of that time in the upbringing of children, on account of factors like caste, kinship, age, gender and the like, rulers like Ashoka (268-31 B.C.), Chandragupta Vikramaditya (*c.* A.D. 375-415) tried to propound moral edicts as a counter-balance in which obedience towards parents and respect for elders was extolled. In nutshell, the point driven home was that loyalty and obedience to one's elders, was not only moral but also socially approved and valued behaviour.

For an account of children and childhood in the Indian literary tradition, let us also take a look at the classical Sanskrit literature. Here, the child curiouslyseems to have appeared as a wish — that is, in the context of a couple's, or more often a father's, longing for offspring — or as the fulfilment of the wish— in descriptions of parental happiness when a child was born and in lyrical accounts of parental love, usually of a father for his son. On the whole, children rarely figured as individuals in their own right, with activities, reactions and feelings separate from those of their all-powerful parents. Bhavabhuti's description of Rama's love for Lava and Kusha, and Banbhatta's rhapsodization over Prabhakarvardhan's love for his son, Harsha, are two well-known examples that could be cited here. Kalidasa, the greatest of all Sanskrit poets, too was lyrical in his descriptions about the father's feeling for his son, but at the same time he sensitively portrayed, with much empathy, the sage Kaṇva's love for his daughter

Shakuntala. Needless to mention, the classics of the regional languages are also replete with rich accounts of children and childhood. It would be useful to mention here the medieval Hindi literature associated with the Bhakti movement, especially the songs of Surdasa on Krishna's childhood and that of Tulsidasa on Rama's childhood. The verses of these songs, till date, are a rich source for Hindu ideals of childhood and for delineating the topography of a culturally approved utopia of childhood. Besides, the Bhakti poetry laid enormous emphasis on the loving relationship between mother and child. Analogous to the motherchild interplay, or rather as its extension, we find a third theme in Bhakti literature in which the child is at the centre of an admiring circle of adults. If the mother is in the foreground, then the background consists of the adults in the community– the *gopis* of Gokul, the citizens of Ayodhya – milling around him. This particular theme reveals the child's primary need to be central to his world, rather than exist forlornly at its outskirts, to cause a glow in the eyes of adults rather than be looked at with indifference.

In traditional India, thus, in comparison to the West, it was early childhood rather than adulthood that was considered to be the 'golden age' in individual's life history. Shashi Pande has distinguished Western and Indian social relations by suggesting that in the West, intimacy in a relationship develops out of some shared activity, as when a father takes his son on hunting and fishing trips as a means of developing (or proving) a mutual trust and camaraderie, whereas no such 'hidden agenda' is needed for a cultivation of a relationship in Indian society. However, before getting lost in any selfcongratulatory adulation, we must also note that the gravest drawback of the Indian tradition was the inferior status accorded to girl children. For girls, in comparison to boys, learning the mandatory skills of household work, cooking and childcare, etc. constituted the daily activities around which their lives revolved. In this, of course, the mother, grandmother, aunts, sisters and sistersin-laws, her allies against the discriminations and inequities of the existent patriarchal order and values groomed her. In fact, late childhood marked the beginning of an Indian girl's deliberate training in how to be a 'good woman', and hence the conscious inculcation of culturally designated feminine roles. M.N. Srinivas, in his book, *Marriage and Family in Mysore* writes that "It is the mother's duty to train her daughter up to be an absolute docile daughter-inlaw...' (Srinivas, 1942: 195). Girls were also married at an early age, which invariably marked the end of their childhood. The low status accorded to the girl child was perhaps one of the reasons for the prevalence of female infanticide in traditional India which continues to exist even today. With the coming of the Arabs, Turks, Afghans and the Mughals, the medieval period stretching across from the eleventh to seventeenth centuries almost, saw an all-round impoverishment and degeneration in India. The foreign invasions not only plundered but completely destroyed the wealth and sociocultural ethos of India. Due to the overall economic deterioration experienced by the people, the children too faced adverse vicissitudes. Imposition of foreign culture had a profound impact at all levels. Families, and particularly those of the preponderant rural population, could no longer afford wholesome food and amenities for their children. Emphasis on elementary education gradually withered away which was quite widespread earlier. Among the Hindus, elementary education was mostly confined to the higher castes like Brahmins, Rajputs and Vaishyas. Elementary education among the Muslims was given to those who belonged to aristocratic and rich families at home through the Maulvis. Others had to go to the *maktabs* situated in mosques. Girls, on the other hand, were seldom given education and their status in comparison to boys remained inferior.

The rulers or the people took no remedial steps either. During this period, in India too, the early legal statements were conspicuously silent on children's rights. The Ten Commandments, arguably the most influential of all legal codes, contains a clear normative pronouncement on parent-child relations but it is in terms of respect for parents and is silent on the obligation of parents to love and nurture children. One of the earliest recognitions of children's rights perhaps is found in the Massachusetts *Body of Liberties* of 1641 where parents are told not to choose their children's mates and not to use unnatural severity against their children. Children, furthermore, were given 'free liberty to complain to the Authorities for redress'. But this was also the law that prescribed the death penalty for children over 16 who disobeyed parents. There is no evidence though that children did successfully litigate against their parents but nor is there any that disobedient children were executed. The document, nevertheless, remains interesting in showing, as it does, that even some 365 years ago protection of children went hand in hand with adding the power of the State to parental authority.

The eighteenth century as well can hardly be said to be identified with children's rights. It is pertinent to remark that the documents emanating from the great libertarian revolutions, the American and the French, have nothing specifically to say about children.

The nineteenth century, however, saw the birth of the child-saving movement, the growth of the orphanage, the development of child protection legislations, schooling and the construction of separate institutions, including the juvenile courts, for delinquent children, in different parts of the Western world. One of the reasons for this kind of development was that in the wake of Industrial Revolution there was severe exploitation of many working-class children who were widely employed in textiles, mining, agriculture, domestic service, docks and navigation.

Moreover, the so-called 'advances' of industrialisation and urbanisation had serious consequences. Displacement of communities, unemployment and sociopolitical unrest resulted in marginalization and abandonment of many children whose 'opportunities' were restricted to petty offending as means of survival. These children were left to their fate to fend for themselves. At this point of time, the British ruled India. Being a colony of the British, the plight of its children especially those belonging to the lower strata of society was certainly gloomy. As Britain was negotiating its place within a new emerging economic, social and political world order, it was a time of great uncertainty for India and this inevitably affected its children too. Despite all this, moral panic and political reaction of that time dovetailed into the already existing reform and philanthropic efforts towards children which mobilised charity crusades and inspired voluntary effort. But, all this took a back seat in the face of growing imperialism of that time that had taken one of its worst forms. This development spelled doom for children as they were thought of as 'Bricks for Empire Building' and like others continued to be exploited in different ways. The ensuing freedom struggle, that nearly spread over 100 years – from mid-nineteenth to the midtwentieth century– aimed not merely at achieving political independence from the

British rule, but also at reinvigorating the debilitated sunken society of India which under decades of slavery had lost its initiative, values and vitality.

It was the endeavour of leaders like Raja Ram Mohan Ray, Mahatma Gandhi and others to awaken the people and rouse them to overcome their backwardness, be it in the shape of illiteracy or socio-cultural practices like child marriage or neglect in the upbringing of children, etc. As a result, the long years of struggle for freedom saw an all-round spate of activities which may be termed as 'social action' so to come out of the prevailing weaknesses in society and to build selfreliance in the people. Consequently, the care of the child came to be viewed upon as a vital element in the resurrection of the nation. Mahatma Gandhi and later Pt. Jawaharlal Nehru, in person, gave much of their time to inculcate social concern for the citizens of tomorrow – the children. Advancing literacy, in Western societies, to a large extent, helped to change attitudes towards children. The resultant effect of all this was that a large number of dedicated visionaries, charitable and voluntary organisations moved by the harrowing tales of children, worked relentlessly to improve the overall position of children in society along with that of women. All of them invested their time, knowledge and resources towards better health, education, and growth of the weaker children. It was during this period that some of the oldest voluntary organizations such as 'The Children's Aid Society' and '*Balkan Ji Bari*' came into being in 1920s in the service of children belonging to the poor, uneducated and helpless families. The entire century of freedom struggle may well be termed as the Evanescent Dawn of Voluntary Action when people learnt to pool their common resources to remove social ills rather than rely upon an alien regime which had no State Policy nor a programme to meet the needs of children. This was also the beginning of a spirit of independence at the group social action level. This period also witnessed the enactment of laws such as the Apprentices Act, Reformatory Schools Act and Factories Act which became important factors in the shaping and structuring of a new childhood.

The period immediately following the First World War, posed a variety of challenges to Britain and other countries of Europe and North America. These were mainly connected to the question of how they could create a society which would preclude the cataclysm of violence and upheaval through which they had just passed. It would be worthwhile to mention that partly as a result of the ravages of war on the civilians in affected countries, and partly in response to the growing concern in most countries of Europe and North America for the protection of children, the newly formed League of Nations established a Committee on Child Welfare in 1919.

Interestingly, private agencies felt the need to provide broad social standards for the protection of children. Of particular importance was the Save the Children International Union, inspired largely by the work of an English woman, Eglantyne Jebb, who had founded Save the Children in response to her own experience with child victims of war in the Balkans. In 1923, the Save the Children International Union adopted as its charter a five-point declaration which described the basic conditions a society should meet in order to provide adequate protection and care for its children. The next year, the Union persuaded the League of Nations to adopt the same declaration. Since the League of Nations held its meetings in Geneva, this 1924 Declaration of the Rights of the Child came to be known as the "Declaration of Geneva". Recognising that 'mankind owes to the child the best that it has to give', the five simple principles of the Declaration established the basis of child rights in terms of both protection of the weak and vulnerable and promotion of the child's development. The Declaration also made it clear that the care and protection of children was no longer the exclusive responsibility of families or communities or even individual countries; the world as a whole had a legitimate interest in the welfare of all children.

The League of Nations, as we all know, was not able to prevent another world war. The Second World War engulfed the entire planet, and caused even greater suffering for non-combatants, particularly children. In 1945, the United Nations Organisation replaced the League of Nations. In 1946, the Economic and Social Council of the United Nations recommended that the Geneva Declaration be reaffirmed as a sign of commitment to the cause of children. The same year, the United Nations established a specialised agency — UNICEF with a mandate to care for the world's children. Initially known as the United Nations

International Children's Emergency Fund, it provided assistance to children in Europe and elsewhere who had lost homes, family, and opportunity as a result of the war. Its mandate was later redefined so as to give the agency responsibility for long-term assistance to children who suffered from deprivation caused by economic and political conditions, as well as the effects of war. The present nomenclature of UNICEF is United Nations Children's Fund.

It would be seen from the above that the primary purpose of this chapter has been to provide a broad overview about children as well as provoke a rethinking of settled ideas about children and childhood so as to interrogate dominant notions which are underpinned by naturalistic and biologically determined conceptualizations.

We all know that there is no universal picture of children or for that matter childhood. Moreover, for understanding childhood it is important to demystify the glory of any one class, caste, region, gender or time. The need of the hour is to unpack the manner in which children and childhood so far have been understood. Who would wish to beg or grovel, to be the recipient of *noblesse oblige* or charity when they can demand what is their due? Rights are entitlements; they are trumps; they are valuable commodities. And they are also, as we now learn, weapons to undermine power. A rights strategy is one way in which the hitherto excluded can be included, within the community and within the socioeconomic and political structure.

"Declaration of Geneva"

- Child must be given the means needed for its normal development, both materially and spiritually.
- Hungry child should be fed; sick child should be helped; erring child should be reclaimed; and the orphan and the homeless child should be sheltered and succoured.
- Child must be first to receive relief in times of distress.
- Child must be put in a position to earn a livelihood and must be protected against every form of exploitation.
- Child must be brought up in the consciousness that its best qualities are to be used in the service of its fellow men.

Milestones: National and International

We all know that India became independent on 15 August 1947. Independence ushered in a new era for children. The historical process, and its social, economic and political priorities from mid-nineteenth to mid-twentieth century, paved the way for shaping a more coherent concept of childhood located within the family as the principal institutional influence and as the prime site for socialization.

Further, it determined the nature of the relationship between the child, the family and the State and thus created the essential foundations of a national childhood for all children. Correspondingly, the Constitution of India, which came into force in January 1950, contains provisions for survival, development and protection of children.

These are included both in Part III and Part IV of the Constitution pertaining to 'Fundamental Rights' and 'Directive Principles of State Policy'. Being one of the world's largest democracy, India has a federal system of government, with the States having their own democratically elected governments. The relative jurisdiction of the Central and State Governments over different matters has been indicated in the Seventh Schedule of the Constitution of India under the Union, State and Concurrent Lists.

The survival, development and protection of children fall either in the Concurrent or in the State List. However, the implementation of schemes, including those of the Central Government, is carried out by the States. The 73rd and 74th constitutional amendments have recognised a third tier, below that of the State Government, viz., *Panchayati Raj Institutions* (PRIs), given them financial and administrative powers, and listed the subjects falling in their area of activities, a number of which relate to those services which have a direct bearing on children.

Major Constitutional Provisions Fundamental Rights

- Article 14: ... shall not deny to any person equality before the law or the equal protection of the laws within the territory of India.
- Article 15: ... shall not discriminate against any citizen... (3) Nothing in this article shall prevent the State from

making special provision for women and children. (4) Nothing ... shall prevent the State from making any special provision for the advancement of any socially and educationally backward classes of citizens or for the Scheduled Castes and the Scheduled Tribes.

- Article 17: "Untouchability" is abolished and its practice in any form is forbidden. ...
- Article 19: (1) All citizens shall have the right – (a) to freedom of speech and expression; ... (c) to form associations or unions; (d) to move freely throughout the territory of India; (e) to reside and settle in any part of the territory of India.
- Article 21: No person shall be deprived of his life or personal liberty except according to procedure established by law.
- Article 21 A: ... shall provide free and compulsory education to all children of the age of six to fourteen years...
- Article 23: Traffic in human beings and begar and other similar forms of forced labour are prohibited...
- Article 24: No child below the age of fourteen years shall be employed to work in any factory or mine or engaged in any other hazardous employment.

Directive Principles of State Policy

- Article 39: ... (e) ... the tender age of children are not abused... and not forced by economic necessity to enter avocations unsuited to their age or strength; (f) that children are given opportunities and facilities to develop in a healthy manner and in conditions of freedom and dignity and that childhood... protected against exploitation and against moral and material abandonment.
- Article 45: ...provide early childhood care and education for all children until they complete the age of six years.
- Article 46: ...shall promote with special care the educational and economic interests of the weaker sections of the people, and, in particular, of the Scheduled Castes and the Scheduled Tribes,...

- Article 47: ...raising of the level of nutrition and the standard of living of its people and the improvement of public health...
- Article 51: The State shall endeavour to – ... (c) foster respect for international law and treaty obligations ...
- Article 51A: ... (k) ... parent or guardian to provide opportunities for education to his child or, as the case may be, ward between the age of six and fourteen years.

Development programmes in the country, including those for children, are carried out within the framework of the Five-Year Plans. Some of these programmes are wholly funded by the Central Government, some by both Central and State Governments, and some entirely by the State Government, depending on whether the programmes are classified as Central, centrally sponsored or State sector schemes. In addition, a wide variety of programmes are also being implemented in collaboration with international organisations and non-governmental organisations, which are now growing as a vibrant sector in the development and empowerment of children. In the ensuing paragraphs, let us now see themilestones achieved by India on the whole ever since it achieved independence with regard to survival, development, protection and participation of children both at the national and international level.

The *First Five-Year Plan (1951-56)* took a comprehensive review of resources and needs of children along with women to meet the problems that had emanated out of the *Second World War* and the partition of the country. Health, nutrition and education of children were identified as special areas of concern. In order to focus attention on these areas, it was decided to forge a viable partnership with the voluntary sector. Correspondingly, in 1953, the *Central Social Welfare Board* (CSWB) was constituted with the object especially of assisting voluntary agencies in organising welfare programmes for children, women and handicapped persons. The Board assisted 591 child welfare organisations during the First Five-Year Plan. Besides, in collaboration with State Governments, the Board setup *State Welfare Boards* throughout the country. In 1954, *Welfare Extension Projects* were started to reach children and women in rural areas through the creation of *balwadis* and *mahila mandals*. Special programmes were also taken up to meet the needs of delinquents, destitute, handicapped and other groups of children. For this, extensive training was provided to childcare functionaries engaged in carrying out different kinds of programmes for children. In addition, the Government of India passed the *Protection of Civil Rights Act, 1955* and ratified the *International Labour Organization (ILO) Convention No. 5 of 1919* on minimum age of work in industry.

The *Second Five-Year Plan (1956-61)* aimed at stabilising the child welfare system. As such, the activities of CSWB were further strengthened. In 1956, the *Suppression of Immoral Traffic in Women and Girls Act (SITA)* was enacted in pursuance of Government of India's ratification of the United Nations Convention for the Suppression of the Traffic in Persons and the Exploitation of the Prostitution of *Others* in the year 1950. Some of the other legislations enacted in the year 1956 were the *Hindu Adoption and Maintenance Act, Hindu Minority and Guardianship Act, Women's and Children's Institutions (Licensing) Act* and *Young Persons (Harmful Publications) Act*. In 1957, the Welfare Extension Projects were reviewed. This led to the launching of *Coordinated Welfare Extension Projects* in 1958. The Central and State Governments also stepped in to share the responsibility of implementing the schemes and programmes for destitutes and delinquents under the *Children's Act, 1960*. Special programmes were also undertaken for education, training and rehabilitation of handicapped children. During the Plan period, existing health, nutrition and education services were further strengthened and expanded. In 1957, the *National Bravery Award Scheme* was instituted and 14 November, which also happens to be the birthday of our first Prime Minister, Pt. Jawaharlal Nehru was declared as *Universal Children's Day*.

At the international level, the United Nations General Assembly adopted the *Declaration of the Rights of the Child* on 20 November, 1959. Prior to this, in 1948, the United Nations General Assembly had adopted the *Universal Declaration of Human Rights* (UDHR). The UDHR contains three specific references about children and their rights. Article 25 states that "Motherhood and childhood are entitled to special care and assistance", and adds that "All children, whether born in or out of wedlock, shall enjoy the same social protection". In Article 26, which deals with the right to education, provision is made to ensure that "Parents have a prior right to choose the kind of education that shall be given to their children".

Thus, when the UDHR was adopted, it was assumed that children's rights had been taken care of on the whole. But, this was, however, not found to be fully adequate to the situation of children in the post-Second World War era. Children were recognised as a particularly vulnerable group, who needed specific measures directed towards their protection and the provision of rights that would permit their full and healthy development. It was in this background that the *General Assembly* adopted the *Declaration of the Rights of the Child* mentioned above.

The 1959 Declaration expanded the five principles of the Geneva Declaration to ten basic principles. Like its predecessor, the 1959 Declaration was no more than a statement of good intentions. For, there was no way to bind the Member States of the United Nations in order to put the principles of the Declaration into practice. Besides, the Declaration looked at children purely as an investment. It did not accord any recognition to their autonomy, or for that matter to the importance of their wishes and feelings, nor any appreciation to their empowerment. The child only remained as an object of concern, rather than a person with self-determination.

However, much before the 1959 Declaration came into existence, Indian Constitution had reflected all these 10 principles including the articles contained in the UDHR. Nonetheless, the Government of India subscribed to the principles enshrined in the Declaration and ensured that adequate steps were taken to guarantee these rights to children. It thus moved ahead with its *Third Five-Year Plan (1961-66)* with increased emphasis on intersectoral coordination of services for children. An attempt was simultaneously made to coordinate health, education and welfare services. The Third Plan also recognised that the child was a human being with special needs. A significant achievement was the establishment of the *Department of Social Security* in June 1964, so as to give concerted attention to the problems and needs of children. This Department was later renamed as the *Department of Social Welfare* in January 1966, and was finally elevated to the status of an independent *Ministry of Social Welfare* in August 1979. This Ministry is today known by the nomenclature of *Social Justice and Empowerment*. To counter poor levels of nutrition, *Applied Nutrition Programme* was introduced in 1963. Later, in the year

1965, *Food and Nutrition Board* was set-up in the Department of Food. Recognising the need to rectify the existent imbalance of educational facilities at the primary, middle and high school levels and the fact that the State was unable to fulfil its constitutional obligation of providing free and compulsory education to all children within a period of ten years, the Third Plan set-up an *Education Commission.*

UN Declaration of the Rights of the Child

- Non-discrimination.
- Special protection, opportunities and facilities to develop physically, mentally, morally, spiritually and socially in a healthy and normal manner and in conditions of freedom and dignity.
- The right to a name and nationality.
- The right to social security, adequate nutrition, housing, recreation and medical services.
- The differently-abled child to be given special treatment, education and care.
- The need for love and understanding so that the child grows in the care and responsibility of his/her parents, and in an atmosphere of affection and moral and material security.
- Entitlement to education, which should be free and compulsory, at least in the elementary stages.
- The child should be among the first to receive protection and relief in all circumstances.
- Protection against all forms of neglect, cruelty and exploitation, including that associated with employment.
- Protection from practices that may foster racial, religious and other forms of discrimination.

Under the chairmanship of Dr. D.S. Kothari to find out possible solutions. The recommendations of the Kothari Commission led to the formulation of the *National Education Policy* in 1968 which in a way gave fillip to the efforts being made in the education sector. A *Committee on Child Care* was also constituted whose recommendations gave way to a comprehensive *Scheme of Family and Child Welfare* in 1967 thereby providing integrated services to pre-school children in villages and basic training to women in craft, health education, nutrition and child care. The *Fourth Five-Year Plan (1969-74)* focussed on development of a package of basic minimum services for children. It also drew attention to the problems of neglected and destitute children and introduced a *Scheme for Children in Need for Care and Protection*. In 1974, the *National Policy for Children* was adopted.

The Policy Resolution recognised children as the nation's supremely important asset and declared that it is the responsibility of the State to nurture them. It further emphasised that it shall be the duty of the State to "provide adequate services to children, both before and after birth and through the period of growth, to ensure their full physical, mental and social development." And that the "State shall progressively increase the scope of such services so that within a reasonable time, all children in the country enjoy optimum conditions for their balanced growth."

To achieve these objectives, it called for the adoption of following measures – comprehensive health programme; provision of nutritional services, nutrition and nutrition education to expectant and nursing mothers; free and compulsory education to all children up to the age of 14 years; provision of non-formal education, promotion of physical education and other types of recreational as well as cultural and scientific activities in schools and community centres; provision of special assistance to children belonging to the weaker sections of society; upliftment of children in distress; protection against neglect, cruelty and exploitation of children; protection against child labour; provision of special facilities for children ailing from various kinds of disabilities and encouragement and assistance to gifted children especially those belonging to the weaker sections of the society. In achieving the above, the Policy gave special recognition to the role of voluntary organisations.

Right to health being a basic human right, the Fourth Plan accorded high priority to *Mother and Child Health Programme (MCH)*. The *Special Nutrition Programme, Balwadi Nutrition Programme* and *Prophylaxis Scheme against Blindness due to Vitamin A Deficiency among Children* were also introduced in 1970-71. The voluntary organisations too continued to work in partnership with the Government and some on their own.

The *Fifth Five-Year Plan (1974-79)* saw a shift in focus from child welfare to child development wherein emphasis was laid on further integration and coordination of services, increased allocations and introduction of new schemes for children. The adoption of National Policy for Children led to the constitution of the *National Children's Board* in December, 1974 under the presidentship of the Prime Minister for planning, reviewing and coordination of services and programmes to meet the needs of children. The scheme of *Integrated Child Development Services* (ICDS) was launched on 2 October 1975. Launching of the ICDS was a logical culmination of efforts pursued through the earlier four Five-Year Plans. In 1975, the Government ratified the *ILO Convention No. 123 of 1965* relating to minimum age for underground work. The *Minimum Needs Programme* was also launched in order to enhance the capacity of families and communities.

The ICDS scheme is considered to be one of the largest outreach programmes for children in the world. It presently covers almost all the development blocks in India. The scheme adopts a multi-sectoral approach to child well-being, incorporating health, education and nutrition interventions, and is implemented through a network of *anganwadi* centres (AWCs) at the community level. At these centres, *anganwadi* workers and their helpers provide eight key services to 0-6 year old children along with expectant and nursing mothers, covering supplementary nutrition, immunisation, health check-ups and referral services, health and nutrition education to adult women, micronutrient supplementation and pre-school education for 3 to 6 year old children. As the programme has developed over the years, it has expanded its range of interventions to include components focussed on adolescent girls' nutrition, health, awareness and skills development, as well as income generation schemes for women.

The year 1979 holds great significance in the history of child welfare and development. Being designated as the *International Year of the Child* (IYC) by the United Nations General Assembly, number of activities and programmes were undertaken throughout the world in this year. In India, a *National Plan of Action* was prepared *to observe the IYC*. The main theme of the National Plan of Action was 'Reaching the Deprived Children'. Based on the model of National Plan of Action, many State Governments in

India as well as non-governmental organisations formulated their own plans of action with specific programmes and activities to be taken up during the year in their respective areas. All this gave a great impetus to the on-going programmes related to children in India. The year also saw the United Nations Commission on Human Rights starting work on the drafting of the *Convention on the Rights of the Child (CRC)*. The initiative to draft the Convention came from Poland and the Commission responded by setting-up a multi-country Working Group.

In India, another important achievement during the year was setting-up of the *National Children's Fund* to provide assistance to voluntary organisations. During IYC, the *National Awards for Child Welfare* was instituted. In the health sector, the Government of India signed the *Alma Ata Declaration* of 1978 and committed itself to the goal of 'Health for All by 2000 A.D'.. The *Expanded Programme of Immunisation* was also introduced in 1978. In the area of nutrition, various nutrition intervention programmes being implemented were strengthened and expanded including the *Prophylaxis against Iron and Vitamin A Deficiency Programmes*. In 1975, the *Scheme of Crèches/Day Care Centres for Children of Working and Ailing Mothers* was launched by the CSWB. In 1976, the Child Marriage Restraint Act of 1929 was amended and in 1978, the SITA enacted in 1956 was modified. In 1976, the *Bonded Labour (System) Abolition Act* was enacted.

The *Sixth Five-Year Plan (1980-85)* reiterated the approach and strategy adopted for children during the Fifth Plan and further promoted integration and strengthening of child welfare and development programmes started earlier. During the *International Year of Disabled* in 1981 vigorous efforts were made to implement various education, training and rehabilitation programmes for the physically handicapped children. Preventive and development services of domiciliary nature were accorded priority over institutional care for destitutes, delinquents and handicapped children. The problem of working children and their welfare simultaneously received attention of the planners for the first time during the Sixth Five-Year Plan and appropriate programmes were undertaken to improve the health, nutrition and educational status of working children. In 1981, the *Central Child Labour Advisory Board* was set-up to review implementation of existing laws concerning child labour. In 1982, the *Scheme of Early Childhood Education* was introduced as a strategy to reduce dropout rate and improve the rate of retention in schools. The *Development of Women and Children in Rural Areas* was another scheme that was introduced in the year 1982. Another important milestone in the Sixth Plan period was the formulation of the *National Health Policy* in the year 1983. The same year, the Government of India recognised the *International Code on the Marketing of Breast Milk Substitutes* that was adopted by the World Health Assembly and formulated the *Indian National Code for Protection and Promotion of Breast Feeding*. ICDS was used as a major nutrition intervention programme as well as a vehicle for promoting elementary education among children.

The *Seventh Five-Year Plan (1985-90)* led to spatial expansion and enrichment of child development services. In order to give focussed attention and direction to child development, a separate *Department of Women and Child Development* was set-up for the first time in the Ministry of Human Resource Development in September 1985. Its status was elevated to that of an independent *Ministry of Women and Child Development* in 2006 and issues concerning children that were earlier being dealt by the Ministry of Social Justice and Empowerment have now been transferred to it. The ICDS continued to be the main integrated national programme for early childhood survival and development during the Seventh Plan period.

To deal effectively with the problem of neglected children and children in conflict with law, the *Juvenile Justice Act, 1986* was legislated, repealing the then Children's Act of 1960. To implement the provisions of the 1986 Act, a *Scheme of* Prevention and Control of Social *Maladjustment* was initiated in 1986-87. The Government also enacted the *Child Labour (Prohibition and Regulation) Act, 1986.* In 1987, the *National Policy on Child Labour* was announced. *National Child Labour Projects* were started in areas where there was high concentration of child labour. Simultaneously, efforts were made to expand crèche services for children of working women. The main thrust in the programmes for children who were handicapped was on prevention of disabilities and development of their functional skills. In 1985, the *Scheme of District Rehabilitation Centres* was introduced as a Pilot Project. In 1986, the Government further modified the SITA and also changed the name of the Act to *Immoral*

Traffic (Prevention) Act to cover all persons, whether male or female, who were exploited sexually for commercial purposes. These apart, stringent punishments were prescribed for offences involving children. Another notable milestone of the Seventh Plan was setting up of a *Central Adoption Resource Agency (CARA)* in 1990 to deal with matters relating to adoption. Later, during the Eighth Five-Year Plan, the Government pioneered a *Scheme of Assistance to Homes for Infants (Shishu Greh) to Promote In-country Adoption.* Under the MCH programme, efforts were made to reduce Infant Mortality Rate (IMR) and Maternal Mortality Rate (MMR). In the year 1985, the *Universal Immunisation Programme* was launched under the MCH programme to protect children from six major diseases which affected early childhood mortality and morbidity, viz., diptheria, whooping cough, tetanus, polio, measles and childhood tuberculosis.

Functions of CARA

CARA grants recognition to Indian placement agencies on the recommendations of the State Government for processing inter-country adoption. It also accords enlistment to foreign agencies that are engaged in sponsoring applications of foreign prospective adoptive parents. These agencies are licensed by the appropriate Government Department in their country of origin to mediate incountry and inter-country adoptions and their applications for enlistment/renewal are forwarded and recommended by India's Diplomatic Mission. At present, there are 74 recognised placement agencies in the country and 158 foreign enlisted agencies. laid on *Oral Rehydration Therapy Programme* to prevent diarrhoeal deaths among children. The *National Diarrhoeal Disease Control Programme* was made part of the MCH Programme.

In the education sector, the strategies of the Seventh Plan underwent a change in the middle of the Plan period with the adoption of a new *National Policy on Education (NPE)* in 1986. Taking a holistic view, the NPE visualised education as a dynamic, cumulative, life-long process, providing diversity of learning opportunities to all segments of society. It's main purpose was to fulfil the objective of *"Education for All"* by providing early childhood care and education, universalising elementary education through formal and non-formal methods, reducing wastage and involving the local community in the management of early education. As a result, new schemes were implemented like the *District Primary Education Programme* in 1986 and the *Operation Black Board* in 1987. Besides, the *Scheme of Non-formal Education* was revised. Few of the other important initiatives taken by the Government in selected areas especially in educationally backward States, were the *Shiksha Karmi Project* and *Lok Jumbish Project* in Rajasthan, *Bihar Education Project* and the *Andhra Pradesh Primary Education Project*. The NPE in its own way tried to provide scope for equal access to education to all, irrespective of class, caste, creed or gender. In addition, it envisaged a common educational structure like 10+2+3 and common core curriculum throughout the country. It also sought to remove disparities by catering to the needs of Scheduled Castes, Scheduled Tribes, the handicapped and other minority groups. To look into the problems of street children, the Ministry of Social Justice and Empowerment introduced the *Integrated Programme for Street Children*.

At the regional level, India actively promoted and supported the 1986 decision of *South Asian Association for Regional Cooperation (SAARC)* to take up the issue of children as a summit concern, and to declare first a year and then a decade for the girl child (1990-2000). At the international level, the Convention on the Rights of the Child (CRC) was approved by the General Assembly of the United Nations on 20 November 1989 (the thirtieth anniversary of the adoption of the Declaration of the Rights of the Child).

This Convention was formally opened for signature and ratification on 26 January 1990, and various nations vied to be the first to sign and ratify, a race that was won by Ghana when the Secretary General of the United Nations received that country's instrument of ratification on 5 February 1990. Previous United Nations human rights treaties had taken several years to receive the minimum number of ratifications necessary for their entry into force.

The CRC had behind it the full resources of UNICEF which, having decided that the Convention was in the best interest of the child, determined to achieve the target of universal ratification as a top priority. Allied with UNICEF in this effort was a worldwide network of non-governmental organisations, focussed in the NGO Group on the Convention. These included Save the Children Alliance, which had a long standing claim of priority in the field of child rights, and Defence for Children International, which chaired the NGO Ad-hoc Group that worked on the negotiation of the Convention.

Many of the proposals made by the NGO Ad-hoc Group for the Convention were adopted by the Government representatives on the Working Group, and are reflected in the final text of the Convention. The resultant effect of all this was that in virtually every country there was a coherent and concerted pressure for ratification applied by UNICEF, from the outside, and by national non-governmental coalitions or coordinating committees for child rights, from the inside. The net outcome was that, by 2 September 1990, just over 8 months after the Convention had been opened for signature, the twentieth ratification had been received and the Convention came into effect – more quickly than any other human rights treaty. The previous record for this kind was held by the Convention on the Elimination of All Forms of Discrimination Against Women (CEDAW), which also had a strong non-governmental lobby pushing for its ratification in many countries, but it took almost three times as long as the CRC to come into effect. When a country ratifies a UN Convention, it becomes law within its territory.

To monitor progress achieved in the realisation of children's rights, the CRC has established an international expert body, the *Committee on the Rights of the Child,* which provides awareness and understanding of the principles and provisions of this treaty. The CRC Committee consists of ten experts which ensures that the law is being enforced.

The Government of India ratified the CRC on 11 December 1992. As of now, except for Somalia and the United States of America, all the countries around the world have ratified the CRC. The latter, however, has signed the Convention, thereby indicating general support for its principles and an intention not to take actions that would actively undermine those principles.

The CRC is "the most complete statement of child rights ever made". It takes the ten principles of the 1959 Declaration of the Rights of the Child, and expands them to 54 articles, of which 41 relate specifically to the rights of children, covering almost every aspect of a child's life. It is indeed an innovative document in overall human rights theory and practice.

In fact, it is the first United Nations human rights instrument since the UDHR which brings together as inextricable elements of the life of an individual human being the full range of civil and political rights, and economic, social and cultural rights. It can do this because it treats children as complete individuals, rather than as elements in an economic or sociopolitical system.

The Convention aims to create a balance between the rights of children and those of the parents or adults responsible for their survival, development and protection. This is achieved by according children the right to participate in decisions concerning them and their future. It is, thus, a holistic document for each article is intertwined with the others. Not only this, the various articles exert an influence on the interpretation and implementation of each other. In other words, the rights defined in the Convention are *interdependent*; as none of the articles can be dealt in isolation. They have to be applied and implemented simultaneously if at all the rights of every child is to be respected.

CRC at a Glance Preamble

Part I: Operational Articles

Article 1 Defines child as a person who is below the age of 18 years.

Article 2 Non-discrimination

Article 3 Best interest of the child

Article 4 Measures for implementation of rights

Article 5 Parents, family, community rights and responsibilities

Article 6 Right to life

Article 7 Right to name and nationality

Article 8 Preservation of identity

Article 9 Non-separation from parents

Article 10 Family reunification

Article 11 Illicit transfer and non-return of children abroad

Article 12 Expression of opinion

Article 13 Freedom of expression and information

Article 14 Freedom of thought, conscience and religion

Article 15 Freedom of association and peaceful assembly

Article 16 Privacy, honour, reputation

Article 17 Access to information and media

Article 18 Parental responsibility

Article 19 Abuse and neglect (while in family or in care)

Article 20 Protection of child who is deprived (temporarily or permanently) of family environment

Article 21 Adoption

Article 22 Refugee children

Article 23 Disabled children

Article 24 Health care

Article 25 Periodic review of children in care

Article 26 Social security

Article 27 Standard of living

Article 28 Education

Article 29 Aims of education

Article 30 Children of minorities, indigenous children

Article 31 Play, recreation and participation in cultural life and the arts

Article 32 Economic exploitation

Article 33 Protection from narcotic and psychotropic substances abuse

Article 34 Sexual exploitation

Article 35 Abduction/sale/trafficking of children

Article 36 Other forms of exploitation

Article 37 Torture, capital punishment, deprivation of liberty

Article 38 Armed conflicts

Article 39 Recovery and reintegration (following abuse, torture, armed conflicts etc.)

Article 40 Juvenile Justice

Article 41 Rights in other national or international instruments.

Part II: Enforcement

Article 42 Dissemination of the principles and provisions of the Convention

Article 43 Establishment of the Committee

Article 44 Reports from States Parties

Article 45 Method of work of the Committee.

Part III: Administrative Issues

Article 46 Signature

Article 47 Ratification

Article 48 Accession

Article 49 Entry into force

Article 50 Amendments

Article 51 Reservations

Article 52 Denunciation

Article 53 Depositary

Article 54 Authentic texts.

Article 43 sets out the criteria for the establishment of the United Nations Committee on the Rights of the Child, which receives and reviews reports prepared by States Parties about their progress in implementing the Convention as required by Article 44. Unlike other international initiatives that have been taken on behalf of children, in particular, the *Declaration and Plan of Action* that emerged out of the *World Summit for Children* that was held at New York in September 1990, there is no requirement *per se* that the Convention is to be fully implemented by all countries within a stipulated date. Instead, all countries are required to make constant progress towards its implementation, but at a rate that suits their economic and political situation within the resources that are available to them. In nutshell, the CRC does not have a time limit nor does it have an expiry date. The obligations on countries to live up to the rights of children will not cease, but will continue to require action and attention of each one of us, including the Government, to take the onus of protecting and respecting rights of children not because of an international agreement but because "that's just the way children are to be treated". A *Special Rapporteur* has also been appointed on the *Sale of Children, Child Prostitution and Child Pornography* by the United Nations General Assembly who analyses instances of sexual exploitation of children in various countries.

The focus in the *Eighth Five-Year Plan (1992-97)* was on human development through advocacy, mobilisation and community empowerment and it accorded high priority to survival and development of children. The ICDS continued to be the basic strategy for child survival and development focussing on areas predominantly inhabited by the tribal people, Scheduled Castes as well as drought-prone regions and urban slums. In fact, the scheme of ICDS was universalised covering all the Community Development Blocks and major slums in the country. As has been pointed out earlier, the Government of India ratified the CRC in the year 1992. This provided a strong base for initiating necessary legal and other developmental measures for protecting and promoting the rights of children in consonance with the CRC.

During 1993-94, the *National Crèche Fund (NCF)* was set-up to meet the growing demand for crèches. The NCF extended financial assistance for the opening of crèches besides conversion of the existing *Anganwadis-cum-Crèches*. Concerted efforts were simultaneously made to tackle the problem of social deviance, juvenile delinquency and juvenile crime through preventive, correctional and rehabilitative services. On 15 August 1994, a programme to *Eliminate Child Labour in Hazardous Employment* by 2000 was announced. Prior to this, in Government of India joined the *International Programme on Elimination of Child Labour* launched by ILO. Subsequently, the *National Authority for Elimination of Child Labour* was constituted on 26 September 1994 to lay down policies and programmes for elimination of child labour. The enforcement of Child Labour (Prohibition and Regulation) Act, 1986 was also strengthened. In pursuance of the National Policy on Child Labour, specific projects were undertaken in industries where the incidents of child labour were found to be very high. Measures were taken to cover families of child labourers under income generation schemes. Public opinion on the evils of child labour was mobilised through investigative journalism, use of electronic media and the support of activists' groups. In the "Health for All" strategy, health for underprivileged including children was promoted consistently. The *Child Survival and Safe Motherhood (CSSM)* programme was launched during the year 1992-93 to strengthen MCH services. Other measures promoted were: greater access for mothers to pre-natal care; training of midwives so that a larger percentage of births took place with the aid of trained attendants; and spreading of awareness in families about the special health and nutrition needs of pregnant women. With a view to regulate and prevent the misuse of modern pre-natal diagnostic techniques, particularly abortion of female foetuses, *Pre-natal Diagnostic Techniques (Regulation and Prevention of Misuse) Act, 1994* was introduced. Prior to this, the *Infant Milk Substitutes, Feeding Bottles and Infant Foods (Regulation and Production, Supply and Distribution), Act* was formulated in 1992. This came into force on 1 August 1993. During the Eighth Five-Year Plan, the *National AIDS Control Organisation* was established under the Ministry of Health and Family Welfare to strengthen the management capacity for prevention and control of HIV/AIDS. In the year 1993, the *National Nutrition Policy* was adopted to combat the problem of malnutrition. The *Pulse Polio Immunisation Programme* was also started in the year 1995.

In the education sector, the main strategy for achieving the target of "Education for All by 2000 A.D." was adoption of a decentralised approach to planning. In pursuance of the revised National Policy on Education, 1992 and the Programme of Action, various steps were taken to expand early childhood care and education activities, and universalise elementary education. An *NGO Cell* was specifically set-up in 1994 to facilitate networking with NGOs on varied issues concerning children. In the year 1994, *District Primary Education Programme (DPEP)* was launched as a centrally sponsored scheme in 42 districts of seven States, with the aim of revitalizing and strengthening the existing system, tackling problem areas, developing innovative approaches with the district as a unit of planning.

In adopting a holistic approach, emphasis was laid on converting existent programmes and services, and encouraging community participation.

The Eighth Plan specifically recognised the 'Girl Child' as an important target group, demanding attention of the Government for her development and to fight against the prevailing gender discrimination. The Eighth Plan marked the adoption of two *National Plans of Action* in 1992 – one for children and the other exclusively for the girl child. These Plans of Action committed themselves to achieve the goals pronounced in the 1990 World Summit on Survival, Protection and Development of Children. In conformity with these National Plans, many States prepared their own *State Plan of Action for Children/for the Girl Child*. Two separate *Inter-Departmental Coordination Committees* reviewed the progress of the implementation of these two Plans of Action at regular intervals. A few States also embarked upon specific schemes to improve the plight of the girl child. For example, Haryana instituted the '*Apni Beti Apna Dhan*' *Scheme*, Tamil Nadu initiated the '*Cradle Scheme*', Rajasthan introduced the '*Raj Lakshmi Scheme*' and Madhya Pradesh the '*Bhagyalakshmi*' *Scheme*. Another very important Act enacted by the Government of India in this Plan period was the *Persons with Disabilities (Equal Opportunities, Protection of Rights and Full Participation) Act, 1995* that came into force in February 1996. This law is an important landmark and is a significant step in the direction of ensuring equal opportunities for people with disabilities and their full participation in the nation-building.

At the international front, the *World Conference on Human Rights* was held in Vienna in the year 1993. The *Vienna Declaration and Programme of Action* urged States to ratify and implement promptly the CRC and the CEDAW. Taking a cue from all these developments, the Government of India submitted *India's Initial State Party Report on CRC* to the Committee on the Rights of the Child in March 1997. This Report was due for submission in 1995. In the year 1995, however, a four Member team of the CRC Committee visited India in October to make on the spot assessment about the specific problems of children in India. The CRC Committee as mentioned above, is made up of ten independent experts. Governments that ratify the Convention must report to the Committee, first within two years of ratification, and then every five-years.

The Committee has circulated detailed guidelines to States Parties as to what their reports should cover as the process of reporting involves a rigorous review of actions taken by them. It encourages "popular participation and public scrutiny of Government policies", which goes on to show that States Parties are publicly and internationally accountable for the treatment meted out to their children. Another important milestone of the Eighth Five-Year Plan was that during the *1995 Beijing World Conference on Women*, India was successful in convincing others to have a separate section on the girl child incorporated in the *Beijing Platform for Action for the Advancement of Women*.

In the *Ninth Five-Year Plan (1997-2002)*, efforts were made to expedite effective implementation and achievement of the goals set in the two Plans of Action besides instituting a *National Charter for Children* to ensure that no child remains illiterate, hungry or lacks medical care. To ensure the 'survival, protection and development' of children, especially that of the girl child, the Ninth Plan concentrated on arresting the problem of declining sex-ratio as well as its other related problems of female foeticide and infanticide.

These problems were attacked through a two-pronged strategy of both direct and indirect measures. While the direct measures included effective implementation of the existing legislation, the indirect measures were directed to change the mindset of the people in favour of the girl child, besides empowering women to exercise their reproductive rights and choices.

In this endeavour, UNICEF made special efforts to launch a 10-year old cartoon character named *Meena* along with her pet parrot Mithu and brother Raju. The Meena Initiative, popular till date with both adults and children, uses the CRC and the CEDAW as tools with which to advocate for the rights of the girl child in South Asia.

Meena makes a claim for the rights of all children and highlights the duties of families and obligations of States to realize those rights. Meena's questioning and reasoning seeks to enable families and communities to come up with positive solutions to deep-rooted discrimination, answers that are realistic and culturally sensitive. Special efforts were made to ensure effective enforcement of the Pre-natal Diagnostic Techniques (Regulation and Prevention of Misuse) Act, 1994.

In order to fulfil the birth right of every child to 'development', especially of those belonging to the disadvantaged and deprived groups as well as those with special needs, the Ninth Plan continued to focus on three major areas of child development, viz. health, nutrition and education.

In the field of 'Health', the scope of the erstwhile programme of CSSM was further widened into a comprehensive programme of *Reproductive and Child Health (RCH)* that laid special emphasis on child survival and other related measures. Continued emphasis was laid on the ICDS.

Under the Universal Immunisation Programme, significant achievements were made to arrest the problem of diphtheria, pertussis, neonatal tetanus, tuberculosis, poliomyelitis and measles. The special drive of Pulse Polio launched during 1995-96 was continued to eliminate the problem of poliomyelitis. All this had a definite impact in reducing the Infant Mortality Rate. The Government of India also committed to provide safe drinking water and sanitation facilities to every village to achieve the goal of 'Health for All'.

In the field of 'Nutrition', children below the age of 6 years along with expectant and nursing mothers, received highest priority in line with the provisions of the National Nutrition Policy, 1993 and the National Plan of Action on Nutrition, 1995. Despite the shortfalls that were recorded in terms of feeding and funding by the State Governments, the coverage under Special Nutrition Programme reached 31.5 million children in the age group of 0-6 years.

Similarly, the coverage under the National Programme of Nutritional Support to Primary Education commonly known as *Mid-day Meals* reached 105 million school children in the age group of 6-14 years by the end of the Ninth Plan. In the field of 'Education', in consonance with the National Policy on Education as revised in 1992 and the Programme of Action, special thrust was given to the measures of Universal Primary Education. As a result of this, the country made impressive achievements whereby the number of schools increased four-fold from 2.31 lakh in 1950-51 to 9.88 lakh in 1999-2000, while the enrolment at the primary level jumped up by about six times from 19.2 million to 113.6 million. In 2001-02, the *Sarva Shiksha Abhiyan (SSA)* was launched with the aim of providing quality elementary education to all children in the 6-14 age group by 2010, besides bridging all gender and social category gaps at primary stage by 2007. Concerted efforts were made to eliminate all forms of discrimination and violations against the rights of the girl child. The Ninth Plan also provided special incentives to the mother and the girl child so that the birth of a girl child in a family was rejoiced. To this effect, in the year 1997, *Balika Samriddhi Yojana (BSY)* was launched whereby a special package consisting of Rs.500/-to the mother and annual scholarship ranging from Rs.300/-to Rs.1,000/-for education of girl children from class 1 to 10 was provided to all those families living below the poverty line to ensure that all girl children went to schools.

The incentive of Rs.500/-to the mother on the delivery of a girl child was limited to two girl children only. Similar initiatives were also launched by other State Governments. In 1999, the BSY was reviewed and recast to make it more effective. In 1998, the Government with the support of UNICEF launched a special service for children called *Childline*.

This is a free phone service that can be accessed by a child or anyone on his/her behalf simply by dialling the number 1098. At present, Childline is working in 68 cities through a network of NGOs which not only responds to the needs of children but also plays a major role in crises intervention, long term care and rehabilitation.

Realizing the need for an effective service delivery to children in need of care and protection, a *National Initiative for Child Protection* was launched through the National Institute of Social Defence and Childline India Foundation. It aimed at building partnerships with the State Departments of Social/Child Welfare, Childline Service and allied systems for protection and promotion of children's rights.

In 1998, the Government of India instituted a *Plan of Action to Combat Trafficking and Commercial Sexual Exploitation of Women and Children*. Strong regulatory and administrative measures were taken to prevent exploitation of child labour.

A thorough review of the Juvenile Justice Act, 1986 was undertaken whereby the Act was repealed by the *Juvenile Justice (Care and Protection of Children) Act, 2000*. Likewise, a review of major existing child-specific and child related legislations was also undertaken to plug the loopholes in their implementation, viz. the Child Marriage Restraint Act, 1929; the Immoral Traffic (Prevention) Act, 1956; the Child Labour (Prohibition and Regulation) Act, 1986; and the Pre-Natal Diagnostic Techniques (Regulation and Prevention of Misuse) Act, 1994.

As per the commitment made by the Government of India to the CRC Committee, a Bill for setting up of a *National Commission for Children* to safeguard their rights was drafted in 2001. Prior to this, a Special Expert Committee chaired by Justice Shri V.R. Krishna Iyer prepared a *Children's Code Bill 2000*. The UNICEF India Country Office facilitated this entire exercise. But this venture proved to be futile as the Ministry of Women and Child Development felt that it was an independent exercise where the Government was not consulted at all. The 2001 draft Bill thus never saw the light of the day.

Efforts were concurrently made to develop a national level '*Information Network System*' for women and children with emphasis on collection of gender-specific data with the objective of preparing a *Gender Development Index* so as to assess the socioeconomic status of women and children on a continuing basis. A scheme entitled *Kishori Shakti Yojana (KSY)* was introduced as an enriched version of the *Scheme for Adolescent Girls* that was being implemented as part of the ICDS, to improve the nutritional and health status of girls in the age group of 11-18 years as well as equip them with vocational skills so that they could be gainfully engaged.

In January 2000, the CRC Committee reviewed the Initial State Party Report that had been submitted by the Government of India and gave its *Concluding Observations and Recommendations. India's First Periodic Report (Second Report) on CRC Implementation* was due for submission in 2000. However, the Government of India could only submit the Report in 2001.

The 2001 Report made all out efforts to address the Observations and Recommendations that were given by the CRC Committee in connection with India's Initial Report. The CRC Committee at its 932nd & 933rd meeting held on 21 January 2004 considered India's First Periodic Report and gave its Concluding Observations and also recommended that India should submit its next Periodic Report by 10 July 2008. Further, the due Report should combine the Third and Fourth Periodic Reports. Thereafter, the Committee expects India to report every five years as foreseen by the Convention.

In the ongoing *Tenth Five-Year Plan (2002 – 2007)*, overall emphasis has been on a rights-based approach with regard to 'survival, development and protection' of children. Accordingly, focussed attention is being given to arrest the problem of declining sex ratio including its offshoots – female foeticide and female infanticide. Special efforts are being made to ensure effective enforcement of related legislations to prevent and eradicate the problem of female foeticide and female infanticide. In this context, in the year 2003, the Pre-natal Diagnostic Techniques (Regulation and Prevention of Misuse) Act, 1994 was amended. The amended Act is now called the *Pre-Conception & Pre-Natal Diagnostic Techniques (Prohibition of Sex Selection) Act*. Emphasis is simultaneously being laid on *compulsory registration of births and deaths*, as visualised in the *National Population Policy (NPP) 2000*.

To ensure 'development' of children, especially those belonging to the disadvantaged and deprived groups, focussed attention is being given once again on three core sectors, viz. health, nutrition and education. All out efforts are being made to improve the coverage levels in respect of the six vaccinepreventable diseases. Special efforts are being made to improve the coverage levels through the Universal Immunisation Programme which is being implemented as part of the RCH programme.

Attempts, in particular, are being made to assess the health needs of all children at PHC level so as to undertake area-specific micro planning whereby all their needs are met through high quality RCH services. Further, it is being ensured that the *Child Survival Programme* of RCH will entail universal screening of all pregnant women so as to identify and manage those at high risk from the point of view of bringing about reduction in the pre-natal and neo-natal mortality and morbidity. In addition, the NPP and the revised *National Health Policy, 2002* are expected to extend both policy and programmatic support with definite targets to ensure child survival.

Along with the above, the two on-going direct feeding programmes of Special Nutrition as part of the ICDS and the *National Programme for Nutrition Support to Primary Education* have been streamlined and strengthened. Moreover, as a follow-up of the announcement made by the Prime Minister in his Independence Day Speech of 2001, a *National Nutrition Mission* was set-up in 2002 with an overall responsibility of reducing/eliminating both macro and micro nutritional deficiencies in the country. The overall approach adopted for the holistic development of children through the ICDS has since continued along with the on-going scheme for the Adolescent Girls, viz. KSY. Recognising the increasing need for support services of crèches/day care centres for the children of working/ailing mothers, especially in the present day context where more and more women are coming out for employment both in the organised and unorganised sectors, the NCF has been further strengthened to provide a wide network of crèches all over the country.

With regard to education, the *Constitution (86th Amendment) Act* was notified in December 2002, making free and compulsory education a Fundamental Right for all children in the age group of 6-14 years.

The fact that Article 21A was added to the Constitution for recognising right to primary education implies that right to personal liberty guaranteed by Article 21 is now also the basis for a general right to education. Correspondingly, Article 45 of the Constitution has been substituted so as to provide for early childhood care and education for all children till they complete the age of 6 years.

Article 51A was further modified by adding a clause – (k)– stating that it is the duty of the parents guardians to provide opportunities for education to their children/ward between the age of six and fourteen years. Ever since education became a Fundamental Right, the Tenth Plan adopted a new approach towards achieving the goal of *Universalisation of Elementary Education (UEE).*

As pointed out earlier since most of the programmes in the field of elementary education were disjointed in nature, Sarva Shiksha Abhiyan was launched in 2001-02 for providing comprehensive elementary education to all children. The SSA is seen as a major vehicle for achieving the goals of UEE in the Tenth Plan period.

SSA is xpected to solve the present problems of low rates of enrolment and retention, besides high drop-out rates, especially amongst the girl children belonging to the Scheduled Castes, Scheduled Tribes, Other Backward Classes and Minorities. Through this programme, the Government aims to cover children who have never enrolled or those who have dropped-out without completing eight years of elementary schooling.

In terms of pre-school education, the *Early Child Care Education* component of ICDS continues to be a significant input for providing a sound foundation for development as well as the first step in the education ladder. Focussed attention is now being given to strengthening the early joyful period of play and learning in the young child's life to ensure a harmonious transition from the family environment to the primary school.

In its quest to guarantee quality basic education through-out the country, the Government of India, in the year 2004, imposed an *Education Cess* @ 2 per cent on direct and indirect Central Taxes. At the international level, it adopted the *Dakar Framework for Action on Education for All.*

The Framework identifies six goals, which includes, *inter alia,* progressive expansion of Early Childhood Care and Education, Universalization of Elementary Education by 2015, achieving Gender Equality in Education by 2015, and improvement in the quality of education. Another very prominent legislation passed in the interest of children during the Tenth Five-Year Plan was the *Goa Children's Act, 2003.*

The Act ensures protection for children and the young against exploitation of all kinds and against moral and material abandonment. In 2003, the Government of India ratified the *1993 Convention for the Protecticn of Children and Cooperation for Inter-country Adoption (The Hague Convention).* The Juvenile Justice Act of 2000 was also modified. This Act is now known as the *Juvenile Justice (Care and Protection of Children) Amendment Act, 2006.*

The year 2006 has been especially significant as the *Commission for Protection of Child Rights Bill, 2005* was passed by the Parliament though the *Child Rights Commission* is yet to be set up. This is a big achievement not only for the children of the country but also for the Government for it was able to fulfil its commitment made to the CRC Committee for setting-up a Child Rights Commission. The children and the people of the country would now have to wait and see how this Commission really functions. At the international level, the *UN General Assembly's Special Session on Children* was held in May 2002.

It attracted 69 Summit-level participants and 190 highlevel national delegations apart from delegates representing NGOs from countries all over the world. It was for the first time in the history of UN meetings that more than 400 children participated as delegates. This Special Session dealt at length with the *Millennium*

Development Goals and set forward quantitative and qualitative goals for children to be achieved by all United Nations Member States by the year 2015. Having accepted the *Millennium Summit Declaration* of 2000 and in order to achieve the targets set by the UN General Assembly, the Ministry of Women and Child Development subsequently drew up a fresh *National Plan of Action for Children* in the year 2005 with a hope that it would provide a roadmap for steps to be taken for bringing about improvement in the lives of Indian children.

The year 2005 was noteworthy as the Government of India ratified the two Optional Protocols to the CRC, viz. the *Optional Protocol to the Convention on the Rights of the Child on the Sale of Children, Child Prostitution and Child Pornography*; and the *Optional Protocol to the Convention on the Rights of the Child on the Involvement of Children in Armed Conflict*. The UN General Assembly on 25 May 2000 had adopted both these Protocols.

The former came into force on 18 January 2002 while the latter on 12 February 2002. It would be worthwhile to mention here that in the year 2002 the Government of India also signed the *Protocol to Prevent, Suppress and Punish Trafficking in Persons, Especially Women* and Children supplementing the United Nations Convention against Transnational *Organized Crime, 2000*. In addition to this, in 2002, the Government of India endorsed the *SAARC Convention on Preventing and Combating Trafficking in Women and Children for Prostitution* and the *SAARC Convention on Regional Arrangements* for the Promotion of Child Welfare in South Asia.

In 2006, the Committee on the Rights of the Child issued *General Comments No. 8 & 9* relating to the *Right of the Child to Protection from Corporal Punishment and Other Cruel or Degrading Forms of Punishment* and the *Rights of Children with Disabilities*. Prior to this, in the year 2005, it had issued *General Comments No. 6 & 7* pertaining to *Treatment of Unaccompanied and Separated Children Outside their Country of Origin* and *Implementing Child Rights in Early Childhood*.

In the year 2003, the Committee had issued *General Comments No. 3, 4 & 5* relating to *HIV/AIDS and the Rights of the Child, Adolescent Health and Development in the Context of the CRC* and *General Measures of Implementation of the Convention on the Rights of the Child*. Before this, in the year 2002, it had issued *General*

Comment No. 2 on the subject of the *Role of Independent Human Rights Institutions*.

General Comment No. 1 was issued in the year 2001 that deals with the *Aims of Education*. From the Seventh Five-Year Plan onwards, the judiciary and the Supreme Court too have played an active role in upholding the rights of the child. The Supreme Court of India has developed the concept of jurisdiction under which any individual can approach the Court with regard to the violation of a fundamental right.

The Supreme Court has also modified traditional concepts by allowing groups of persons or organizations to intervene in cases relating to violations of fundamental rights even though they may not have been affected personally in the matter. This concept of 'social action litigation' in India represents an effort to use the legal system to ensure action to realize constitutionally guaranteed rights.

7

Mental Health Services

Mental health is increasingly recognised as a significant aspect relating to the overall well-being of the individual. This year World Mental Health Day, which falls on October 10, has been dedicated to "Mental Health in Primary Care: Enhancing Treatment and Promoting Mental Health". Mental health issues are a global priority and it is absolutely necessary to address issues pertaining to it at the earliest and in an effective and efficacious manner. The World Health Organization has identified the following 7 reasons for integrating mental health into the primary care setting:

- The burden of mental disorders is great. They create a substantial personal burden for affected individuals and their families, and they produce significant economic and social hardships that affect society as a whole.
- Mental and physical health problems are interwoven. Integrated primary care services help ensure that people are treated in a holistic manner.
- The treatment gap for mental disorders is enormous. There is a significant gap between the prevalence of mental disorders and the number of people receiving treatment.
- Primary care for mental health enhances access. When mental health is integrated into primary care, people can access mental health services closer to their homes. It also facilitates community outreach and mental health promotion.

- Primary care for mental health promotes respect of human rights.
- Primary care for mental health is affordable and cost effective. Primary care services for mental health are less expensive than psychiatric hospitals, for patients, communities and governments alike.
- Primary care for mental health generates good health outcomes. The majority of people with mental disorders treated in primary care have good outcomes, particularly when linked to a network of services at secondary level and in the community.

At present, if we look at the Indian scenario we need to keep in mind the population of our country and the fact that maximal population resides not in the metropolitan cities but in the smaller cities, towns, and villages. Surveys have clearly reflected the predominant availability of mental health professionals – psychiatrists, psychologists, psychiatric social workers – in metropolitan cities. Thus there is a glaring disparity between the availability of mental health services in the larger cities and those available in other parts of the country.

Furthermore, there is also a recognition of the general inadequacy of the number of available professionals. Documentation of the number of available psychiatrists and psychologists has revealed that there is a 330% shortage of psychologists and a 200% shortage of psychiatrists in our country. As a result, the number of patients that need to be seen and that are actually seen is not concordant.

It has been suggested that the integration of mental health services within the purview of the primary health care setting be initiated. It is felt that this integration of services would help align diagnosis, treatment, care, and rehabilitation of the individual. This would also help ensure that the same amount of significance is accorded to both these aspects of overall health and the associated stigma is also alleviated with the passage of time. Furthermore, there is an understanding that both mental and physical health have a reciprocal interaction and influence each other.

Given the present scenario in our country, it is easily recognisable that the maximum numbers of people tend to reach the general practitioners and medical professionals who work at the grassroots level. It is thus important for us to impart skills and competencies along with a good understanding to identify mental health related problems and provide the first line of treatment to the general practitioners who are working in the field of medicine. At the same time non-medical professionals such as village health workers, anganwaadi workers, non-governmental organisations, community based social workers and volunteers, and even teachers and school counsellors play a significant role in the early identification of any problems and concerns and thus help direct individuals in need to the right professionals who could help them resolve these issues.

It is thus necessary for us to ensure that through the integration of mental health within the primary care setting there can be more effective:

- Screening for psychiatric disorders leads to improved patient outcomes only when appropriate care follows detection.
- Physician education.
- Enhancing referrals to specialty behavioural health providers with additional supports may lead to improved follow-through and outcomes.
- Care needs to be co-ordinated and based in evidence-based approaches.

At the same time it is important to ensure that there are clearly delineated principles and steps regarding the line of treatment that should be provided to the general practitioners and primary care workers. Following the initial treatment by primary workers further referrals for difficult mental health problems and those that are not easily resolvable can be referred to specialist psychiatrists and psychologists.

Thus, policies are required to be designed and implemented by the government. This would mean that legislation is required and these issues need to be integrated into the general health policy which should be inclusive of not just medical or physical health but also psychological or mental health concerns. As a result, advocacy is required and is an important aspect of mental health. We would need to sensitise the leadership, health authorities, management and primary care workers about the necessity of integration of these two aspects of health. It is understandable that integration is a process and it would take time and it is absolutely essential to attain collaboration between the governmental sectors, governmental non-health sectors, non-governmental organisations, village and community health workers and volunteers. This can be summarised as follows as has also been suggested by the WHO as strategies for integrating mental health in primary care:

- Policy and plans need to incorporate primary care for mental health.
- Advocacy is an absolute essential.
- Adequate training needs to be imparted along with allocation of tasks that are doable.
- Sensitisation at different levels is an essential aspect.
- Collaboration is required between governmental and non-governmental organisations which work in the primary health care setting.
- There needs to be adequate allocation of financial resources and human resources to ensure the availability of services to maximum number of people.

Early and cost effective interventions need to be given primary importance. Some of the interventions that need to be incorporated include the following:

- Early intervention within schools by school counsellors and by paediatricians.
- Provision of support to children through life skills education and skill building programmes.
- Mental health promotion activities in school.
- Specialised supportive services for women and elderly that cater to their needs and requirements.
- Mental health activities at the work place given the current levels of stress, impact on interpersonal relations, social functioning, levels of attrition and absenteeism.
- Community programmes to generate awareness and remove stigma associated with mental health related problems.

The recognition of the need for integration of services is particularly applicable within the context of a large and populous country like India, where due to the paucity of professionals there are millions of people who are not receiving the treatment that they urgently require. A step in the direction of integration would be beneficial to all – patients, their families, medical professionals, mental health professionals, non medical and non-governmental organisations working in the field for the promotion of the overall health and well-being of the individual and thus the community at large.

Moving Away from Mental Institutions-Towards Community Mental Health Care

Mental disorders figure among the leading causes of disease and disability the world over. Depressive disorders are already the fourth-leading cause of the global disease burden; they are expected to rank second by 2020, behind Ischaemic heart disease. Meta-analysis studies indicated high prevalence rate of mental disorders in the community (58.2 per thousand). Mental disorders affect one in four persons.

The year 2001 was a landmark in the development of mental health services. Since the problem of mentally challenged is a global problem, WHO has chosen the theme: "Mental Health: stop exclusion-Dare to Care" during the year 2001, to focus worldwide attention on the issues related to mental health. The past, in the history of mental health services has been a gloomy, but nevertheless it has taught us many lessons. Past experience of mental health built a strong myth and perception in the community and the common man perceived mental illnesses as stigma, admission in asylum or mental hospital, electric shocks and confinement in institution with subhuman conditions. The picture has changed drastically and the modern mental health care goes far beyond the institutions and in a way it is trying to restore and build confidence of common man and by changing his/her perception through educational programme. Mass media continues to focus on miserable conditions of asylums and mental hospitals and subhuman conditions of these hospitals, to draw the attention of authorities for improving these conditions. Directives of Honourable Supreme Court have made substantial contribution in the area of mental health programme. Similarly, the derogatory Indian Lunacy Act of 1912 which was based on earlier English Lunacy Act of 1890 has been replaced by 1987 Mental Health Act with a focus to improve the quality of services/care and protect the rights of mentally ill. Mental health act has been a very important milestone in the development of modern psychiatric services in the country, hopefully, the act is made patient friendly. The State Governments took a long lead time to establish mental health authority and to implement this act.

National Mental Health Programme initiated in 1981 has ultimately come out with community based approach for sustainability of actions as also enhanced accessibility. Development of district mental health programme is a step in the right direction, but the progress and coverage is too slow to make any mark on amelioration of the problem. Nodal agency has been identified in each state to undertake in-service training programme of the Medical Officers and paramedical workers as also to provide technical support to district training programme; it adheres to prescribed manual by NIMHANS, Bangalore. Two weeks training programme is being perused at the level of Medical College by the department of Psychiatry (a tertiary level of care). This decision undermines the capacity of district health agencies or district training teams developed recently as a training institution for continuing education programme of medical and paramedical personnel.

It is recognized that effective delivery of primary health care including mental health care would largely depend upon the nature of education and appropriate orientation towards community health of all categories of medical and health personnel and their capacity to function as an integrated team. Basic training curriculi of all categories should incorporate sufficient time for building essential skills of medical and paramedical personnel so that they are able to deal with the problem of mental health within the framework of primary health care. In general, we must address the issues of quality of medical education for undergraduates and specifically to the training of students in the discipline of Psychiatry, to lay firm foundation for development of mental health services at primary health care level. This should be considered as real investment in development of psychiatric health services in the community. Training of Trainers (TOT) is essential to impart need based and relevant training on the key areas of mental health and counselling. Training needs assessment and pursuing the hands on the training with case material and community should become the primary focus with trainers of medical and paramedical personnel. Medical education cell and State Institute of Health and Family Welfare can be entrusted with the task of training of trainers. National Health Policy and programme on mental health and its key strategies must be made available to the trainers. To maintain the uniform standard of training, manuals prepared by NIMHANS, Bangalore be distributed in local languages.

In-service training manual prepared by NIMHANS focuses largely on technical subjects and hospital based training, confirming an established impression that the solution to mental health problem lies in big hospitals and nothing worthwhile can be done/ achieved at the community level. Substantial part of training of Medical Officers and paramedical personnel should be at the community level to focus on critical areas like role of community, institutions, family and individual to tackle mental health problems.

Focus of the training of necessity should be on the methods of interviewing and contact with the individuals and families, skills of listening to clients, assessing their needs, counselling and identification of high risk families and clients as also group meetings and dynamics besides community organization and mobilization of resources. Continuing education should be part of routine meetings. Health teams (multipurpose health workers, anganwadi workers, gram sewikas and health guides) should be trained together for better understanding of each other's role and responsibility. Awareness generation and mental health literacy drives at the level of community through active involvement of Panchayati Raj Institutions, influential groups, non-formal leaders and other organized groups on regular basis can be most productive. Awareness generation campaign must have the support of district mental health services, Community Health Centre, Primary Health Centre and Subcentre system.

Ownership of the programme by district health orgnization and the area is essential for sustainability and endurance. If the training programme and development of strategies are evolved far away from the real situation, this may create a negative impact and generate a sense of dependency and kills local initiatives. Building district capacity for training and continuing education as also for developing services should be the real role of nodal agency.

If one looks at the basic curriculum of MBBS students and paramedicals (multipurpose health workers male and female) one finds that subject of Mental Health is covered adequately but the implementation thereof is questionable.

Even the available services for mental disorders are being poorly utilized. Nearly two third of persons with known mental disorders never seek help from health professionals and most clients utilize the services of other agencies and resort to harmful practices and keep on visiting faith healers and delay the treatment till the condition deteriorates which compels them to seek the treatment from established government institutions. Stigma, discrimination and neglect prevent care and treatment reaching people. Mental health literacy needs to be built strongly in the community to scale up the utilization of available mental health services.

In the first instance, the services and infrastructure for mental health services in public sector are inadequate and mostly confined to bigger cities and hospitals. Distt. programme of Mental Health Services has just taken off, primary health care infrastructure on the other hand is reasonably well developed and is almost universally accessible to rural and urban areas. Minimum package of mental health services for all can be best delivered through primary health care system. Preventive and promotive programme along with awareness generation can be undertaken on sustainable basis through this infrastructure.

System of Integrated Child Development Services (ICDS) which is poised for universal coverage has played a pivotal role for mother and child development in rural, urban and tribal areas. Non-formal education component and early childhood stimulation through play way activities have laid down firm physical, mental and psychological development foundation.

In a way, the institution of anganwadis has been recognized as sheet anchor in personality development of young children. This is one of the finest examples of development of positive mind and mental health. International programme developed by WHO to stimulate mother-child interactions has much more chances for success if persued actively in the family through ICDS system. This system involves families in total child development through integrated services of nutrition, health and education and relies on inter-sectoral co-ordination. NIMHANS has rightly picked up ICDS system to involve them in National Mental Health Programme through District Mental Health Services. They are being imparted 5 days training programme at distt. level. Their training would be critical, as these workers will serve as link workers between community and the formal health services system. Since anganwadi workers are locally resident voluntary workers, deeply rooted in the community they can be most effective in dissemination of knowledge on mental health programme besides identification of clients at the earliest stage of morbidity, because of their continuous contact with families. Strengthening of this institution can be most rewarding and will have high payoff effects in the long run. National Population Policy envisages enlarging the sphere of ICDS to cover school going children upto the age of 9 years. Continuous on the job training of anganwadi workers through supervisory support can further enrich the non-formal education programme. The in-service training on mental health should be undertaken by supervisors or trained Child Development Programme Officers and it should focus on child development, personality development and learning by play way activities.

Adolescent boys and girls who are the future parents need greater degree of mental health services to develop value based learning and balanced personality. Teachers training programme for balanced development of physical, mental and social faculties of school going children is essential for healthy life styles. Teachers along with parents can shape balanced personality. District Mental Health Services Programme should have incorporated this programme very strongly and entrust the responsibility of teachers training to district health teams. Though the teachers are trained during their teachers training programme on Child Psychology but they need continuous education on balanced personality development of child. District mental health programme shouid not lose the opportunity, as it would be a real investment in preventive, promotive and positive mental health or extended community mental health. The outreach district mental health services should embody this component of the programme on sustainable basis.

WHO's "Life Skills" educational curriculum which attempts learning of wide range of skills amongst school children to improve their psycho-social competency through problem solving, critical thinking, communication, equity, tolerance, interpersonal skills, empathy and methods to cope with emotions can be made effective through school teachers and parents teachers interaction on continuous basis and much more through "child friendly schools".

Government or Public Mental Services is just one resource for mental health services, Private sector and Non-Governmental Organizations, as also diverse health care providers such as practitioners of Indian System of Medicine should be considered as potential resource for primary health care including mental health services.

Their involvement can increase the base of accessibility of services to masses. Some of the technologies of Indian System of Medicine can be exploited for treatment of mental disorders. District programme of mental health services may be given liberty to utilize the services of these agencies. Resource mapping for primary health care, as also mental health care should not lose sight of other available organizations contributing to the care or services related to mental health programme. Partnership between government and private sector is an important area for development of mental health services programme at community level.

It is widely acclaimed that community care is more effective as well as more humane than in-patient stays in mental hospitals. It is, therefore, essential to develop mental health services in the community settings as an integral part of primary health care; to root out stigma, myths and misconceptions and discrimination against mental disorders. The World Mental Health report 2001 advocates community based mental health programmes and active involvement of families and consumers and community in the delivery of programme.

People and the community are the biggest resources available in India. Many of the problems in the area of mental health can be effectively dealt with by the people and within resources available close to them. Large-scale dissemination of knowledge and simple skills to people and health volunteers should be addressed through primary health care. Capacity of family must be built and primary health care infrastructure should support the family to build their capacity to prevent and manage the mental health problems within the available means.

What people do with their lives and those of their children affects their health far more than anything that government does. Building knowledge and awareness of families can make the real difference. Health guides, anganwadi workers and health workers as also Non-Governmental Organizations (NGOs) should raise the level of awareness of people on sound mind in sound body and attainment of positive mental health, through their own actions and practices as also utilization of available services.

Operational research studies on community based mental health services are called for. We have just two models evolved long back at Chandigarh and Bangalore in 1975 which are indeed insufficient. These two models limited their approach to curative services at the community level through primary health care. District mental health programme was initiated at Bellary (Karnataka). Success of operations in programme conditions at the ground level needs to be documented further. Outcome and impact of district training programme in terms of coverage of mental health services and awareness level; of community needs to be explored through operational research studies.

The task can be undertaken by nodal agency or independent institution can be entrusted this task. Built in system of monitoring and evolving parameters of mental health in the community could be another area of interest. Similarly, longitudinal follow-up of preschool children and school children for personality development could be another worthwhile area of research. Many more interventional studies can be evaluated in adolescents in and out of schools in community settings, Delineation of role of NGOs, Panchayati Raj Institutions and partnership of public and private sector in delivery of mental health services can be throught of as an area of exploration. Working of drug de-addiction centres, their cost benefit ratio and impact should form part of community based operational research.

Social Security

Social security is primarily a social insurance program providing social protection, or protection against socially recognized conditions, including poverty, old age, disability, unemployment and others. Social security may refer to:

- social insurance, where people receive benefits or services in recognition of contributions to an insurance scheme. These services typically include provision for retirement pensions, disability insurance, survivor benefits and unemployment insurance.
- income maintenance—mainly the distribution of cash in the event of interruption of employment, including retirement, disability and unemployment
- services provided by administrations responsible for social security. In different countries this may include medical care, aspects of social work and even industrial relations.
- More rarely, the term is also used to refer to basic security, a term roughly equivalent to access to basic necessities—things such as food, clothing, shelter, education and medical care.

Social Insurance

Actuaries define social insurance as a government-sponsored insurance program that is defined by statute, serves a defined population, and is funded through premiums or taxes paid by or on behalf of participants.

Participation is either compulsory or the program is subsidized heavily enough that most eligible individuals choose to participate. In the U.S., programs that meet this definition include Social Security, Medicare, the PBGC program, the railroad retirement program and state-sponsored unemployment insurance programs.

Income Maintenance

This policy is usually applied through various programs designed to provide a population with income at times when they are unable to care for themselves. Income maintenance is based in a combination of five main types of program:

- social insurance, considered above

- means-tested benefits. This is financial assistance provided for those who are unable to cover basic needs, such as food, clothing and housing, due to poverty or lack of income because of unemployment, sickness, disability, or caring for children. While assistance is often in the form of financial payments, those eligible for social welfare can usually access health and educational services free of charge. The amount of support is enough to cover basic needs and eligibility is often subject to a comprehensive and complex assessment of an applicant's social and financial situation.
- non-contributory benefits. Several countries have special schemes, administered with no requirement for contributions and no means test, for people in certain categories of need-for example, veterans of armed forces, people with disabilities and very old people.
- discretionary benefits. Some schemes are based on the discretion of an official, such as a social worker.
- universal or categorical benefits, also known as demogrants. These are non-contributory benefits given for whole sections of the population without a test of means or need, such as family allowances or the public pension in New Zealand (known as New Zealand Superannuation).

Social Protection

Social protection refers to a set of benefits available (or not available) from the state, market, civil society and households, or through a combination of these agencies, to the individual/ households to reduce multidimensional deprivation. This multidimensional deprivation could be affecting less active poor persons (e.g. the elderly, disabled) and active poor persons (e.g. unemployed). This broad framework makes this concept more acceptable in developing countries than the concept of social security. Social security is more applicable in the conditions, where large numbers of citizens depend on the formal economy for their livelihood. Through a defined contribution, this social security may be managed. But, in the context of wide spread informal economy, formal social security arrangements are almost absent for the vast majority of the working population. Besides, in developing countries, the state's capacity to reach the vast majority of the poor people may be limited because of its limited resources. In such a context, multiple agencies that could provide for social protection is important for policy consideration. The framework of social protection is thus capable of holding the state responsible to provide for the poorest sections by regulating non-state agencies.

Collaborative research from the Institute of Development Studies debating Social Protection from a global perspective, suggests that advocates for social protection fall into two broad categories: 'instrumentalists' and 'activists'. 'Instrumentalists' argue that extreme poverty, inequality and vulnerability, is dysfunctional in the achievement of development targets (e.g. the MDGs). In this view social protection is about putting in place risk management mechanisms that will compensate for incomplete or missing insurance (and other) markets, until a time that private insurance can play a more prominent role in that society. 'Activist' arguments view the persistence of extreme poverty, inequality and vulnerability, as symptoms of social injustice and structural inequality and see social protection as a right of citizenship. Targeted welfare is a necessary step between humanitarianism and the ideal of a 'guaranteed social minimum' where entitlement extends beyond cash or food transfers and is based on citizenship, not philanthropy.

Since inception of the Civilization man explored better ways of living (starting from Shelter, Family, Group, Society, Group of Societies, Geographical Boundaries, Tools of Material) through the resources continuously provided by nature. After this success, the need of governance for the management of resources and geographical boundaries was brought in existence. Thus the concept of religion, government, state, country was formed by Society.

As we observe that the existing System of Administration in India has been unable to deliver the prosperity to most of the Indian People due to small number of vested interest Political Ideologies that have segregated the society in different wings. Most importantly-None of these ideologies work for the benefit of Common People of India or the universe. The ideologies such as "Independence Movements" "Garibi Hatao", "Ram Mandir", "North East Movements", "Violent Movements", "Samajwadi Movements", "Separatist Movements", "Communism

Movements", "Religious Movements" "Dalit movements" and numerous others have not been able to achieve prosperity and justice to the common man of India. Though, with the help of these popular ideologies, their leaders are successful to achieve desired political platforms of vested interests.

Can we realize that "what does a common man expects in a living environment?" We may not find that a common man needs more than the basic life security, family security, health care, education, employment, housing, water, electricity, roads, corruption free administration. It seems amazing that after 60 years of independence, none of the basic measure or accountability of the livelihood for millions of Indians has been secured by any administration. More amazingly this serious matter of urgency is not the agenda of any people group or political group!

This fact has inspired the group behind Indian Social Security to lay down actions of Truth, courage and never ending effort. Therefore a Pro People system such as 'Social Security System' or a similar system that enables the country India to provide Social & Economic Security to all citizen's through mutually accountable & Pro-People Governance should be in Place.

Social Security is not a new concept but on behalf of all people of India, the System which keeps India on the path of Prosperity has to be implemented. 52 countries have been observed where Social Security is the best method of providing the allocated Food Security, Housing Security, best Health care, best Education, Self employed Society run by 'Pro People Government System' Therefore we stand committed to get the similar System of Social Security to all Indians. We hope that one day the common man of India becomes aware of his rights, we hope that one day the political parties work for the prosperity of each common citizen of our land, we hope that happiness and good livelihood exist for all people of India and this unique universe.

Social Security System – S3 (Proposed Terminology in Three Phases)

Definition of Social Security System : Social Security System is an Organized Structure Designed to the needs of the Government & the People for mutual Contributions for the Welfare of Society & the State

Why Social SecurityOverall Mechanism Concept

There is a vast need of Singular & Secular Methodology to link all Citizen's in one National Entity.

The External & Internal Security has to be induced at the Highest form of Humanitarian & Nationalism Grounds.

The Country has to be governed by an accountable Welfare State structure as well as Citizen's have to be Participant of Fundamental duties to attain an equilibrium of Social & Economic Justice to all Citizen of India.

To evolve India as the Nation of apostle of Peace & source of knowledge to the world.

Phase–1 : National Database System

In this System a Single National Database Number will be tagged to every single Citizen of the Country. The National Data will be controlled by the Central Governance and will be accessible to Several Administrative bodies of the Public Affairs according to their respective Needs and Rights.

Mechanism of National Database System :

Following Stages of the Life of a Citizen will be registered under his National Database Number:

1. MCD/Citizenship Records of Birth
2. School Admission
3. University Admission
4. Permanent/Rented Address Record
5. Bank Accounts/Bank Loan Record
6. Property/Land Records
7. Passport Records
8. Vehicle Record
9. Telephone Subscriptions Record
10. Police/Court Record.
11. Internet Record
12. Voting Record
13. Personal Income Tax/Other Income Record
14. Business & Assets Record
15. Mortgage of Property Record

16. Employment (Govt. or Private)/Occupation Record
17. Subsidies/Health Benefits/Record
18. Pension Records
19. Collaborating Data of Business income (TIN) Records
20. Category of Citizen Record ie; Handicap, SC/ST, etc.
21. Marriage/Children Data Linked Records
22. Country Migration Record.

Ecological Security Issues

1. Air
2. Water
3. Food
4. Energy
5. Power
6. Roads
7. Rivers
8. Health Care
9. Education Policies
10. Sports Policies
11. Prevention of Diseases
12. Green Environment
13. Effects of Pesticides
14. Use of Hybrid Seed in Farming
15. Concrete Environment
16. Agriculture Produce Equilibrium
17. Forest Policy
18. Pollutants in Commodities.

The Practical Implementation & the Continuous upgradation of People Centric Welfare measures for Citizen & the State is the main role of Citizen & Environment Policy.

As the Concept of Social Security System is a Combination of 03 Phase Structure, Therefore after the first Phase, National Database System is implemented, The Phase 02; Citizen & Environment Policy can be Co-ordinated to its full force for the exact Number of Area wise Population with their Demographic or Living needs. The Unique Strategies of Facts from National

Database System will form a Practical Vision of Policy Implementation under this Process.

Citizen & Environment Policy Process is a Continuous Process for analyzing the Basic needs of a Citizen, a Family & the Collective Society for Series of Developments to achieve Ecological Security, Humanitarian value's structure & Economic Security in a country.

Human Value Structure

1. Secularism by eliminating divide & rule policy
2. Honesty at governance level
3. Patriotism by sense of responsibility by state in favour of citizen
4. Compulsory education for all
5. Sense of Equality by state starting from education standards
6. Sense of belongingness towards Family, Society & Nation
7. Brotherhood by mutual social initiative
8. Compulsory child care education for all women
9. No influence of fascism in education
10. Skill oriented education
11. Knowledge of values of Democracy & fundamental duties
12. Declaration of corruption as anti national activity
13. Knowledge of healthcare in education
14. Discipline mandate in all citizen as the basic value
15. Encouragement for sports during education
16. Ambition values towards upliftment of nation
17. Enhancement of creativity & reduction in burden of education
18. Social work & leadership values in Education.

Economic Security Issues

1. Right For Food
2. Old Age Public Pension
3. Health & Life Insurance of Citizen's & Dependents
4. Un Employment Insurance
5. Worker Accident Insurance

6. Negative Impact of Free International Trade Policies
7. Migration from Village to Urban
8. Eradication of Poverty Cause
9. Displacement Security
10. Crop Wastage due to in Sufficient Management
11. Crop Price Assessment Policy
12. Use of Machine for Collective Benefit
13. Fair Distribution of Per Capita Income
14. Handicap Grants & Reservations
15. Demographic & Natural Calamity Management
16. Social Saving Schemes
17. Equal Opportunity Policy in Education & Employment
18. Opportunities to Women for Economic Development.

Social Security is a federal benefits program the United States developed in 1935. While the program encompasses disability income, veterans' pensions, public housing and even the food stamp program, it is most commonly associated with retirement benefits. However, if you still have many working years ahead of you, you may not be able to depend on these benefits as a source of income. In this article, we go over how the Social Security system works and why it is predicted to fail in the future.

The Social Security system is funded through payroll taxes. The Federal Insurance Contributions Act (FICA) mandates a 12.4% levy on the first $94,200 (2006 limit) of each individual's earned income each year. The employer pays 6.2% and the employee pays 6.2%. Self-employed individuals pay the full 12.4%.

Contrary to popular belief, this money is not put in trust for the individual employees who are paying into the system, but is used to pay existing retirees. Any excess is invested in U.S. Treasury bonds.

Earning Credits

Eligibility for Social Security benefits is accrued over time. Prior to 1978, workers were required to earn $50 in a three-month quarter in order to receive one Social Security credit. The achievement of 40 credits, accrued over 10 years of working, provided eligibility. Today, employers report earnings once per year instead of quarterly. Credits are accrued based on your earnings, not on a quarterly basis, so it is possible to earn all four credits for the year even if you only work a short amount of time each year. In 2006, workers will be required to earn $970 per credit.

Benefits

The amount of your Social Security benefit is calculated by averaging the earnings from your 35 highest income-generating years. The maximum monthly Social Security check that you can earn is $2,053 per month in 2006. To sign up for Social Security benefits, it is recommended that you apply three months prior to your retirement date.

8

Psycho-medical Illnesses Among the Senior Citizens

Life expectancy in Indiahas been improving. However, this has also thrown up challenges in dealing with geriatric population that is on the rise. Indiais yet to fully develop an end-to-end health care system for senior citizens. This, coupled with increasing structural changes in the societal matrix – from the conventional joint family to more urbanized nuclear family, migration and changes in economic activity – are all leaving the old people at the receiving end. Healthcare assumes one of the top most priorities for them.

With technology penetrating deep into the rural hinterland, it may now be possible to evolve a method for addressing the concerns of the senior citizens in a better manner, especially in the rural areas. Information and Communication Technology (ICT) can easily become an enabler for such schemes. The setting up of the common service centres (CSCs) promises a ray of hope as it will be able to provide surplus capacity to act as the last mile point of access to the rural citizens for elementary healthcare and support. This could also act as the last tier of a multi-tier health referral system. Once established, the system can also accommodate other related value added services meant for senior citizens such as health insurance and old age welfare schemes from the state.

There have been several welcome developments in extending the welfare net to senior citizens, who for a long time remained as a neglected segment within the civil society. Starting with fare concessions on travel to better rate of returns on deposits with banks, the right noises have been made at the policy level in acknowledging the senior citizens. Yet much needs to be done in making public health care accessible to them, which logically speaking, should take precedence over other services. Based on the 2001 census, there are about 80 million senior citizens in the country and this will be over 120 million by 2020.

This papers attempts to identify ways in which Information and Communication Technologies (ICT) can act as enablers to provide senior citizens easy access to health care, which otherwise is a challenge for this segment. The paper tries to establish that ICT can act as the backbone for broad spectrum public health care for the aged with the Accessibility, Acceptability and Affordability principle.

The paper also tries to examine the challenges and possible conflicts involved when technology plays a central role in a domain like health care. It finally concludes by suggesting a loose architecture for the public health care for the aged and a business model that may be considered for ensuring sustainability and replicability. Furthermore, the paper tries to establish the possible linkages between robust geriatric health profiling and transparent health insurance schemes. It also envisages the possibility of linking existing senior citizen schemes such as old age pension, widow pension etc. to the senior citizen health record.

Background

India along with other WHO member Nations pledged to ensure 'Health for All by the Year 2000' at Alma-Ata in 1978; and in the same year signed the International Covenant for Economic, Social and Cultural Rights – Article 12, in which the State is obliged to achieve the highest attainable standard of health. However the health scenario in Indiais abysmal.

The number of people over the age of 60 is expected to triple by 2050, according to a 2006 revision of 'World Population Prospects' by the UN Department of Economic and Social Affairs Population Division. And India, Nigeria, Pakistan, the Democratic Republic of Congo, Ethiopia, the US, Bangladesh and China will account for half of the world's 2.5 billion extra people by 2050.

The United Nations broadly classified societies into 'young' (4% or less of those aged 60+), 'matured' (4-7%) and 'ageing' (7%

and above). India, which falls under the 'matured' society category, has moved further into the 'ageing' society.

The age-wise segments within the growing population are increasing at different rates, the fastest growing segment being the 60-plus bracket. As a result the percentage of population of the elderly is likely to grow steadily. According to United Nation's estimates there are 427 million aged persons in the world today, which constitute about 8.8 per cent of the total. However, by the year 2025, the population of the aged is likely to reach 1171 millions, which will constitute a staggering 21.9 per cent of the total population. It is estimated that by the year 2010 the elderly population of Indiamay be around 124 million, constituting over 10 per cent of the total population.

Beyond the statistics, there are several socio psycho implications for the geriatric segment that need to be considered. In the Indian context, concepts of old age homes and Third Party Geriatric Care are yet to mature. Existing social system looks down at the proposition of sending ageing parents/relatives to "Homes." However, the increasing pace of life among the younger generation has resulted in a widening gap between them and their seniors. Economic non-productivity, failing physical abilities all add to the complexities that already exist with the geriatrics. Partners in Development Initiatives, an NGO working on health has pointed fingers at "loneliness" as a debilitating factor among the senior citizens. A study on geriatrics in Kashmir speaks about depression as a serious ailment that often goes unnoticed. The paper also correlates the possibility of depression to family care and support. Adding up all the socioeconomic factors, it becomes evident that this 10 per cent segment of ageing citizens requires equal or more attention than the new born and infants at the other end of the social spectrum. Needless to say, a significant part of such an intervention must happen from public spending.

The Government has attempted to give a boost to public health care by raising public health spending from the current 0.8 per cent to an estimated 3 per cent of the GDP (approximately INR 250 billion) by 2012 through a large program called the National Rural Health Mission (NRHM). NRHM is a comprehensive programme that seeks to improve rural health through decentralized planning and interventions. NRHM is being operationalized throughout the country with special focus on 18 states-Bihar, Jharkhand, Madhya Pradesh, Chhattisgarh, Uttar Pradesh, Uttaranchal, Orissa and Rajasthan, 8 North-East States, Himachal Pradesh and Jammu & Kashmir. NRHM, together with the states' own health reform plans, is expected to push public spending in the health sector for better results. The main aim of NRHM is to provide accessible, affordable, accountable, effective and reliable primary health care facilities, especially, to the poor and vulnerable sections of the population. NRHM seeks to strengthen Public Health delivery services at all levels. The interventions/initiatives launched under the NRHM aim to reduce mortality and morbidity, and consequently improve life expectancy.

While NRHM seeks to widen the coverage of healthcare through "innovation" and "public private partnerships", role of technology is not expressed as forcefully as it could, however implicit it may be. Thus, a situation has arisen where there is a substantially large ageing population on the one side and there is an overarching "affordable, accountable, effective and reliable" health policy on the other side with a connecting link in between. Use of Information and Communication Technologies (ICT) can be an effective enabler in this context. Health is a state subject; however, it is under the overarching reach of the National Rural Health Mission (NRHM). There are several avenues in the NRHM that can be extended to benefit the senior citizen of the rural areas. Some of the measures that we propose are:

- Mapping primary data of citizens
- Use of telecenters as collection points
- Convergence of data with the Village Health Plan, and making this data available to Rogi Kalyan Samitis (RKS)
- Use of sub centres (SCs) as the first level of data processing
- Use of Primary Health Centres (PHCs) as the repository for localized health information
- Develop two-way information flow from PHCs to Community Health Centres (CHCs), medical colleges and research institutions
- Develop public private partnership for research and evidence-based promotive, curative and preventive care at the state medical department/headquarters level.

Mapping Primary Data

Mapping and profiling of senior citizens at the local level is the single most important task in this exercise. Ageing and ageing-related ailments generally relate to disabilities affecting vision and locomotor movements, urogenital disorders and gastrointestinal disorders claiming the highest rate of prevalence. The Department for Community Medicine at the All India Institute of Medical Sciences (AIIMS) has suggested the following set of parameters that can be applied to geriatrics. The entire matrix can be filled through a combination of efforts by the Accredited Social Health Activist and the Gram Panchayat.

Parameters for Preparation of a Health Profile for the Elderly

Physical Profile

- Weight
- Hemoglobin (is an important factor which can trace a lot of diseases; a non-medico can also carry out the test)
- Diabetes
- Blood pressure and case sheet of a patient in the hospital
- Diabetes
- Hyper tension
- Cardiac (Smoking/drinking/exercise pattern)
- Ocular mobility (cataract, blindness test).

Disability

- Ortho
- Hearing
- Vision.

Social Issues

- Widows
- Support system.

Availability of Health Services

- Mapping of health infrastructure in the district (Distance traveled to access service, services available, referral system)
- Willingness to pay and how much.

Other Indicators

- Radiological
- Pathological
- Clinical
- Epidemiological
- Nutritional
- Disease trend, pattern and consequences.

Source: Department of Community Diseases, All India Institute of Medical Sciences.

Use of Telecenters as Collection Points

Under the National e-Governance Plan (NeGP) of the Government of India, 100,000 rural telecenters and another 10,000 urban/semi urban telecenters running on broadband connectivity and offering government services will be established. The telecenters will presumably have surplus capacity to act as collection points for geriatric health profiles. ASHA/MPWs with sufficient training can use the centres (there will be a minimum of one telecenter for a cluster of six villages) to upload the non-GP data. Senior citizens can be identified with the help of census data or through physical verification by the health workers. The profile once recorded fully, will generate a reference number that will be retained by the citizen.

Convergence of Data on to Village Health Plan

NRHM envisages the development of a village health plan that is aimed at capturing the salient health parameters of the region. The geriatric health mapping could be a component of the village health plan. Further, this data could be used for reference by the Rogi Kalyan Samiti, a participatory committee formed at the district level.

Localisation of Data for Decentralized Administration

One of the unique features of the data capturing and retention at the local level is the reverse engineering impact it can have on health administration. As data at the grassroots level gets pushed upwards, it will also throw up region-wise demand for medical interventions and supply of drugs. A case in point is the decentralization of medical treatment for snake bites, effected by the Health Department of Goa. The Goa experiment shows how deaths from snake bites could be minimized through capacity building at the local level and decentralization of anti venom administration. Similarly, health care for senior citizens must be addressed by first mapping the generic needs of this segment, and then effecting it through a process-driven health support system.

Reduction in Deaths from Snake Bites through LocalizedCapacityBuilding and Decentralization of Anti Venom Administration in Goa.

Mining is a major economic activity in Goa. The activity calls for substantial deforestation, which results in the straying of the forest inhabitants into human habitats. Cobra and krait are two commonly found reptiles in these parts and these snakes found their shelters in the houses and barns of the neighbouring villages.

This has resulted in increased number of snake bite reporting in the villages neighbouring the mining belt. Both snakes inject lethal neuro toxins into their objects which results in the breakdown of the nervous system and subsequent death. Only district hospitals stored the anti-venom for such snake bites and the delay in reaching the victims to the district hospitals invariably resulted in the loss of life.

A significant turnaround to this situation was effected with the collective efforts of the Health Department of Goa and an NGO. The Volunteers NGO worked with the youth and trained them to catch snakes when anyone reported having sighted them. Instead of creating a pandemonium out of fear, the villagers would seek the help of the volunteers to catch the snake from houses or barns. The snakes are then let out into their own natural habitat by the volunteers.

The Health Department, on the other hand, used the volunteers to sensitize the common people about snake bites and the essential first aid to be administered. The department also trained the medical and paramedical staff at the PHCs, CHCs and SCs in the mining belt to store anti-venom vials. This has helped to significantly reduce the loss of human life in the region.

The Public Health Care System follows an elaborate process of reporting. However, in practice, these reports are erroneous, unreliable and far removed from truth. This apart, these monthly dispatches are executed with a lag at village, block and district levels resulting in a wasteful exercise.

Thus, the present system defeats the very purpose of accurate and clean data collection. With the proposed health care revamp using ICT, the village level telecenters can act as points for the primary level data collection. Data that is digitally fed in can be sent to multiple recipients without any time lapse. MPWs, ASHAs and Anganwadi workers who normally get intimidated by the amount of file work for such reporting can pass on the information to telecenter operators who would be responsible for entering and updating data.

Today, the data received from the field is kept with scant respect at the state headquarters. Often such files are looked at only when questions about a particular disease or a pandemic outbreak are raised in the legislative assembly or in Parliament. However, digital data updated at the village level can be converted into a wealth of primary information with respect to the general health profile of each and every region.

The data can be used by not only the Directorate of Health Services in the state but also Institutes of Nutrition, Virology, Immunology, Communicable Diseases etc. to analyse and study commonly occurring deficiencies and the diet pattern of the people in a particular region; and to work on the possibility of supplementary nutrition etc.

The Tripura Experience

In Tripura, the government is experimenting with the use of ICT in healthcare on a large scale. The government has embarked upon a plan to link major government hospitals in the state with PHCs with CSCs. This model is replicable as well as scalable in the rest of the country too. A work flow chart of the program is given below.

Earlier, the people of Tripura had to travel long distances to access health care services. Now, this is no longer required– at least in the case of eye sight related problems. The Vision Centre project, initiated by the Department of Health, provides quality eye care services to rural patients in an integrated manner whereby every case is accounted for, classified and closed with a solution. 41 vision centres for providing tele-ophthalmic services are being rolled out across the state. The vision centres in rural villages are connected to the mini data centre at IGM Hospitalin the city for maintaining electronic medical records and connectivity with an ICT enabled real time consulting facility at the ophthalmology-OPD counter at IGM.

The project is being deployed in phases and caters to a population of about 3.4 million people spread across 38 blocks of four districts in Tripura. The first and second phases have been successfully completed with more than 5,000 patients having been screened in 11 locations. The third phase is currently on for the remaining locations in the state.

The Tripura model proves that a reliable network of primary data collection centres (telecenters) could be put to good use to link up with a multi-tiered health referral system finally terminating at the speciality and super speciality hospitals in possible far off areas. This hub-and-spokes model has the potential to include other services related to health care, such as health insurance and old age pension.

Data Synthesis and Way Forward

Some states have taken the step of connecting the front and back ends of the hospital administration. Since health is a state subject, the progress of interlinking medical establishments within and outside the states varies. However, concepts like Electronic Health Records (EHR) and Hospital Management Information Systems (HMIS) are being implemented at several places. Similarly, back-end supply chain management programmes are also being embarked upon. The proposed health profiling for the senior citizens can compliment the ongoing reforms and modernization in the public healthcare sphere.

The senior citizens' health mapping needs to be backed by a regular institutional support system which may be fee-based. The operational success of the scheme relies heavily on post-data support. The mapping done at the telecenters will be rendered useless soon enough unless it is regularly updated and followed up with through an institutional backing. The proposed plan is to widen the net of healthcare support through home visits by ASHA/MPWs and if required, the village postman. Thus, the designated telecenter in the region acts as a data entry point for the entire catchment area surrounding it. The (non-clinical) data is captured into a designated template by the ASHA/MPW and sent to the SC or PHC. Citizens, who are in receipt of the reference number from the telecenter, can present themselves at the Sub Centre or PHC for examination by the general physician (GP). The GP can access the template of the patient by feeding in the reference number and complete the clinical parameters of the patient. This completes the health profile of the rural citizen.

Using the health profile as a reference, the GP can flag areas of concern and send the template back to the telecenter. The telecenter manager acts as the coordinator for the region and uses the network of ASHAs/MPWs or even village postmen to track patients who require medication, care and support. Health profile card holders, in turn, pay a pre-designated amount for the service.

Enhancing Value Delivered to Stakeholders

The data collected at the grassroots level pertaining to this segment of the society is priceless. Research institutions such as the National Institute of Immunology or Institute for Tropical Medicine may find data updated at regular intervals to be extremely important. On the commercial front, health insurance companies stand to gain significantly as they could get authentic information regarding citizen's health. This information is also very useful to pharmaceutical companies and manufacturers of personal hygiene products wishing to target this segment.

From the welfare point of view, there are already several schemes running in the country that use chip-embedded plastic cards for data storage. NREGA scheme inBihar, Women Economic Empowerment Scheme in Rajasthan, Employees State Insurance Scheme by the Ministry of Labour, Government of India are all examples where personal information is stored and distributed on plastic cards for easy mobility, transferability and authenticity. Therefore, it should not come as a surprise if a willing state introduces SMART health cards for its rural citizens that can be read at the Sub Centre level and upwards.

Global Aging and International Social Work Practice: A Developing Country Perspective

The aging population within industrialized countries is expected to surge in the next 30 years. The long-term financing challenges of adequate insurance and healthcare for the burgeoning number of older adults have accentuated policy concerns regarding the aging population in industrialized countries. These concerns are statistically rooted. In 2000, people over 60 years of age composed roughly 10% of the world's population. By 2050, that percentage is projected to increase to 21% (Sowers & Rowe, 2007). Moreover, the worldwide life expectancy is expected to rise by eleven years. Sowers and Rowe (2007) further reported that in 2005, 1 out of every 12 people in developing countries was over 60; by 2050, that number will be raised to 1 out of every 5 people. Developing countries will experience almost two thirds of this growth spurt in the aging population (Dhar Chakraborti, 2004). This phenomenon is simply known in the literature as global aging (Healy, 2008). However, the current state of gerontological social work practice, especially in the developing world, lacks the training of social workers and adequate funding to attend to the great challenges of aging population (HelpAge India Foundation, 2008). Therefore, it is important to assess the challenges that such a demographic splurge will entail on global social work practice as it relates to the developing world. There are several key questions that seek answers: How will global aging affect the international donor agencies' capacity to meet the demand of gerontological social workers in developing nations? What kind of strategies should global policy practice adopt to influence national and international approaches to global aging? This article explores the implications of global aging on social work practice in developing countries.

Academic and practice literature tend to focus singularly on strategic discourse on future challenges to population aging within developed countries, without taking into consideration the simultaneous impact it might have on developing countries. This article compares aging trends in developing countries to those in developed nations through the use of available literature and the United Nations international data on aging. The article argues that economic globalization has necessitated global interdependence, which must be acknowledged and taken into consideration when researching the effects of an aging population. The article asserts that an exclusion of developing countries' perspectives on research and strategies regarding this demographic deluge can create limitations in the approaches taken by developed nations concerning this issue. The article also examines the role of international gerontontological social work practice as a possible conduit between aging research in developed and developing countries.

The need for an international consensus on gerontological social work was first felt during the World Conference on Aging in Vienna, organized in 1982 by the United Nations. The conference identified several key variables contributing to the increased longevity in society, including advances in preventive medicine and controls on human fertility. The baby boom generation is expected to live longer than their predecessors, which could put enormous pressure on the state infrastructure in the United States and several Western European countries.

Alongside this projected age inflation in developed countries are the predictions by population scientists that the growth in the percentage of the elderly population in relation to that of working adults could have long-term implications on international immigration policies.

Working-age immigrants from population-rich countries, such as China and India, are expected to swamp the shores of those developed nations with dwindling working populations and a burgeoning number of dependent older adults (Friedman, 2006). Notably, the argument above is predicated on an inherent assumption that the developing countries are generally characterized by a growing number of high-skilled young adults.

The purpose of this article is to challenge this notion and to argue that population aging is as much a challenge for developing countries as it is for developed ones. Because of globalization, there have been some fundamental changes in the cultural practices and traditional social norms and values across many developing societies, thereby weakening the social status of older adults. The article traces these social vulnerabilities and establishes the need for international social work intervention to specifically address the protection of at risk older adults across developing regions.

Population Aging in Developing Countries

Developing nations have witnessed sustained economic growth, yet have consistently scored low on the Human

Development Index (HDI), have relatively low per-capita income, and have underdeveloped tertiary or service sectors within their economy.

Developing countries are experiencing a geometric growth in the service industries and per capita income due to a surge in the Business Processing Outsourcing (BPO) contracts between developed countries, such as the United States, United Kingdom, Germany, and Australia, and developing countries such as India, Brazil, China, and the Philippines. However, the gross domestic contribution from the service sector is nominal at best. It is important to note that many developing countries are also emerging economies, which means that, not too long ago, they made the transition from regulated to open market economies (Bhagwati, 2004).

Along with the economic changes, developing countries are witnessing a significant increase in the proportion of the older population (Takamura, 2007). In 2007, 66% of the total population of developing nations were over 55 years old, which is a 59% increase from 2000. The United Nations' report on "World population aging 2000-2050," which predicts that the underdeveloped regions in Asia, Africa, and Latin America will constitute 81 percent of the worlds' elderly population by 2050, with 53% of that increase taking place in Asia alone. This would make developing countries such as India, Pakistan, Bangladesh, Nepal, the Philippines, and Myanmar especially vulnerable to the looming socioeconomic challenges of aging (Dhar Chakrabarti, 2004).

Among the developing regions, Asia would witness the largest increase of older adults, and countries like China and India-with more than 2 billion people between them-would have a combined 600 million people over the age of 60 by 2020 (U.S. Administration on Aging, 2005). Moreover, within different cohorts of older persons, the number of individuals who are 80 years of age or older has been predicted to grow faster than any other cohort, raising additional challenges for long-term care facilities. Developing countries like Singapore, Costa-Rica, Colombia, and Malaysia would each witness more than a 200% increase in their aging population.

Aging and the Moral Economy

Initially, there were three factors that influenced the global aging population during the 19th Century: the Industrial Revolution, the rural-urban migration and the development of the working class (Bhagwati, 2004). The industrial revolution was initially fueled by the wealth amassed by the Western European countries through their economic occupation of Asian and African regions during the colonial era.

As a result, Western European countries, along with their 'new land' in the Americas, were well positioned to invest in mass-scale industries and simultaneously encouraged migration from rural to urban areas, creating a working class concentrated in the cities. These developments during the early 1800s joined social status with economic productivity and associated older adults with economic unproductiveness, leading to a decline in their social status (Yusuf, 2001).

The rise of urban, industrialized societies gave birth to the social and cultural value systems that bestow more importance to individual needs and aspirations over those of the family and community. By the third quarter of the 20th century (1950-1975), the patterns of social expectation in the Western democratic societies required publicly funded state institutions to ensure that elderly populations did not become dependent on their families during retirement. In response to such expectations, the state within many industrial societies implemented policies to provide employment based and publicly funded retirement benefits for older adults called this state involvement with the fiscal responsibility of the aged the beginning of a moral economy.

Aging, in a moral economy, is divided into two phases. The first phase is active retirement supported by Social Security, pensions, and private insurance, while the second phase is characterized by frailty, with financial support being provided by Medicare, Medicaid, and other publicly funded health insurance programs. During the latter half of the 20th century (1950-2000), federal funding for entitlement programs which targeted the elderly had already been institutionalized in the social policy infrastructures of industrialized nations, including the United States. Though economic protection for older adults had dramatically improved in moral economies, they still had to face the rapid pace of urban industrialized lifestyles and cultural resistance to professional social work intervention. As a result, the traditional values of social respect given to the aged and emotional support provided by the family system were dealt a blow by the increasingly fragmented families and the rapid migration to urban areas.

Consequently, the elderly population experienced an increase in social isolation, a decline in social support networks, a higher rate of depression and anxiety, and a susceptibility to elder mistreatment or abuse. In other words, the moral economy, in its attempt to institutionalize economic support, had failed to increase social capital for the elderly.

However, towards the close of the 20th century, the initial shock of industrialization and the rapid melting down of the old order had begun to settle down for the elderly living in developed regions (Yusuf, 2001). Still, modernization has resulted in a loss of identity and social status for older adults and eroded the cultural view that has traditionally supported societal norms of respect for seniors.

In response, a new generation of older adults in developed countries organized around group interests through advocacy organizations, such as the American Association of Retired People (AARP) and SeniorNet. They fought against policies that called for mandatory retirement, age-caps on issuing driver licenses, and high costs of senior healthcare. Strong civil rights groups representing the elderly in developed nations have been working to preserve the rights of older adults, while federal support for older adult welfare has dwindled over time.

On the other hand, the developing countries have had a history of weak or non-existent moral economies. The institutionalization of welfare for the elderly has been limited in these regions. The benefits of industrialization came to developing countries almost half a century after that of more developed countries.

As a result, the dominant value structures in these regions remained more traditional, with older adult populations enjoying considerable social status and cultural capital. Because of this traditional mindset, the role of national government funded initiatives remained minimal throughout developing countries, and the socioeconomic and medical responsibilities of the elderly were borne primarily by family members and the local community.

Globalization, Social Capital, and Aging in Developing Societies

Historically, in developing countries, agrarian economies and family-owned production of goods necessitated a shared lifestyle and collective responsibilities, which instilled norms and values that helped maintain a higher social status for the aging population (Mukherjee, 2008). The family, kinship, and friendship networks played a vital role in sustaining the elderly population within a "joint" or "co-resident" family structure, where older adults lived in the same house with the families of their children.

Co-resident families provided support, dignity, and security for the elderly. These families assumed care giving responsibilities without expecting financial compensation from the state. Thus, the onus of providing minimum social security and medical care had primarily rested on the family, kinship, and friendship networks. Although a small minority of older adults, who were employed by the federal and state government, have benefited from a small monthly state pension, the number was minimal, compared with the overall spectrum of older adults living in developing countries.

In developing countries, dependence on families and informal networks was further accentuated by the lack of resources at the disposal of governments. Furthermore, due to overpopulation, the sheer volume of the elderly people who needed support had been overwhelmingly disproportionate to the resources that were available (Morgan & Kunkel, 2007).

Additionally, it has been well documented that pervasive corruption has long plagued government administrations across developing nations, which has further jeopardized the prospects of implementing effective initiatives for the welfare of the elderly. As a result, a majority of developing countries have historically failed to build comprehensive and sustainable social security and medical social insurance policies similar to that of the United States and the Western Europe (Dixon, 2002).

In the absence of nationally funded entitlement programs, the elderly population in developing countries primarily relied on the social capital in their families and communities (Ghai, 2003). Social capital includes high levels of social support, strong family ties, larger friend networks, trusting and nurturing environments, and higher social statuses for the elderly (Putnam, 2001). Traditionally, the aging population across developing countries enjoyed higher levels of social capital due to the influence of co-resident family structure and the prevalence of cultural norms and values that taught communities to revere seniors.

In the last two decades, the process of globalization has significantly impacted the social order in the developing countries described above. Globalization, for the purposes of this article, refers to unification of economic, socio-cultural, political, and technological forces across the world, primarily through the integration of global markets by the activities of the transnational organizations. Globalization has facilitated the exchange of goods, services, lifestyle norms, and entertainment commodities from the developed to the developing countries, fundamentally altering social cultural norms of life in the hitherto closed communities of developing regions.

As a result, developing countries have observed a steady growth of urban lifestyle and city-based employment that has transformed social norms and institutions, causing a disintegration of co-resident families, as well as necessitating rural to urban migration in many agrarian communities.

Rapid industrialization and the growth of the service-based industries have further increased migration into cities (Dhar Chakraborti, 2004). The gradual but definite shift from agrarian values of interdependence to more global values of individualization has debilitated family and kinship support for seniors across developing societies, thereby eroding the local support based traditionally available to seniors.

Recent studies (Baars et al., 2006) have indicated that values such as individualism, personal responsibility, and the fragmentation of families, as opposed to collectivism, social responsibility, and co-residential family systems, have gradually been influencing the socio-cultural way of life across developing nations. As a result, social capital for older adults is declining. Older adults across developing nations are finding it more difficult to acculturate with the lifestyle of the younger generation dominated by technological finesse.

Moreover, in many developing countries-like India, the Philippines, and Brazil-globalization has brought about employment opportunities that are mostly technologically driven. These jobs are ones with which older adults cannot easily identify. As a result, the social relevance that the elderly population has always enjoyed due to the knowledge and skills they acquire over a lifetime of service, a relevance that continued even after their retirement, appears to have lost its significance.

Declining Potential Support Ratio

The decline in social capital among the elderly has been further marked by the increase in potential support ratio (PSR). PSR is the ratio of people between the ages of 15 and 64 to every person over 65 years. This ratio describes the burden placed on the working population by the non-working elderly population. The PSR is a key macro-economic marker of social and economic support available to non-working older adults.

The social security income maintenance program in the United States has been conceived on the basis of PSR. When social security was created in 1935, the PSR in the United States was 16, which suggests that for every single individual aged 65 and older receiving benefits from the federal government, there were 16 working adults contributing to their retirement support fund. In 2008, the PSR for social security in the US has decreased to 3 working people per retired older adult, and in the next thirty years it is expected to assume a negative ratio.

Implications for Global Social Work Policy Practice

The importance of global aging to social work is clear. However, even with that recognition, how do social workers and policy practitioners respond to these trends through policy and practice intervention designs? Could a global standard be set on intervention techniques that could be adopted across nations? There has been significant writing on the worries caused by the impending global aging. However, unless these discussions move towards integrated practices in a standardized fashion, nothing substantial can be realized on an international level.

In this regard, the role of international social work organizations and entities, such as the International Federation of Social Workers (IFSW), the International Association of Schools of Social Work (IASSW), and the International Council of Social Welfare (ICSW), is imperative. Beyond these social work associations, there is also a need for action on behalf of the aging population by NGOs, FBOs, International Aid Organizations, International Government Organizations, and local groups.

Before social workers even begin thinking about designing transnational policy interventions, they need to have a thorough understanding of the ethical codes that bind them at the national and international levels.

The IFSW code states that social workers should "contribute professional expertise to the development of policies and programs which improve the quality of life in society".

The IFSW code further states that social workers "have a duty to bring to the attention of their employers, policy makers, politicians, and the general public situations where resources are inadequate or where distribution of resources, policies and practices are oppressive, unfair and harmful" (IFSW, 2004).

The need for global social workers to attend to the issues of the global aging and its impact on the affected populations in developing countries is an apt case for the above-referred ethical code from IFSW. The lack of policies focusing on the elderly in developing countries have undermined their human rights and hindered social justice-two of the guiding ethical principles of IFSW (IFSW, 2004).

Recent research has indicated that the surge in global aging could generate tasks for international social workers at both macro and micro levels (Moody, 2006). According to Takamura (2007), the 2002 Madrid International Plan on Aging had identified three crucial issues around which global social work policy practice could be developed: 1) economic security for the elderly, 2) long-term care needs for older adults, and 3) developing strategies for promoting healthy and active aging.

These broad areas of practice are relevant to older adults across developing nations and should be addressed through concerted global policy practice. The next step for global social work practitioners is to prepare and address these crucial issues by developing culturally competent interventions in the global aging field in developing countries. Intervention may be developed in the following five stages:

Intervention Stage One-global Consortium

International consensus regarding agreed upon issues play a major role in influencing national policies. Global social workers should try to use the already existing international diplomatic forums of developing countries to endorse global aging in their policy agenda. Brazil, Russia, India, and China (BRIC) have already formed a forum to work together on relevant issues. Global social work consortiums need to work with the United Nations and international non-governmental organizations (INGOs)-such as Help Age International, which works on aging issues in all 43 developing countries-to form an UN-sponsored global commission on developing countries. The consortium can then develop task forces to influence national policies across developing countries.

Intervention stage two-influencing national policy: Social workers should be equipped with training, skills, and motivation to influence their respective national legislators to adopt policy positions that would provide social security, long-term care needs, and affordable health care services to their native older adults. This may be done through adopting lobbying techniques and media interventions from developed countries. Social workers should understand differences in the policy making process at the global level and identify the differences across nations.

Intervention stage three-transnational electronic lobbying: Electronic lobbying is a supplement to the traditional lobbying tools, such as letter writing, telephoning, radio programming, and television advertising. The development of information communication technologies, like multimedia supported emails, online podcasts and Web 2.0 supported social networking technologies could be used to influence public opinion internationally. There are no legal boundaries on communication protocols across these forums, which make it possible for internationally located social workers to participate electronically in national lobbying activities.

Intervention stage four-resource mobilization: Currently, inadequate resources and trained professionals remain the biggest impediment to policy practice implementation in developing countries. Very few national or international organizations are working in the field of aging, especially in developing regions. Thus, global social workers should get involved in fund raising activities to support such efforts.

Intervention stage five-developing knowledge base: Global social workers should compile culture specific exploratory and descriptive data on best social work practices with older adults, and support practice research to implement them across cultures.

For example, the Older Americans Act (OAA, 1964) in the United States has been designed to produce greater involvement of civil society and community groups in addressing the needs of older adults. Similar models can be implemented in developing societies where families, community-based organizations, and non-governmental organizations can forge partnerships with the state in conceiving, testing, and developing interventions and policies that target the elderly population.

The above mentioned stages to global social work practice with older adults interact with each other and transcend national issues, and thus would need an international perspective to implement.

Conclusion and Future Directions

Aging policies across developing regions should devise strategies to stem the projected decline in social capital (Bhagwati, 2004). Forging partnerships with international organizations, such as Help Age International, could be a beginning of international social work practice with the elderly in the developing world. Without any institutional support from the state, a vast elderly population in the developing world-approximately 800 million by 2020-will need immediate attention from international social workers.

There are several common issues around which global social work strategies between the developed and the developing countries could be forged. These issues include growth of the aging population, shifts in family structure, redefinition of inter-generational relations, loss of social capital and social support, vulnerabilities to poverty and elder abuse, debate over the role of government, interest groups, and multinational organizations in program planning and delivery, and, finally, issues of cultural competency and political economy. Successful policy practice would include implementing interventions among developed and developing nations, thereby promoting international collaborative partnerships. In order to address and fruitfully achieve results across these goals, more comparative research on social policy and population aging across international borders must be supported. Future research on the pervasive influence of culture must be carried out to refine global social work approaches. Moreover, encouraging interdisciplinary partnerships among demographers, gerontologists, social workers, economists, and policy makers can further generate cohesion among international stakeholders and would facilitate knowledge sharing.

Rights of Senior Citizen: Need of the Hour

Ageing is a natural process, which inevitably occurs in human life cycle. It brings with a host of challenges in the life of the elderly, which are mostly engineered by the changes in their body, mind, thought process and the living patterns. Ageing refers to a decline n the functional capacity of the organs of the human body, which occurs mostly due to physiological transformation, it never imply that everything has been finished. The senior citizens constitute a precious reservoir of such human resource as is gifted with knowledge of various sorts, varied experiences and deep insights. May be they have formally retired, yet an overwhelming majority of them are physically fit and mentally alert. Hence, given an appropriate opportunity, they are in a position to make significant contribution to the socioeconomic development of their nation.

Constitutional Protection

Art. 41: Right to work, to education and to public assistance in certain cases: The State shall, within the limits of economic capacity and development, make effective provision for securing the right to work, to education and to public assistance in cases of unemployment, old age, sickness and disablement, and in other cases of undeserved want.

Art. 46: Promotion of educational and economic interests of .... and other weaker sections: The State shall promote with special care the educational and economic interests of the weaker sections of the people.....and shall protect them from social injustice and all forms of exploitation. However, these provision are included in the Chapter IV i.e., Directive Principles of the Indian Constitution. The Directive Principles, as stated in Article 37, are not enforceable by any court of law. But Directive Principles impose positive obligations on the state, i.e., what it should do. The Directive Principles have been declared to be fundamental in the governance of the country and the state has been placed under an obligation to apply them in making laws. The courts however cannot enforce a Directive Principle as it does not create any justiciable right in favour of any individual. It is most unfortunate that state has not made even a single Act which are directly related to the elderly persons.

Legal Protections

Under Personal Laws: The moral duty to maintain parents is recognized by all people. However, so far as law is concerned, the position and extent of such liability varies from community to community.

Hindus Laws: Amongst the Hindus, the obligation of sons to maintain their aged parents, who were not able to maintain themselves out of their own earning and property, was recognized even in early texts. And this obligation was not dependent upon, or in any way qualified, by a reference to the possession of family property. It was a personal legal obligation enforceable by the sovereign or the state. The statutory provision for maintenance of parents under Hindu personal law is contained in Sec 20 of the Hindu Adoption and Maintenance Act, 1956.

This Act is the first personal law statute in India, which imposes an obligation on the children to maintain their parents. As is evident from the wording of the section, the obligation to maintain parents is not confined to sons only, and daughters also have an equal duty towards parents. It is important to note that only those parents who are financially unable to maintain themselves from any source, are entitled to seek maintenance under this Act.

Muslim Law: Children have a duty to maintain their aged parents even under the Muslim law. According to Mulla:

(a) Children in easy circumstances are bound to maintain their poor parents, although the latter may be able to earn something for themselves.

(b) A son though in strained circumstances is bound to maintain his mother, if the mother is poor, though she may not be infirm.

(c) A son, who though poor, is earning something, is bound to support his father who earns nothing.

According to Tyabji, parents and grandparents in indigent circumstances are entitled, under Hanafi law, to maintenance from their children and grandchildren who have the means, even if they are able to earn their livelihood. Both sons and daughters have a duty to maintain their parents under the Muslim law. The obligation, however, is dependent on their having the means to do so.

Christian and Parsi Law

The Christians and Parsis have no personal laws providing for maintenance for the parents. Parents who wish to seek maintenance have to apply under provisions of the Criminal Procedure Code.

Under the Code of Criminal Procedure

Prior to 1973, there was no provision for maintenance of parents under the code. The Law Commission, however, was not in favour of making such provision. According to its report:

The Cr.P.C is not the proper place for such a provision. There will be considerably difficulty in the amount of maintenance awarded to parents apportioning amongst the children in a summary proceeding of this type. It is desirable to leave this matter for adjudication by civil courts. The provision, however, was introduced for the first time in Sec. 125 of the Code of Criminal Procedure in 1973. It is also essential that the parent establishes that the other party has sufficient means and has neglected or refused to maintain his, i.e., the parent, who is unable to maintain himself. It is important to note that Cr.P.C 1973, is a secular law and governs persons belonging to all religions and communities. Daughters, including married daughters, also have a duty to maintain their parents.

Governmental Protections

1. The Government of India approved the National Policy for Older Persons on January 13, 1999 in order to accelerate welfare measures and empowering the elderly in ways beneficial for them. This policy included the following major steps:
   - (i) Setting up of a pension fund for ensuring security for those persons who have been serving in the unorganized sector,
   - (ii) Construction of old age homes and day care centres for every 3-4 districts,
   - (iii) Establishment of resource centres and re-employment bureaus for people above 60 years,
   - (iv) Concessional rail/air fares for travel within and between cities, i.e.,30% discount in train and 50% in Indian Airlines.
   - (v) Enacting legislation for ensuring compulsory geriatric care in all the public hospitals.
2. The Ministry of Justice and Empowerment has announced regarding the setting up of a National Council for Older Person, called agewell Foundation. It will seek opinion of aged on measures to make life easier for them.
3. Attempts to sensitise school children to live and work with the elderly. Setting up of a round the clock help line and discouraging social ostracism of the older persons are being taken up.
4. The government policy encourages a prompt settlement of pension, provident fund (PF), gratuity, etc. in order to save the superannuated persons from any hardships. It also encourages to make the taxation policies elder sensitive.
5. The policy also accords high priority to their health care needs.

6. According to Sec.88-B, 88-D and 88-DDB of Income Tax Act there are discount in tax for the elderly persons.
7. Life Insurance Corporation of India (LIC) has also been providing several scheme for the benefit of aged persons, i.e.,Jeevan Dhara Yojana, Jeevan Akshay Yojana, Senior Citizen Unit Yojana, Medical Insurance Yojana.
8. Former Prime Minister A.B.Bajpai was also launch 'Annapurana Yojana' for the benefit of aged persons. Under this yojana unattended aged persons are being given 10 kg food for every month.
9. It is proposed to allot 10 percent of the houses constructed under government schemes for the urban and rural lower income segments to the older persons on easy loan. The policy mentions:

The layout of the housing colonies will respond to the needs and life styles of the elderly so that there is no physical barriers to their mobility; they are allotted ground floor; and their social interaction with older society members exists. Despite all these attempts, there is need to impress upon the elderly about the need to adjust to the changing circumstances in life and try to live harmoniously with the younger generation as for as possible.

It may be pointed out that recently the Madurai Bench of the Madras High Court has ruled that the benefits conferred on a Government employee, who is disabled during his/her service period, under Section 47 of Persons with Disabilities(equal opportunities, protection of rights and full participation) Act, 1995 cannot be confined only seven types of medical conditions defined as 'disability' in the Act.

The seven medical conditions are blindness, low vision, leprosy-cured, hearing impaired, locomotor disability, mental retardation and mental illness. A Division Bench comprising Justice F.M.Ibrahim and Justice K.Venkataraman said: "We feel that the court cannot shut its eyes if a person knocks at its doors claiming relief under the Act. In a welfare State like India, the benefits of benevolent legislation cannot be denied on the ground of mere hyper technicalities. It may be noted that this Act is not directly related to aged person but seven medical conditions which prescribed in this Act are the common symptom of the aged person.

Need for a Change in Approach

In the older times, after the completion of 50 years of life, one had to detach oneself from the responsibilities of a 'Grihastha' and switch over to the third stage of human life which was known as 'Vanpristha' which referred to the devotion of the next 25 years of life by the 'Vanpristhi' by mana, vachana and karma to the selfless service of the suffering humanity and the larger society in return to the services received form society during the first 50 years of life.

Certain strategies and approaches at different levels of policy making, planning and programming etc. will have to be adopted in order to harness this vast human resource for promoting the involvement and participation of senior citizens in socioeconomic development process on a much larger scale.

This participation must result in an end to their social isolation ad an increase in their general satisfaction with their life. Any attempt to secure the help of the elderly in offering their service to the nation must simultaneously ensure some sort of package of services aimed at arranging for them a better quality of life and a well-designed social security network for the senior citizen. The society and the state in India need to accept the challenge of their effectively focusing their attention on the following twin issues of:

(i) How to provide a fair-deal to the senior citizens so that they are able to peacefully, constructively and satisfactorily pass their lives; and

(ii) How to utilize the vast treasure of knowledge and rich life experience of the older people so that they are able to utilize their remaining energies and contribute to the all round development of their nation.

Palliative Care: Need of the hour: According to a pilot survey, 70% of city's elderly population is undergoing some kind of medication. The average spending per day ranges between Rs. 3 to 200. However, nearly half of the money goes waste. The reason is absence of proper palliative care in the country. World Health

Organization has marked October 7 as a day to create awareness about the importance and need for hospice and palliative care. "Access to the best quality care, while facing terminal illness is a human right. Ironically, many people in the world are denied this right. The bitter side is that government in many countries does not even realize the important of this right" said geriatric physician Dr. Abhishek Shukla.

The Maintenance and Welfare of Parents and Senior Citizens Bill, 2007

THE ACT WILL be enforced by the State government concerned. The date on which the Act will come into force will be notified by the State government concerned in the Official Gazette.

Under Clause 5(1) of the Bill, a senior citizen or a parent may apply for maintenance under Clause 4 of the bill. (A senior citizen is an Indian citizen who is at least 60 years old. A parent could be father or mother, whether biological, adoptive or step father or step mother, whether or not the father or the mother is a senior citizen). If the senior citizen or parent is incapable, any other person or a voluntary organization authorized by the senior citizen or parent can apply for maintenance on their behalf. The Tribunal may take cognizance suo motu (that is, it can act on its own cognizance). These two provisions are welcome since most senior citizens or parents do not have the energy (they do not have the money anyway) to apply for maintenance.

The said Tribunal may, when a proceeding regarding monthly allowance for the maintenance under this section is pending, order such children or relative to pay a monthly allowance for the interim maintenance of the senior citizen including parent. The State government is required to constitute within a period of 6 months from the date of commencement of the law (Act), Tribunals for the purpose of adjudicating and deciding upon the order for maintenance under Clause 5.

According to Clause 4, the senior citizen including parent is entitled to apply for maintenance under Clause 5 if he is unable to maintain himself from his own earnings or out of the property owned by him. A parent or grand-parent can make an application for maintenance against one or more of his children who are majors ('children' includes son, daughter, grandson and granddaughter). The obligation of the children to maintain his or her parent extends to the needs of such parent either father or mother or both, as the case may be, so that such parent may lead a normal life. A childless senior citizen, on the other hand, can make an application against his relative ("relative" means any legal heir of the childless senior citizen who is a major and is in possession of or would inherit the property after the childless senior citizen's death; property means property of any kind, whether movable or immovable, ancestral or self-acquired, tangible or intangible and includes rights or interests in such property).

Thus Clause 4 makes a reference to grand-parent while Clause 5 does not. In other words, Clause 5 is silent about how the application for maintenance should be made by a grand-parent (who is not yet 60) under Clause 4. I wish the learned lawmakers took notice of this inconsistency lest vested interests should exploit this well-intended provision.

If the senior citizen has transferred by way of gift or otherwise, his property, subject to the condition that the relative shall provide the basic amenities and basic physical needs to the senior citizen and such relative refuses or fails to provide such amenities and physical needs, Clause 23 (1) says the said transfer of property shall be declared void by the Tribunal, if the senior citizen so desires. This is a welcome provision since it protects naïve senior citizens from exploitation by relatives who intend to renege on their promise subsequently.

The State government is also required to prescribe a comprehensive action plan for protecting the life and property of senior citizens. This is also a welcome provision since the vulnerable senior citizen can be easily harmed or hurt. In fact the senior citizen may be even carted away somewhere to ensure that none else including the voluntary organization and the Tribunal come to know of their whereabouts. Fortunately Clause 24 of the Bill takes care of this aspect. According to this Clause, 'Whoever, having the care or protection of senior citizen leaves, such senior citizen in any place with the intention of wholly abandoning such senior citizen, shall be punishable with imprisonment of either description for a term which may extend to three months or fine which may extend to five thousands rupees or with both'. I suggest registration of senior citizens with the jurisdictional police station be mandated. The NGO concerned may be requested to visit senior citizens at least every quarter under intimation to the jurisdictional police station.

Obviously, the Bill, in its present form, will meet the needs of only parents and senior citizens from educated families, propertied classes and the urban areas. It cannot cater to the needs of parents and senior citizens belonging to the poorer sections of society or hailing from villages. One may find three generations living in the same village and at times even under the same roof! If the son is also indigent, how can he maintain his parent and grand parent? How would the Tribunal adjudicate such disputes? The son will be only too happy if he is put behind bars because he is at least assured of two square meals a day!

Understandably, given its limited resources, one cannot expect the government to do a thorough job here. But it can at least ameliorate the situation. How? It should allow income tax sops to those who take care of parents/grand-parents/senior citizens. This is only fair because if tax is collected from citizens, they should be provided social security by the government when they grow old.

When the government is not able to provide social security, it should at least encourage the citizens to provide it by allowing income tax sops. After all, a citizen taking care of his aged parents or senior citizens is providing them social security which strictly speaking the government should have provided. Our government taxes individuals a la the US government but unlike the US government does not provide social security to all citizens. I have pointed out this anomaly in my article, "Why Tirupur has raced ahead of Ludhiana?" dated, Nov 20, 2007. All that the government has to do is rob Peter and pay Paul.

It is also unfortunate that the government has not made any serious attempt to cover the senior citizens under "Group Health Insurance Scheme". It believes that insurance coverage is mostly required in critical illness and at places where adequately-equipped hospitals are not available (!). Well, for a start, let the government convince me that AIIMS, New Delhi, is adequately equipped to treat indigent senior citizens.

The Bill does not cover old age pension perhaps because State governments are implementing the Old Age Pension Scheme. But the amount of pension and the eligibility criteria are not uniform across the States, under the said Scheme. The Bill should have mandated the State governments to pay old age pension to the senior citizens adequately and uniformly across the country. This should not be difficult because all that the government has to do is rob Peter and pay Paul. It has to deny income tax sops to those who do not maintain parents/grand parents/relatives; it has to deny old age pension to those parents/grand parents/relatives who are being maintained by their children/relatives.

Lastly, the government, while drafting Bills, uses the word 'may' (instead of the word 'shall') even where provisions of a mandatory nature are involved. What leads to this howler? Is it ignorance or lack of conviction on the part of the government?

A Critique of the Maintenance of Parents Bill 2007

On May 8, 2007, the Indian Express carried a critique of the UPA government's Maintenance and Welfare of Parents and Senior Citizens Bill 2007, which was introduced in the Lok Sabha in March. M. R. Madhavan, who works with the PRS Legislative Research at the Centre for Policy Research focuses on larger policy problems with the Bill, while also zeroing in on specific provisions that arouse his concern:

"The Maintenance and Welfare of Parents and Senior Citizens Bill, 2007, which was introduced in Lok Sabha in March, aims "to provide for more effective provisions for the maintenance and welfare of parents and senior citizens guaranteed and recognised under the Constitution and for matters connected therewith or incidental thereto." While it is difficult to contest the objective of ensuring a comfortable life for senior citizens, a number of provisions in the Bill may not be easy to implement.

The Bill neatly sidesteps the directive in the Constitution, which directs the state to provide public assistance in cases of old age. The Bill does state that, "The state government may establish and maintain such number of old age homes at accessible places, as it may deem necessary, in a phased manner, beginning with at least one in each district to accommodate in such homes a minimum of one hundred fifty senior citizens who are indigent". Note the use of "may" instead of "shall" – there is no obligation on the state governments to establish these. Even without this clause, there was never any prohibition on them from providing old age homes. Also, one wonders why a Bill should specify details such as the minimum size of an old age home. Instead, the Bill places the obligation of maintaining a senior citizen on his or her children, grandchildren or any legal heirs. The process and amount differs from the existing provision in the Code of Criminal Procedure, under which a first class magistrate may order a person to provide a monthly maintenance to his parents (or wife, including divorced wife or children), limited to Rs 500.

The Bill provides that the children of a senior citizen have the obligation to maintain a senior citizen to the extent that he "may lead a normal life". In case of a childless senior citizen, the obligation is on a relative who is in possession of the senior citizen's property or who would inherit his property. The maximum monthly allowance is to be specified by state governments, subject to a limit of Rs 10,000.

Some of the definitions in the Bill are confusing. Senior citizens are defined as "any person being a citizen of India, who has attained the age of sixty years or above and includes parent whether or not a senior citizen". This implies that every parent, including those below sixty years of age, would be considered a "senior citizen". Relative "means any legal heir of the childless senior citizen who is not a minor and is in possession of or would inherit his property after his death." How does one determine who would inherit the property? Does this mean that the senior citizen has to reveal the contents of his will, and does not have the freedom to change it later? If he is allowed to change his will, consider the case of the person who is initially named in the will, forced to provide a maintenance, and who finds on the death of the senior citizen that there is another will that disinherits him.

So what does a senior citizen do if he wants maintenance? He applies to the 'Maintenance Tribunal'. The application may also be made by any other person or organisation authorized by him.

However, the Bill clarifies that such an "organisation" means "any voluntary organisation registered under the Societies Registration Act, 1860, or any other law for the time being in force". It seems to ignore the fact that the Societies Registration Act does not define "voluntary organisation".

One might be tempted to believe that the purpose of permitting such organisations is to assist a senior citizen. However, the Bill makes it clear that "no party to a proceeding before a tribunal or appellate tribunal shall be represented by a legal practitioner". That is, one may not use the services of a legally qualified person in obtaining one's legal entitlements under this law. Regarding the maintenance tribunal, the Bill states that "the state government may... constitute for each subdivision one or more tribunals... The tribunal shall be presided over by an officer not below the rank of sub-divisional officer of a state". There are two points to note here. First, the use of "may", leaving the state governments the option of not forming such tribunals. Second, the job is entrusted to the SDO, who has a number of other responsibilities.

To conclude, one is not arguing against the idea of providing a safety net for senior citizens. The point is that any law that provides for such a net should be implement able. Other than the various loopholes discussed, the big issue is whether parents would take their children to the tribunal, given various social pressures. A better approach may be to design a social security system, including financial products such as pension schemes and reverse mortgages that enable the elderly to live a dignified life."

This is a powerful critique of the Bill, which is scheduled to be debated during the current session of Parliament. To my mind, there is only one existing precedent for such a law, which is the Singaporean Maintenance of Parents Act. Significantly, that law is backed by governmental programmes of pension, healthcare and other forms of support for the elderly, which adds weight to Madhavan's core argument. Hopefully, these issues will be aired during the Parliamentary debates on this law.

Anonymous said...This bill has provisions where the chances of misuse are greater than beneficial use. What if a particular heir or children live out side India or other than the place where the Senior citizen resides? Will that give the Senior citizen a right to live with the heir/children? Will the order of Magistrate be implantable in a foreign jurisdiction to bring him back to fulfil his obligations? What if the senior citizen is the cause of discord, will that still be the reason to keep that person with him/her? What happens to parents with daughters only and no son? Will the law make it compulsory even for the son-in-law to take care of the senior citizen? How many such senior citizen one shall be responsible to take care of?

The law is designed simply to avoid the State's responsibility to provide a better social security system for its citizen and putting the onus on the citizen for such responsibility while the State and its guardians-the executives and legislators wish away the hard earned tax payers money in such wishful bills and squander the same on their own security.

Conclusions: It may be conclude by saying that the problem of the elderly must be addressed to urgently and with utmost care. There is urgent need to amend the Constitution for the special provision to protection of aged person and bring it in the periphery of fundamental right. With the degeneration of joint family system, dislocation of familiar bonds and loss of respect for the aged person, the family in modern times should not be thought to be a secure place for them. Thus, it should be the Constitutional duty of the State to make an Act for the welfare and extra protection of the senior citizen including palliative care.

9

Managing Social Workers

The Leadership and Management sub group of the Review 1 was set up to consider how leadership and management should be strengthened across social work services and to make recommendations on a leadership and management development strategy for the social work services. The remit required the group to develop a draft strategy by September 2005. The group concluded that this was not achievable in the time available primarily due to the need to ensure that its work took account of, and was sufficiently aligned with, the emerging findings of the review. This paper therefore sets out 5 key recommendations for strengthening leadership and management across social work services.

The group took account of other aspects of the review since many of its strands are overlapping and complementary. In particular the role of social worker and performance improvement sub groups have significant implications for leadership and management and which were picked up by the group in its deliberations. This report makes reference to many of the issues identified by the review but does not restate them in detail.

The group met on 6 occasions April to September. To support its work it considered a range of evidence drawn from front line staff, managers, other professional groups and key stakeholders including the views of users and carers.

The work was informed by research undertaken both previously and specifically for the review by the Scottish Leadership Foundation. It also considered the evaluation of Cohort 1 of Leading to Deliver, a leadership development programme funded by the

Scottish Executive. This report draws together the thinking of the group and makes recommendations on the way forward for developing and strengthening leadership and management in social work services.

Since the group has concluded its work the report by Audit Scotland "Leadership Development: How Government Works" has been published. The main conclusions of that report echo many of the recommendations drawn by the sub group although Audit Scotland were looking at leadership development in a public sector context only.

Context and Challenges for Leadership and Management in Social Work Services

Current and future demands on the provision of social work services requires change. The review makes clear that doing more of the same will not deliver what is required for the future. Increasing demand, greater complexity and rising expectations mean that the current situation is not sustainable. The focus for services will need to be on engaging people as active participants; on what actually improves outcomes for service users and ensuring that these are done consistently. It will require finding new ways of designing and delivering services in ways that make best use of skills across the public sector workforce with professionals, services and agencies working together. The focus of services is shifting away from welfare based approaches to services to those that promote wellbeing both for individuals and communities.

Professionals and services are under considerable pressure. There are often competing and conflicting demands made on social services and leaders and managers in that context – accountability and flexibility, choice and protection amongst others. They are also increasingly provided in a context of changing needs and opportunities. Good professional and practice leadership does exist and whilst there are many strengths from which to build, the scale of the challenges – demographic, social and political-that influence future design and delivery of services are such that the delivery of the vision set out by the 21st century review, particularly improving outcomes for users and carers and communities, must be underpinned by enabling and empowering leadership and effective management.

The 21st century review highlights certain key issues which have implications for leadership and management. These include:

- Need for effective professional leadership at all levels
- Strengthened local political leadership
- Enhanced culture of continuous professional development that balances need for generic competence and specialist knowledge and skills
- Development of career pathways in practice and in leadership and management
- Development of an accountability framework that builds from the SSSC Codes of Practice for employees and employers
- Increased delegation of decision-making and devolved budgets
- Empowered frontline staff
- Development of a learning culture and organisations learning from what works as well as "near misses"
- The drive to greater service user involvement in design and delivery of services
- Greater personalisation of services
- The need for increased capacity and skills in service redesign
- Increasing provision by multi disciplinary teams
- Greater partnership working
- Enhanced skills and capacity in strategic planning.

These are not exhaustive but give an indication of the range of issues emerging from the 21st century review which were considered in thinking about how leadership and management in social work services should be strengthened. They can be characterised as a need to build the capacity of social work services at all levels and across all sectors for sustainable change. These are the challenges that current and future leaders and managers in social work services will face.

The group also considered the wider context and its implications for how work might be managed and organised in future. The work of the "Tomorrow Project" accords with the findings of the review emphasising the need to develop people rather than control them and that the task of leadership and management will be to enable workers through the creation of the right culture and climate and by giving them the tools to work effectively. This will mean that leaders and managers will have to manage the tension between professional autonomy and the need for accountability within a focus on outcomes rather than task.

What do we Mean by Leadership and Management?

The terms leadership and management are often used interchangeably and assumptions made that leadership only exists within management positions and that leadership can only be exercised by those at the very top of organisational structures.

Leadership whilst similar to management in many ways – for example both involve influence and achieving goals-is also different. The overriding function of management has been to provide order and consistency to organisations – transactional skills. Leadership is most often construed as seeking adaptive and constructive change – transformational skills.

Leadership is necessary at all levels of organisations – not just the top. As a result, effective organisations need to nourish both competent management and skilled leadership at all levels. Leadership needs to be visible across the whole organisation and wherever social work services are delivered and to articulate the vision of that organisation and how it will go about fulfilling that vision. Leadership at the top of organisations is critical – the styles and behaviours of those at the top set the tone for the culture, attitudes and behaviours of others across the organisation. They must provide effective models for the rest of the organisation.

Thus what is required is both empowering, enabling leadership and effective management.

Climate for Change

A major challenge for leadership and management across social work services is one of change management. To deliver the vision set out in the 21st Century Social Work Review requires transforming how we think about services, how we deliver those services and a shared view of what the changes we are seeking to make should deliver. Establishing the right culture and climate for change to implement the review effectively is critical to its success.

This will mean individuals and organisations taking ownership of the change agenda across the sector and committing to making this happen. The experience of other sectors – notably the NHS 7 in implementing major change within their services has identified a critical need to build ownership and capacity within organisations in order to do this effectively. This means addressing for individuals, skills in change management, identifying the required behaviours and attitudes to create a climate in which change can flourish – a "can do" approach, as well as developing the capacity of organisations to develop and flex and adapt to changing needs and expectations. The shift needed is in leadership and management style to embrace a partnership approach that empowers staff, users and managers to participate in developing creative solutions, developing positive, supportive behaviours and environments to sustain leadership and management development in social work services.

In addition to building the right climate in which enabling and empowering leadership and effective management can flourish it is important that other factors which may be a barrier to success are addressed. This includes considering how leaders and managers could be best supported as they seek to implement the findings of the review. The research by SLF identified a fragmented and inconsistent approach to leadership and management development across the sector. Consideration should be given to bringing leaders and managers from all sectors together-nationally and locally-as a way of both helping to develop, and sustain, leadership and management development initiatives. The forums offered to participants of Leading to Deliver post completion of the programme have proved a useful continuing support mechanism with participants identifying its value in helping to sustain the behaviours and learning from the programme itself once back in the workplace. However, to be effective the active support of managers and leaders at all levels is needed to sustain individual and organisational change and development.

Issues of access to leadership and management development also need careful consideration. The vision for 21st century services– multi professional and provided on a cross sector, cross organisational basis means that initiatives for strengthening leadership and management need to be applicable and available to not just local authorities but independent sectors and take account of integrated models of service provision. In taking forward strengthening leadership and management care must also be taken to ensure that developments are appropriately phased so that the necessary foundations are in place from which to build sustainable change.

The Role of Leadership and Management

The group identified that leaders and managers need to:

- have vision, which is informed by involving service users and other partners
- lead and support staff to work with service users and their carers to influence service developments and outcomes
- take responsibility and be accountable for good practice
- influence a wide range of stakeholders to promote a social model of care and its values
- be able to deal with the conflicts, tensions and gate-keeping roles in managing social work services, taking account of individual and community needs.

Professional leaders also have a clear role in developing and maintaining practice, which is self-aware, critically reflective, founded on, informed by, and capable of being judged against a clear value base.

Leadership and management practice should actively:

- inspire staff
- promote and meet service aims, objectives and goals
- develop joint working/partnerships that are purposeful
- empower staff and service users to develop services people want
- value people, recognise and actively develop potential
- develop and maintain awareness and keep in touch with service users and staff
- provide an environment and time in which to develop reflective practice, professional skills and the ability to make judgements in complex situations
- take responsibility for the continuing professional development of self and others.

Social work services have built on values such as choice and self-determination to develop practice that is person-centred and emphasises social inclusion, advocacy, engagement and partnership with service users. It is based on a social model, which underpins a range of interventions from skills in assessment, planning and review, supporting independent living and alternative care, networking, communication and partnership. Leaders and managers need to support staff to develop good practice as an integral part of achieving good services.

Contribution of Leadership and Management

'This paper covers some of the key features and elements of how strengthening leadership and management capacity across social work services should be taken forward as part of implementing the 21st Century Social Work Review.

A framework for leadership and management should be developed and located within a common approach to leadership and management development across public services, not just social work services and that integrates individual and organisational needs. It can be applied to all leaders and managers and any size of organisation across local authority and voluntary and private sectors. It must facilitate changing the current, inconsistent and fragmented approach to leadership and management development. It will expect individuals, teams and organisations to regularly assess and address learning needs and evaluate the impact this has on service delivery. This process should contribute to the development of learning organisations and enable employers to take responsibility for meeting learning needs in the most effective way.

The aim of strengthening leadership and management across social work services is to ensure there are sufficient effective and competent leaders and managers in the social service workforce. Lord Laming highlighted the issues in *The Victoria Climbié Inquiry: Summary Report of an Inquiry* (DH, 2003) when he said:

"What is needed are managers with a clear set of values about the role of public services, particularly in relation to addressing the needs of vulnerable people, combined with the ability to 'lead from the front'."

A leadership and management development framework will have to take account of:

- The current and future policy drivers for social work services in the context of cross-service boundaries with health, education, housing, police and other agencies including the voluntary and private sector
- The implementation of new inspection and performance improvement structures and processes
- Current developments in management and leadership standards and training, such as the revised SVQ's and the Management Standards Council standards for leadership and management
- Approaches being taken to leadership and management development in other sectors such as health, education, police as well as by SOLACE and the Improvement Service to locate it within a wider public service approach to development
- Current understanding about leadership and management functions and development in the sector, what is actually happening in practice to determine what now requires to happen.

A number of key principles provide a starting point:

- the approach to leadership and management needs to be systematic and consistent, integrating individual, team and organisational development
- leadership and management should be seen as distinct but overlapping activities
- continuing professional development will be a core part of every leader's and manager's responsibility in the future.

We recognise that there are common behaviours, skills and knowledge required for leaders and managers across the public sector. The framework should make explicit common qualities and behaviours that are required of all leaders and managers in a public sector context but also identify whether there are additional or specific needs for the social service context.

Professional Autonomy, Accountability and Governance

A framework for leadership and management development must set out clearly what is meant by good governance, provide clarity about accountability and be underpinned by values and ethical considerations. The report "Good Governance Standard for Public Services (2004) outlines six core principles of good governance, each with a set of supporting principles.

The report describes the function of governance as ensuring: "that an organisation or partnership fulfils its overall purpose, achieves its intended outcomes for citizens and service users, and operates in an effective, efficient and ethical manner. This principle should guide all governance activity." and outlines the six core principles of good governance as follows:

1. Focusing on the organisation's purpose and on outcomes for citizens and service users;
2. Performing effectively in clearly defined functions and roles;
3. Promoting values for the whole organisation and demonstrating the value of good governance through behaviour;
4. Taking informed, transparent decisions and managing risk;
5. Developing the capacity and capability of the governing body to be effective;
6. Engaging stakeholders and making accountability real.

Increased political and media interest in the effectiveness of social work services in recent years has been mirrored by increased public expectation of services. This scrutiny can negatively affect the confidence of all those within organisations. Clarity of roles, the accountability of both individuals and organisations and their respective responsibilities are particularly important within this environment. Increasingly, since the establishment of the SSSC and publication of the Codes of Practice, social work services are moving from committing voluntarily to standards, ethics and values on an individual basis to a professional and organisational environment that is firmly and explicitly embedded within a clearly stated legal and statutory context. Recent inquiries highlighted particular issues for leaders and managers. The SLF report comments on the O' Brien Inquiry that:

> *"Again the underlying theme for leadership and management is about securing not just the development of a vision for services but also leadership behaviours that will instil a culture of challenge, learning and sharing supported by robust*

management systems. These systems should be created and actively managed both within each of the agencies and across agency boundaries, with clear protocols on sharing information, communicating, assessing and managing risk, decision making and accountability."

Practice across the broad range of social work services brings with it complex and challenging situations, which demand a high level of analytical and ethical skills by all leaders and managers. The ability to take on board a range of different and possibly conflicting perspectives, to frame the problem with a depth of understanding and to communicate this in a transparent manner is an indication of good governance by a confident and competent leader and manager.

The framework should give consideration to ensuring that issues of governance form part of the contractual obligations for all staff working in social work services.

All of this must be underpinned by clear frameworks of accountability which set out the responsibilities of individuals, including managers at all levels as well as the organisation itself in order to provide clarity about what is meant by individual professional autonomy, management and organisational accountability. Consideration should also be given as whether we could learn from the experience of the NHS in developing clinical governance and its applicability for developing sound professional governance.

Framework for Delivery

A framework for leadership and management development needs to be broad in its scope given the breadth of change that is already taking place across social work services and the demands this creates for effective leadership and management. The framework should therefore address the following areas:

- Professional and Practice Leadership
- Political Leadership
- Strategic Leadership
- Operational management
- Academic Leadership
- Citizen Leadership.

Professional and Practice Leadership

Professional leadership is a key issue within the 21st century review. For social workers this means developing social work as a strong profession underpinned by a clear evidence base and development of social workers exercising professional autonomy within a clear framework of accountability – individual and organisational. To support this social workers require effective professional support which focuses on 3 core elements – performance management including accountability, staff development and staff support. It must deal with all these aspects and ensure that staff are enabled to deliver high standards of practice and enhanced outcomes for service users. This will be critical as multi professional teams become further established and social workers are increasingly employed in a range of different settings. Evidence from other sectors suggests that if you want to achieve sustainable service change and continuous improvement then this requires clear professional leadership.

Professional and practice leadership demands critical self evaluation and evaluation against benchmarks. It has to be supported by a learning culture which enables individuals to develop their skills, knowledge and expertise as part of a commitment to continuous improvement. There is a need for practitioner career pathways which allow for social workers to develop roles as consultant practitioners and so provide practice leadership to others within social work services as well as those in other professions. This however needs to be supported by building the evidence base to no underpin practice in social work services, based on evaluative research and knowledge building.

This will require a greater partnership between employers, practitioners and academics to build the required knowledge base for the practice and professional leadership that is now needed. The higher education sector should provide leadership in taking this forward and in ensuring that the social work degree equips social workers from early on with a clear understanding of professional and practice leadership. Every front line practitioner must understand the need for, and demonstrate in practice, professional leadership.

The group also considered the role of the Chief Social Work Officer within local authorities in the context of professional leadership. The Local Government Act 1994 (Scotland) required local authorities to appoint a chief social work officer to oversee social work services and fulfil other specific responsibilities. However, clarity as to what the role meant in practice was not evident and what level the role occupies within organisations varies across Scotland.

To enhance senior professional leadership in social work services the Chief Social Work Officer has a key role to play in ensuring that standards of professional practice are maintained and developed within local authorities and that this includes identification of adherence to the SSSC Codes of Practice. The Chief Social Work Officer role should be held by a single person in each authority reporting directly to Chief Executives and elected members for the quality of all social work services – whether provided directly or commissioned on behalf of the local authority. The role of the Chief Social Work Officer should be further examined to provide clarity and consensus about their responsibilities and accountability, the needs of Chief Executive's, elected members and others such as partner organisations and partner providers for standards of professional practice, service delivery and workforce development at all levels. This should then be set out in guidance defining the rights, responsibilities required competencies and accountabilities. The Chief Social Work Officer must be a visible, credible social work professional – one who has the time and resources to fulfil this important role effectively.

Political Leadership

Developing a practical and critical understanding of the leadership and management challenges faced by social work services will need visible and committed political leadership and support at a national and local level. The shift from representative democracy to more participative democracy will bring increased challenges and demand greater leadership at local levels. The capacity of elected members to provide effective leadership to transform the provision of social work services, to deliver improved outcomes for users and carers and to effectively involve users and carers in this also needs to be developed. Elected members have a key role to play and their needs should not be overlooked in developing a framework for leadership and management development. The framework should identify how best to assist enhanced understanding of the key drivers and barriers to change across social work services and its partners. This model operates elsewhere in Europe, e.g. Germany where those wishing to be an elected member at a federal level are expected to undertake a course. However, there is a need for leaders and managers to be politically aware and skilled in order to better understand, anticipate issues and build strategic alliances as necessary.

Strategic Leadership

A key issue identified by the experience of Leading to Deliver and identified within the review itself is the need to enhance the capacity for, and understanding of, strategic leadership and management at all levels across social work services. This should include key areas such as setting direction, service redesign, organisational development, capacity to lead change, performance management and building and leading effective partnerships. It should also cover issues of governance and accountability particularly in multi - service structures. Whilst some understanding of these key issues is critical across all levels of an organisation a key priority for development in this regard should be senior managers as they will need to address the implications of the 21st century review particularly in service redesign, complex partnerships (including collaborative leadership and leadership without formal authority) and personalisation of services. Such skills will be particularly critical as local authorities develop their role in community planning with an emphasis on social models of need and risk. This will also be influential in taking forward more collaborative models of commissioning with the voluntary and private sector and in placing users centre stage. Particular attention should be paid to succession planning and strategic leadership skills across all sectors-public, private and voluntary – to ensure that leaders are prepared and have the skills necessary to operate in complex partnership environments.

Operational Management

A move to management should be a positive decision and one for which individuals are prepared and can acquire the skills and knowledge needed as they progress. This is not the case currently and where management development programmes exist within local authorities and voluntary and private sectors their focus is often on orientating the individual to the procedures and processes of that organisation and not on wider leadership and management skills and behaviours that meet both individual and organisational needs. Managers have little access to opportunities to understand the management role and develop their skills. Therefore more attention needs to be paid to induction into management and transitions across management levels. This highlights the need for effective systems for continuing professional development and the development of specific career pathways for those moving into management roles. Management development at this level must pay particular attention to management of people, management of resources and management of procedures and processes.

The move to integrated service delivery with greater emphasis on multi professional teams and increased skill mix requires a broader approach to leadership and management development at all levels. It should also encompass what it means to lead without formal authority. In this context both leaders and managers need to know how to devolve responsibility, empower staff and understand how to work effectively to improve outcomes for service users through promoting effective practice. It should also have a focus on accountability, governance and performance management.

The development of standards for leadership and management should be used to underpin this development and which would allow for local flexibility of delivery and tailoring to local circumstance but set against a consistent framework of standards. This would allow for cross sector recognition of experience and qualifications held by individuals and enable greater movement between sectors. It is vital that the leadership and management standards capture the importance of leading and managing complexity and diversity; this may be across agencies, in integrated services and through contracts. Any leadership and management standards/competences framework should promote:

- flexible career pathways across integrated services
- transferable skills across agencies
- applicability to diverse organisations and individuals.

Systems also need to be in place for leaders and managers to have access to support and mentoring as part of their development and to ensure accountability for service delivery. Occupational standards and competences for specific roles and functions need to reflect the wider organisational business and workforce plans. Competences need to be reviewed regularly to ensure the leader or manager has the appropriate knowledge and skills as roles and plans change. Effective operational management is critical as the challenges of managing complex services and service delivery increase.

Academic Leadership

Identified above is the need for greater partnership between employers, practitioners and academics to build the required knowledge base for the practice and professional leadership. It also identified that the higher education sector should provide leadership in taking this forward and in ensuring that the social work degree equips social workers from early on with a clear understanding of professional and practice leadership. Academic leaders therefore have a vital contribution to make. They must assist professional leadership by taking social work services forward in the 21st century – helping to shape future practice and service delivery and embracing the involvement of users and carers in that process. They must influence through rigorous evaluation improving our understanding of what constitutes effective practice. Attention should also be paid to developing future academic leaders. This requires thinking creatively about improved partnerships between practice and academia and enabling career pathways that assist those that wish to move between direct practice and educating future practitioners.

Citizen Leadership

The shift from welfare models of provision to one which promotes wellbeing and inclusion needs to be underpinned by the effective engagement of those who use services to help shape the design, delivery and quality of services. Increased personalisation of services and the shift to viewing users as partners will mean that users also need to be identified as leaders in the co-creation of services that meet their needs. At its simplest it means seeing users as experts in their own needs but also that leadership can be found amongst those who use services and the carers and not just from within professional ranks of social work services. This means the meaningful engagement of users and carers at an individual, operational and strategic level. For example, users and carers should contribute to designing, delivering, evaluating and inspecting social work services. Users and carers should also have a role in developing professional leadership within social work services through active involvement in the delivery of training.

Other Issues

The framework should also encompass a range of development tools and techniques as part of an overall approach to leadership and management development. The group was clear that leadership and management development is not about training programmes alone. It requires a whole systems approach – one which is closely tied to the development of learning organisations and the embedding of a learning culture. There are a number of approaches. They include action learning, mentoring, coaching, stretch assignments/projects and secondments. Such approaches should form part of an overall strategy for leadership and management development. We need to develop a clearer understanding of what kinds of learning and development are most effective in supporting leaders and managers better understand what works best and when. This is critical to achieving a balance between authoritative and adaptive leadership responses. In addition the use of IT to support the provision of leadership and management development needs further consideration. The use of IT through e-learning has gained ground but works best when part of a blended learning approach which includes some face to face teaching and peer review. IT should also be used in the support of ongoing development for leaders and managers such as online peer networks and advice forums.

Implementation

The recommendations from the leadership and management group will form part of the overall report of the 21st century review of social work. Further detailed work will be needed to implement the recommendations. Resources to underpin it and to ensure that the key features can be effectively implemented should be identified as part of the implementation plan. This plan must identify priorities for action, including short as well as medium to longer term goals. Action will be required at a number of different levels – local, regional and national and learning from elsewhere suggests that leadership and management development must be owned by the sector itself. Establishing a clear understanding and support across the sector of what needs to be done to strengthen leadership and management is a pre-requisite in order to take forward the other developments.

Evaluation of the framework for leadership and management development as it is implemented is also recommended to ensure that it achieves the aims identified, meets the identified needs and that it continues to be relevant. Evaluation will be critical to understanding what is successful and where blockages occur. This will assist in identifying what further action is needed to ensure empowering and enabling leadership and effective management is in place to deliver improved outcomes for users and carers in the 21st century.

In the interim, consideration should be given to continued provision of Leading to Deliver across the social service sector. Key aspects of the programme may need rethought to take account of the recommendations from the 21st century review, but as the SLF report makes clear it is by and large the only major development programme currently taking place for the sector that is addressing many of the challenges identified by the review and which is positively regarded and achieving results at an individual and organisational level. The potential time lag between the 21st century review reporting and development of the framework for leadership and management development should not give rise to a hiatus for the sector in addressing key leadership and management challenges that exist now.

Similarly, the Collaborative Leadership Programme being piloted by SLF and Lancaster University and targeted at senior managers across the public sector is unique in Scotland. It will be an important source of learning as it is delivered and evaluated and should be used to inform thinking on the need for cross service/cross organisational development, particularly in the context of community planning and working in complex partnerships, for senior managers.

The programme only commenced in June 2005 and was not a stage where the leadership and management group could make detailed recommendations about this particular programme. The costs of this programme per individual participant at this pilot stage would also need examined to ensure that if the programme were continued issues of costs and equity of access are properly considered.

However, it is clear skills in leading collaboratively will be highly relevant to shaping the future design and delivery of social work services.

Recommendations

Action will be required at a number of levels to ensure that enabling leadership and effective management are put in place. These are integral to a culture of continuous improvement focusing on delivery of improved outcomes for service users and carers. The group's recommendations for how leadership and management development for social work services could best be taken forward are set out below.

"Empowering and enabling leadership and effective management should be developed at all levels of social work services:"

(a) Establish national "pan sector" leadership and management forums, to achieve broad sector "buy in", providing equity in terms of access and contribution. Early establishment of a "pan sector" leadership and management steering group to take forward the strengthening of social work services leadership and management.

(b) Develop a national framework for leadership and management development, which supports flexible career pathways across integrated services, and encompasses personal, organisational and professional drivers/ guidance, criteria and competences.

(c) Address the need for cultural and behavioural change, that enables a shift in management styles to include a partnership approach. This would empower staff, users and managers to participate in developing creative solutions, assist development of positive, supportive behaviours and environments to sustain leadership and management development in social work services.

(d) Strengthen strategic professional leadership, including developing leadership capabilities around political and non-executive leaders.

(e) Build organisational development capacity in social work services, to initiate and sustain the change process.

Non-governmental Organization

Non-governmental organization (NGO) is a term that has become widely accepted as referring to a legally constituted, non-governmental organization created by natural or legal persons with no participation or representation of any government. In the cases in which NGOs are funded totally or partially by governments, the NGO maintains its non-governmental status and excludes government representatives from membership in the organization. Unlike the term *intergovernmental organization*, "non-governmental organization" is a term in general use but is not a legal definition. In many jurisdictions these types of organization are defined as "civil society organizations" or referred to by other names.

The number of internationally operating NGOs is estimated at 40,000. National numbers are even higher: Russia has 277,000 NGOs. India is estimated to have between 1 million and 2 million NGOs.

History

National NGOs go back to antiquity. International non-governmental organizations have a history dating back to at least 1839. Rotary, later Rotary International, was founded in 1905. It has been estimated that by 1914 there were 1083 NGOs. International NGOs were important in the anti-slavery movement and the movement for women's suffrage, and reached a peak at the time of the World Disarmament Conference. However, the phrase "non-governmental organization" only came into popular use with the establishment of the United Nations Organization in 1945 with provisions in Article 71 of Chapter 10 of the United Nations Charter for a consultative role for organizations which are neither governments nor member states—see Consultative Status. The definition of "international NGO" (INGO) is first given in resolution 288 (X) of ECOSOC on February 27, 1950: it is defined as "any international organization that is not founded by an international treaty". The vital role of NGOs and other "major groups" in sustainable development was recognized in Chapter 27 of Agenda 21, leading to intense arrangements for a consultative relationship between the United Nations and non-governmental organizations.

Rapid development of the non-governmental sector occurred in western countries as a result of the processes of restructurization of the welfare state. Further globalization of that process occurred after the fall of the communist system and was an important part of the Washington consensus.

Globalization during the 20th century gave rise to the importance of NGOs. Many problems could not be solved within a nation. International treaties and international organizations such as the World Trade Organization were perceived as being too centred on the interests of capitalist enterprises. Some argued that in an attempt to counterbalance this trend, NGOs have developed to emphasize humanitarian issues, developmental aid and sustainable development.

A prominent example of this is the World Social Forum which is a rival convention to the World Economic Forum held annually in January in Davos, Switzerland. The fifth World Social Forum in Porto Alegre, Brazil, in January 2005 was attended by representatives from more than 1,000 NGOs. Some have argued that in forums like these, NGOs take the place of what should belong to popular movements of the poor. Others argue that NGOs are often imperialist in nature, that they sometimes operate in a racialized manner in dominant countries, and that they fulfil a similar function to that of the clergy during the high colonial era. The philosopher Peter Hallward argues that they are an aristocratic form of politics. However, this philosophy would suggest that organizations of indigenous peoples are not represented, which is untrue. Whatever the case, NGO transnational networking is now extensive.

Types of NGOs

Apart from "NGO", often alternative terms are used as for example: independent sector, volunteer sector, civil society, grassroots organizations, transnational social movement organizations, private voluntary organizations, self-help organizations and non-state actors (NSA's).

Non-governmental organizations are a heterogeneous group. A long list of acronyms has developed around the term "NGO".

These include:

- CSO, short for civil society organization;
- DONGO: Donor Organized NGO;
- ENGO: short for environmental NGO, such as Global 2000;
- GONGOs are government-operated NGOs, which may have been set up by governments to look like NGOs in order to qualify for outside aid or promote the interests of the government in question;
- INGO stands for international NGO; Oxfam is an international NGO
- QUANGOs are quasi-autonomous non-governmental organizations, such as the International Organization for Standardization (ISO). (The ISO is actually not purely an NGO, since its membership is by nation, and each nation is represented by what the ISO Council determines to be the 'most broadly representative' standardization body of a nation. That body might itself be a nongovernmental organization; for example, the United States is represented in ISO by the American National Standards Institute, which is independent of the federal government. However, other countries can be represented by national governmental agencies; this is the trend in Europe.)
- TANGO: short for technical assistance NGO;
- GSO: Grassroots Support Organization
- MANGO: short for market advocacy NGO.

There are also numerous classifications of NGOs. The typology the World Bank uses divides them into Operational and Advocacy:

> *The primary purpose of an operational NGO is the design and implementation of development-related projects. One frequently used categorization is the division into* relief-oriented *versus* development-oriented *organizations; they can also be classified according to whether they stress service delivery or participation; or whether they are religious or secular; and whether they are more public or private-oriented. Operational NGOs can be community-based, national or international.*

The primary purpose of an Advocacy NGO is to defend or promote a specific cause. As opposed to operational project management, these organizations typically try to raise awareness, acceptance and knowledge by lobbying, press work and activist events.

USAID refers to NGOs as *private voluntary organisations*. However many scholars have argued that this definition is highly problematic as many NGOs are in fact state and corporate funded and managed projects with professional staff. Furthermore it has often been argued that USAID is in fact a key arm of American imperialism and that it sets up and supports NGOs in order to further imperial agendas.

NGOs exist for a variety of reasons, usually to further the political or social goals of their members or funders. Examples include improving the state of the natural environment, encouraging the observance of human rights, improving the welfare of the disadvantaged, or representing a corporate agenda. However, there are a huge number of such organizations and their goals cover a broad range of political and philosophical positions. This can also easily be applied to private schools and athletic organizations.

Methods

NGOs vary in their methods. Some act primarily as lobbyists, while others primarily conduct programs and activities. For instance, an NGO such as Oxfam, concerned with poverty alleviation, might provide needy people with the equipment and skills to find food and clean drinking water, whereas an NGO like the FFDA helps through investigation and documentation of human rights violations and provides legal assistance to victims of human rights abuses. Others, such as Afghanistan Information Management Services, provide specialized technical products and services to support development activities implemented on the ground by other organizations.

Public Relations

Non-governmental organizations need healthy relationships with the public to meet their goals. Foundations and charities use sophisticated public relations campaigns to raise funds and employ standard lobbying techniques with governments. Interest groups may be of political importance because of their ability to influence social and political outcomes.

Consulting

Project management: There is an increasing awareness that management techniques are crucial to project success in non-governmental organizations. Generally, non-governmental organizations that are private have either a community or environmental focus. They address varieties of issues such as religion, emergency aid, or humanitarian affairs. They mobilize public support and voluntary contributions for aid; they often have strong links with community groups in developing countries, and they often work in areas where government-to-government aid is not possible. NGOs are accepted as a part of the international relations landscape, and while they influence national and multilateral policy-making, increasingly they are more directly involved in local action.

Staffing

Not all people working for non-governmental organizations are volunteers. The reasons people volunteer are not necessarily purely altruistic, and can provide immediate benefits for themselves as well as those they serve, including skills, experience, and contacts.

There is some dispute as to whether expatriates should be sent to developing countries. Frequently this type of personnel is employed to satisfy a donor who wants to see the supported project managed by someone from an industrialized country. However, the expertise these employees or volunteers may have can be counterbalanced by a number of factors: the cost of foreigners is typically higher, they have no grassroot connections in the country they are sent to, and local expertise is often undervalued.

The NGO sector is an important employer in terms of numbers. For example, by the end of 1995, CONCERN worldwide, an international Northern NGO working against poverty, employed 174 expatriates and just over 5,000 national staff working in ten developing countries in Africa and Asia, and in Haiti.

Funding

Large NGOs may have annual budgets in the hundreds of

millions or billions of dollars. For instance, the budget of the American Association of Retired Persons (AARP) was over US$540 million in 1999. Funding such large budgets demands significant fundraising efforts on the part of most NGOs. Major sources of NGO funding include membership dues, the sale of goods and services, grants from international institutions or national governments, and private donations. Several EU-grants provide funds accessible to NGOs.

Even though the term "non-governmental organization" implies independence from governments, most NGOs depend heavily on governments for their funding. A quarter of the US$162 million income in 1998 of the famine-relief organization Oxfam was donated by the British government and the EU. The Christian relief and development organization World Vision collected US$55 million worth of goods in 1998 from the American government. Nobel Prize winner Médecins Sans Frontières (MSF) (known in the USA as Doctors Without Borders) gets 46% of its income from government sources.

Monitoring and Control

In a March 2000 report on United Nations Reform priorities, former U.N. Secretary General Kofi Annan wrote in favour of international humanitarian intervention, arguing that the international community has a "right to protect" citizens of the world against ethnic cleansing, genocide, and crimes against humanity.

On the heels of the report, the Canadian government launched the Responsibility to Protect R2PPDF (434 KiB) project, outlining the issue of humanitarian intervention. While the R2P doctrine has wide applications, among the more controversial has been the Canadian government's use of R2P to justify its intervention and support of the coup in Haiti.

Years after R2P, the World Federalist Movement, an organization which supports "the creation of democratic global structures accountable to the citizens of the world and call for the division of international authority among separate agencies", has launched Responsibility to Protect-Engaging Civil Society (R2PCS). A collaboration between the WFM and the Canadian government, this project aims to bring NGOs into lockstep with the principles outlined under the original R2P project.

The governments of the countries an NGO works or is registered in may require reporting or other monitoring and oversight. Funders generally require reporting and assessment, such information is not necessarily publicly available. There may also be associations and watchdog organizations that research and publish details on the actions of NGOs working in particular geographic or program areas.

In recent years, many large corporations have increased their corporate social responsibility departments in an attempt to preempt NGO campaigns against certain corporate practices. As the logic goes, if corporations work *with* NGOs, NGOs will not work *against* corporations. In December 2007, The United States Department of Defence Assistant Secretary of Defence (Health Affairs) established an International Health Division under Force Health Protection & Readiness.

Part of International Health's mission is to communicate with NGOs in areas of mutual interest. Department of Defence Directive 3000.05, in 2005, requires DoD to regard stability-enhancing activities as a mission of importance equal to warfighting. In compliance with international law, DoD has necessarily built a capacity to improve essential services in areas of conflict such as Iraq, where the customary lead agencies (State Department and USAID) find it difficult to operate. Unlike the "co-option" strategy described for corporations, the OASD(HA) recognizes the neutrality of health as an essential service. International Health cultivates collaborative relationships with NGOs, albeit at arms-length, recognizing their traditional independence, expertise and honest broker status. While the goals of DoD and NGOs may seem incongruent, the DoD's emphasis on stability and security to reduce and prevent conflict suggests, on careful analysis, important mutual interests.

Legal Status

The legal form of NGOs is diverse and depends upon homegrown variations in each country's laws and practices. However, four main family groups of NGOs can be found worldwide:

- Unincorporated and voluntary association
- Trusts, charities and foundations
- Companies not just for profit
- Entities formed or registered under special NGO or nonprofit laws.

NGOs are not subjects of international law, as states are. An exception is the International Committee of the Red Cross, which is subject to certain specific matters, mainly relating to the Geneva Convention.

The Council of Europe in Strasbourg drafted the European Convention on the Recognition of the Legal Personality of International Non-Governmental Organizations in 1986, which sets a common legal basis for the existence and work of NGOs in Europe. Article 11 of the European Convention on Human Rights protects the right to freedom of association, which is also a fundamental norm for NGOs.

Citizen Organization

There is a growing movement within the "non"-profit and "non"-government sector to define itself in a more constructive, accurate way. Instead of being defined by "non" words, organizations are suggesting new terminology to describe the sector. The term "civil society organization" (CSO) has been used by a growing number of organizations, such as the Centre for the Study of Global Governance.

The term "citizen sector organization" (CSO) has also been advocated to describe the sector — as one of citizens, for citizens. This labels and positions the sector as its own entity, without relying on language used for the government or business sectors. However some have argued that this is not particularly helpful given that most NGOs are in fact funded by governments and business and that some NGOs are clearly hostile to independently organized people's organizations.

Non-profit Organization

A nonprofit organization (abbreviated NPO, also not-for-profit) is an organization that does not distribute its surplus funds to owners or shareholders, but instead uses them to help pursue its goals. Examples of NPOs include charities (i.e. charitable organizations), trade unions, and public arts organizations. Most governments and government agencies meet this definition, but in most countries they are considered a separate type of organization and not counted as NPOs.

Non-profit Distinction

Whereas for-profit organizations exist to earn and re-distribute taxable wealth to employees and shareholders, the nonprofit corporation exists solely to provide programs and services that are of self-benefit. Often these programs, services and policies are overlooked and not otherwise executed or enforced by the government.

While they are able to earn a surplus, more accurately called a profit, such earnings must be retained by the organization for its self-preservation, expansion and future plans. Earnings may not benefit individuals or stake-holders. While some nonprofit organizations put substantial funds into hiring and rewarding their internal corporate leadership, middle-management personnel and workers, others employ unpaid volunteers and even executives may work for no compensation.

However, since the late 1980s there has been a growing consensus that nonprofits can achieve their corporate targets more effectively by using some of the same methods developed in for-profit enterprises. These include effective internal management, ensuring accountability for results, and monitoring the performance of different divisions or projects in order to better benefit from their capital and workers.

Those require satisfied management and that, in turn, begins with the organization's mission.

Nature and Goals

NPOs are often charities or service organizations; they may be organized as a not-for-profit corporation or as a trust, a cooperative, or they may be purely informal.

Sometimes they are also called foundations, or endowments that have large stock funds. A very similar organization called the supporting organization operates like a foundation, but they are more complicated to administer, they are more tax favored, and the public charities that receive grants from them must have a specially determined relationship.

Foundations give out grants to other NPOs, or fellowships and direct grants to participants. However, the name *foundations* may be used by any not-for-profit corporation — even volunteer organizations or grass roots groups.

Applying Germanic or Nordic law (e.g., Germany, Sweden, Finland), NPOs typically are voluntary associations, although some have a corporate structure (e.g. housing cooperatives). Usually a voluntary association is founded upon the principle of one-person-one-vote.

Legal Aspects

There is a wide diversity of structures and purposes in the NPO landscape. For legal classification and eventual scrutiny, there are, nevertheless, some structural elements of prime legal importance:

- Economic activity
- Supervision and management provisions
- Representation
- Accountability and Auditing provisions
- Provisions for the amendment of the statutes or articles of incorporation
- Provisions for the dissolution of the entity
- Tax status of corporate and private donors
- Tax status of the foundation.

Some of the above must be, in most jurisdictions, expressed in the document of establishment. Others may be provided by the supervising authority at each particular jurisdiction.

While affiliations will not affect a legal status, they may be taken into consideration in legal proceedings as an indication of purpose.

Most countries have laws which regulate the establishment and management of NPOs, and which require compliance with corporate governance regimes. Most larger organizations are required to publish their financial reports detailing their income and expenditure for the public.

In many aspects they are similar to business entities though there are often significant differences.

Both non-profit and for-profit entities must have board members, steering committee members, or trustees who owe the organization a fiduciary duty of loyalty and trust. A notable exception to this involves churches, which are often not required to disclose finances to anyone, including church members, though most churches remain fiscally transparent with their members.

Formation and Structure

In the United States, nonprofit organizations are formed by incorporating in the state in which they expect to do business. The act of incorporating creates a legal entity enabling the organization to be treated as a corporation under law and to enter into business dealings, form contracts, and own property as any other individual or for-profit corporation may do.

Nonprofits can have members but many do not. The nonprofit may also be a trust or association of members. The organization may be controlled by its members who elect the Board of Directors, Board of Governors or Board of Trustees.

Nonprofits may have a delegate structure to allow for the representation of groups or corporations as members. Alternately, it may be a non-membership organization and the board of directors may elect its own successors.

A primary difference between a nonprofit and a for-profit corporation is that a nonprofit does not issue stock or pay dividends, (for example, The Code of the Commonwealth of Virginia includes the Non-Stock Corporation Act that is used to incorporate nonprofit entities) and may not enrich its directors. However, like for-profit corporations, nonprofits may still have employees and can compensate their directors within reasonable bounds.

The two major types of nonprofit organization structure are membership and board-only. A membership organization elects the board and has regular meetings and power to amend the bylaws. A board-only organization typically has a self-selected board, and a membership whose powers are limited to those delegated to it by the board. A board-only organization's bylaws may even state the organization has no membership, although the organization's literature may refer to its donors as "members"; examples of such structures are Fairvote and the National Organization for the Reform of Marijuana Laws. The Model Nonprofit Corporation Act imposes many complexities and requirements on membership decision-making. Accordingly, many organizations, such as Wikimedia, have formed board-only structures.

The National Association of Parliamentarians has raised concerns about the implications of this trend for the future of openness, accountability, and understanding of grassroots concerns in nonprofit organizations.

Specifically, they note that nonprofit organizations, unlike business corporations, are not subject to market discipline for products and shareholder discipline over their capital; therefore, without membership control of major decisions such as election of the board, there are few inherent safeguards against abuse.

A rebuttal to this might be that as nonprofit organizations grow and seek larger donations, the level of scrutiny rises, including expectations of audited financial statements.

Tax Exemption

In many countries, nonprofits may apply for tax exempt status, so that the organization itself may be exempt from income tax and other taxes. In the United States, to be exempt from federal income taxes the organization must meet the requirements set forth by the Internal Revenue Service.

Canada

In Canada, NPOs may be formed at either the federal or provincial levels. Charities must generally be registered with the Canada Revenue Agency and may issue tax receipts for donations.

Finland

In Finland, "rekisteröity yhdistys", given the abbreviation ry, denotes a registered association. This is done at a cost of 50 Euro. The association is required by law to keep a list of members. It must also hold an AGM and at least 3 members are required to set it up. A secretary, chair and treasurer being the usual formation.

India

In India, NPOs are commonly known as Non-Governmental Organizations (NGOs). They can be registered in four ways, viz. 1. Trust 2. Society 3. Section-25 Company 4. Special Licensing. Registration can be done with the Registrar of Companies(RoC).

The following laws or Constitutional Articles of the Republic of India are relevant to the NGOs:

- Articles 19(1)(c) and 30 of the Constitution of India
- Income Tax Act, 1961
- Public Trusts Acts of various states
- Societies Registration Act, 1860
- Section 25 of the Indian Companies Act, 1956
- Foreign Contribution (Regulation) Act, 1976.

South Africa

In South Africa, charities issue a tax certificate when requested by donors which can be used as a tax deduction by the donor.

United Kingdom

In the UK, many non-profit companies are incorporated as a company limited by guarantee. This means that the company does not have shares or shareholders, but it has the benefits of corporate status. This includes limited liability for its members and being able to enter into contracts and purchase property in its own name. The goals ("objects") of the company are defined in the Memorandum of Association when the company is formed. The profits of the company (also referred to as the trading surplus) must be invested in achieving these goals and not distributed to the company's members.

Alternatively, non-profit companies may be formed as a Community Interest Company. This is in many ways similar to a Limited Liability Company, but is intended specifically to ensure that the profits and assets of the company are used for public good.

A charity is a non-profit organisation that meets stricter criteria regarding its purpose and the way in which it makes decisions and reports its finances.. For example, a charity is generally not allowed to pay its Trustees. In England and Wales, charities may be registered with the Charity Commission. In Scotland, the Office of the Scottish Charity Regulator serves the same function. Other organizations which are classified as non-profit organizations elsewhere, such as trade unions, are subject to separate regulations, and are not regarded as "charities" in the technical sense.

United States

After a recognized type of legal entity has been formed at the state level, it is customary for the nonprofit organization to seek tax exempt status with respect to its income tax obligations. That is typically done by applying to the Internal Revenue Service (IRS), although statutory exemptions exist for limited types of nonprofit organizations. The IRS, after reviewing the application to ensure the organization meets the conditions to be recognized as a tax exempt organization (such as the purpose, limitations on spending, and internal safeguards for a charity), may issue an authorization letter to the nonprofit granting it tax exempt status for income tax payment, filing, and deductibility purposes. The exemption does not apply to other Federal taxes such as employment taxes. Additionally, a tax-exempt organization must pay federal tax on income that is unrelated to their exempt purpose. Failure to maintain operations in conformity to the laws may result in an organization losing its tax exempt status.

Individual states and localities offer nonprofits exemptions from other taxes such as sales tax or property tax. Federal tax-exempt status does not guarantee exemption from state and local taxes, and vice versa. These exemptions generally have separate application processes and their requirements may differ from the IRS requirements. Furthermore, even a tax exempt organization may be required to file annual financial reports (IRS Form 990) at the state and federal level.

Issues Faced by NPOs

Capacity building is an ongoing problem faced by NPOs for a number of reasons. Most rely on external funding (government funds, grants from charitable foundations, direct donations) to maintain their operations and changes in these sources of revenue may influence the reliability or predictability with which the organization can hire and retain staff, sustain facilities, or create programs. In addition, unreliable funding, long hours and low pay can lead to employee burnout and high rates of turnover.

Founder's syndrome is an issue organizations face as they grow. Dynamic founders with a strong vision of how to operate the project try to retain control over the organization, even as new employees or volunteers want to expand the project's scope and try new things.

Examples

In the United States, two of the wealthiest non-profit organizations are the Bill and Melinda Gates Foundation, which has an endowment of $38 billion, and the Howard Hughes Medical Institute, which has an endowment of approximately $14.8 billion. Outside the United States, another large NPO is the British Wellcome Trust, which is a "charity" in British usage. Measuring an NPO by its monetary size has obvious limitations, as the power and significance of NPOs are defined by more qualitative measurements such as effectiveness at carrying out charitable mission and goals.

Some NPOs which are particularly well known, often for the charitable or social nature of their activities conducted over a long period of time, include Amnesty International, the Better Business Bureau, Oxfam, Carnegie Corporation of New York, DEMIRA Deutsche Minenräumer (German Mine Clearers), Goodwill Industries, United Way, The National Rifle Association, ACORN, Habitat for Humanity, Teach For America, the Red Cross and Red Crescent organizations, UNESCO, IEEE, World Wide Fund for Nature, Heifer International, and SOS Children's Villages.

However, there are also millions of smaller NPOs that provide social services and relief efforts on a more focused level (such as Crosswind — Community Outreach Ministry and Literacy Centre West) to people throughout the world. There are more than 1.6 million NPOs in the United States alone.

On the Internet

Many NPOs often use the.org or.us (or the CCTLD of their respective country) or.edu top-level domain (TLD) when selecting a domain name to differentiate themselves from more commercially focused entities which typically use the.com space.

In the traditional domain categories as noted in RFC 1591,.org is for "organizations that didn't fit anywhere else" in the naming system, which implies that it is the proper category for non-commercial organizations if they are not governmental, educational, or one of the other types with a specific TLD. It is not specifically designated for charitable organizations or any specific organizational or tax-law status, however; it encompasses anything that does not fall into another category. Currently, no restrictions are enforced on registration of.com or.org, so you can find organizations of all sorts in either of these domains, as well as other top-level domains including newer, more-specific ones which may fit particular sorts of organizations such as.museum for museums or.coop for cooperatives. Organizations might also register under the appropriate country code top-level domain for their country.

10

The Role of Voluntary Action

As India has the largest population of poor people, community development has assumed high priority. The initial programme aimed at upliftment of the rural poor, covered agriculture, animal husbandry, roads, health, education, housing, employment, social and cultural activities. However, food security being the main cause of concern, agriculture received significant attention.

In 1957, a three-tier-system of rural local Government, called.Panchayati Raj. (Rule by Local Councils) was established. These were Gram Panchayat (Village level), Panchayat Samiti (Block level) and Zilla Parishad (District level). The aim was to decentralise the process of decision making and encourage people.s participation. As the programme could not fulfil the expectations of the rural poor, the Integrated Rural Development Programme (IRDP) was introduced in 1979, with specific focus on the weaker sections of the society. By mid eighties, the Government was able to meet the minimum needs of the poor, which included elementary education, health, water supply, roads, electrification, housing and nutrition.

In 1987, the Planning Commission decided to consider block as the basic unit for development planning. The task of planning at the district level was entrusted to the District Planning and Development Council which had wider representation of the society. Panchayati Raj reforms were introduced through the 73rd Constitutional Amendment to facilitate planning at the micro-level and to strengthen the Gram Sabha (village assembly).

The Government of India has also been encouraging voluntary action to mobilise the rural people. Several initiatives of the non-government organisations in the last two decades have had significant impact on the development. NGOs such as BAIF Development Research Foundation are promoting sustainable livelihood through dairy husbandry, water resource management, wastelands development and various income generation activities in several states.

Farmers in several states have established cooperatives for processing sugarcane, oil-seeds, milk, fruits and vegetables. With professional management and application of modern technologies, these organisations have brought economic stability and eliminated exploitation by intermediary traders. To strengthen people.s organisations, Self Help Groups (SHGs), comprising of poor families have been promoted under the Ninth Five Year Plan (1997-2002). It is only the peoples initiatives and involvement which can sustain the development. The government and political power have the will to support peoples movement and this should promote sustainable rural development in India.

Problems of the Poor

Poverty in Poverty in India is judged by the income generated by the family. Unemployment and underemployment are the major causes of rural poverty. The other factors are small land holdings, harsh agro-climatic conditions, poor infrastructure and limited opportunities for rural industrial development, poor health care, illiteracy, social suppression, addiction to alcohol and exploitation by vested interests.

Land is the major resource in India, which provides livelihood to the rural population.

According to a survey about 11.25% of the rural families are landless and among the land holders, over 69.35% own less than 1 ha (marginal farmers) and 21.25% own between 1 and 2 ha (small farmers). Water is another critical resource required to enhance the agricultural production. Out of the total arable area of 169 million ha, only 28% area is under irrigation and the rest is dependent on rains, where hardly one crop can be grown in a year. About 40% of the cropping area is located in low rainfall regions where the employment opportunity is hardly for 40 to 50 days in a year and crops generally fail twice in five years. Decline in many traditional occupations and poor institutional infrastructures have further reduced job opportunities. Thus about 90% of the rural population, who are deprived of adequate land holding have to look for other means of livelihood for their survival.

Livestock is another important natural resource owned by the poor. Generally the rural families keep 1-2 cows or buffaloes for milk, a pair of bullocks for farming and a few sheep, goats and poultry for supplementary income. Although fodder is in scarcity, most of the poor families maintain large herds and let them graze on common lands. Dairy husbandry has good scope, as there is good demand for milk.

However, most of the important breeds of cattle and buffaloes are genetically eroded and about 80-85% of the livestock are unproductive and cause undue pressure on forest resources while the rural poor are unable to take advantage of these animals. It is feasible to make sustainable use of these natural resources through application of appropriate technologies and use of idle labour.

Apart from inadequate earning for livelihood, the rural people also suffer from poor health arising from starvation, lack of immunisation, hygiene and sanitation. Over 25% villages do not have year-round supply of drinking water and about 75% of the potable water sources are polluted.

Consumption of polluted water is the main source of illness particularly during the rainy season.

Most of the villages have no drainage and sanitation and less than 10% of the rural people use latrines. Medical and immunisation services do not reach remote villages. Illiteracy in rural areas is high particularly among women, varying from 55% to 75%. This has a direct bearing on the population growth, child health and education. With the annual birth rate of 28 per 1000, as compared to 23 in Asia, the family size has been growing without any addition to the income. Unable to meet the growing needs, the rural poor have to depend on money lenders, to meet their emergencies and fall into the debt trap. They often try to forget their problems by consuming alcohol.

While some migrate to cities, others live in chronic poverty. They lose confidence in others as well in their ability to live a decent life. This is a vicious cycle.

Community Development Programme

The concept of community development in India was initiated well before independence. Even during the struggle for independence, under the leadership of Mahatma Gandhi-the Father of the Nation, considerable attention was given to rural upliftment and reconstruction. He emphasized on a nineteen point constructive programme for complete independence by truthful and non-violent means. He often warned the leaders that true independence could be enjoyed only when the rural economy was strengthened and poverty eradicated. He advocated communal harmony, economic equity, social equality, deaddiction from alcohol and narcotics, promotion of khadi (hand spun and hand woven cloth) and village industries, sanitation, health care, education and empowerment of women. The aim was to generate gainful employment in rural areas and to improve the quality of life (Gandhi, 1941).

The Government of India Act, 1935 under the British Rule, while confirming autonomy on the provinces, included rural development as an important programme to be initiated for the welfare of the people. With the outbreak of World War II and Bengal Famine of 1943, food supply was a critical problem in most parts of the country. Emphasis on food production was provided through. Grow More Food Campaign which included the supply of free seeds, subsidies for construction of wells and embankments, supply of manure, fixing a minimum price for grain, etc. However, there was limited scope under the Zamindari. system where a small number of rich farmers owned the agriculture lands and the rest of the villagers worked as labourers.

After the independence of India in 1947, community development assumed high priority. In 1948, a pilot community development project was launched through the Etawah Project. Later in 1952, the Government of India launched 55 Community Development Projects, each covering about 300 villages or a population of 30,000. This programme was multidimensional but the major emphasis was placed on agricultural production, as the areas selected for launching the project were located in irrigated areas or where the rainfall was assured. In 1953, the National Extension Service Project was launched with similar objectives to cover larger areas, including the dry regions. This project of three-year duration, demarcated the blocks of 150-300 villages as manageable units for initiating community development programmes. The objectives and activities of the Project were modified from time to time and continued as a permanent multi-function extension agency in each block. These community development blocks were treated as normal administrative units for planning and development with regular budgetary allocations.

By the end of the First Five Year Plan (1952-57), 1114 blocks covering 163,000 villages were in operation and by sixties, the community development programme covered the entire country. The programme was characterised by the following features: comprehensive in content; economic progress as the core objective; flexible programmes and posting of a multipurpose worker at the village level.

The plan defined the central objective of planning as creation of conditions in which living standards are reasonably high and the citizens have full and equal opportunity for growth and justice (Sachidananda, 1988). The programme aimed at upliftment of the rural poor, covered agriculture, animal husbandry, roads, health, education, housing, employment, social and cultural activities. While aiming at economic development through agriculture and cottage industries, efforts were made to improve literacy, health, sanitation, housing, transport and communication.

To implement the multifacet programme, an extension organisation, headed by a Block Development Officer (BDO) was established at each block or the revenue tehsil, with a team of subject specialists and village level workers (VLW). Each VLW covered a population of 5000-6000, spread over 5-10 villages to implement various development programmes launched by different departments. The VLWs were expected to meet the farmers and persuade them to take part in various development schemes. The BDO was assisted by eight Extension Officers, one each for agriculture, animal husbandry, panchayat, cooperation rural industries, rural engineering, social education and women and child welfare. In addition, a medical officer with support staff was posted in each block to provide medical assistance.

The extension officers reported primarily to the BDO and to their senior as well, in the respective department, based at the district headquarters. The BDOs reported to the District Collector, who is the administrator of the district. The Development

Commissioner, at the state level was responsible for coordinating community development through the District Collectors. At the National level, the administration of the community development programme was entrusted to the Planning Commission.

During the initial phase of community development, the government officials prepared the plan under the guidance of the Planning Commission. There was no opportunity for the community to demand any facilities to solve their problems. As the intention was to ensure peoples participation, advisory committees were subsequently established at various levels. A state level consultative committee consisting of state legislators was constituted for advising on community development.

District development or planning committee consisting of officials and non-officials was formed under the chairmanship of the collector. A block level advisory committee was constituted with block level officers and non-officials, member of the parliament and state legislators, heads of educational institutions, progressive agriculturists and representatives of voluntary organisations. As the nonofficials were generally interested in matters of personal concern, they did not look at their roles in the proper perspective. Furthermore, as the development programmes approved at the central and state level were rigid, the consultation process remained merely an academic exercise (Maheshwari, 1985).

From 1950s till mid 1970s, there was no significant achievement and poverty was on the verge of increasing. The Indian economy had become slower compared to those in the East and South East Asia over the post independence period. The levels of living were unacceptably low for a large section of the population. The Land Reforms Act of 1956 did remove vestiges of the feudal-colonial rule from the scene, but the enactment of the laws did not help the poor and landless to gain control over the land, particularly in North India.

There were fluctuations in the poverty status but the most prominent increase in poverty was observed in the late sixties and early seventies (55%-69%), when rainfall less the programme of agricultural development failed to enhance food production. In early seventies, India was compelled to import foodgrains. Trickling benefits of development were wiped out by the growing population. Improvement in agricultural productivity improvement in the absence of education and infrastructural development was not sustainable. The resources allotted for community development during 1952-67 were also so low that it worked out to hardly Rs.10 per head over this period.

Panchayati Raj Institutions

In 1957, five years after launching the community development programme, the Government appointed the Balvantrai Mehta Committee to suggest measures to remove obstacles in implementing the programme.

The Committee recommended the formation of a three-tier-system of rural local Government, to be called. Panchayati Raj. (Rule by Local Councils). These were Gram Panchayat (Village level), Panchayat Samiti (Block level) and Zilla Parishad (District level). The aim was to decentralise the process of decision making and to shift the decision making centre closer to the people, encourage their participation and place the bureaucracy under the local peoples control.

However, the Panchayati Raj was not able to fulfil all the expectations of the people and planners. A major reason was the domination of socially and economically privileged sections of the local community, who ignored the welfare of the weaker sections. The other reasons were lack of harmony among the elected members due to political fractions and prevalence of corruption and inefficiency (Maheshwari, 1985).

In mid sixties, the national priority was shifted to agricultural production and a distinct technological orientation was given to agriculture. Under the Fourth and Fifth Five Year Plans (1969-74 and 1974-79), the central government introduced independent administrative hierarchies to carry out special programmes, bypassing the Panchayati Raj institutions. Special programmes like Small Farmers. Development Agency (SFDA), Intensive Agricultural Areas Programme (IAAP), Intensive Agricultural District Programme (IADP), Tribal Development Agency (TDA), Marginal, Small Farmers and Agricultural Labourers Development Agency (MFAL) and area development agencies such as Command Area Development, Drought Prone Area and Hill area Development Programmes were financed and operated directly by the Central Government.

Integrated Rural Development Programme

The special programmes to boost the agricultural production in late sixties certainly helped to raise the food production but the benefits were largely reaped by those who had necessary resources. Small and marginal farmers trailed behind, as they were not directly benefited by the Green Revolution. On the contrary, their economic position worsened as the rich farmers declined to offer their lands for shared cropping. Thus to tackle the problems of the rural poor, the Integrated Rural Development Programme (IRDP) was introduced in 1979, with specific focus on the weaker sections of the society, particularly those living in poverty and to involve them in programme implementation. While the earlier programmes emphasized on the delivery systems which suppressed self-reliance, there was good scope for peoples initiatives to build up their economy with dignity.

Heeding to the criticism, further changes were made in the programme during the Seventh and Eighth Plans (1985-1990 and 1992-1997 respectively). These included the linkage between infrastructure and employment schemes, designing of the programme as a credit based self-employment activity, rather than a subsidy distribution and decentralisation of programme implementation through District Rural Development Agency and block authorities. Several sub-schemes such as Development of Women and Children in Rural Areas (DWCRA), Training of Rural Youth for Self-employment (TRYSEM), National Rural Employment

Programme (NREP), Jawahar Rojgar Yojana (JRY) were also launched to target the weaker section of the society.

By mid eighties, the Government was able to meet the minimum needs of the poor, which included elementary education, health, water supply, roads, electrification, housing and nutrition. In 1993-94, about 32.37% of the population in India was poor. The percentage of population living in poverty was high by about 17-22% among the Scheduled Castes and Scheduled Tribes, compared to general categories. This was mainly due to small land holdings, landlessness or illiteracy.

Decentralised Planning for Rural Development

Based on the Sivaraman Committee report, the Planning Commission issued guidelines to all the State Governments in

1987 to consider the block as the unit for planning. The task of planning at the district level was entrusted to the District Planning and Development Council or District Planning Board which had wider representation of the society. This body consisted of elected as well as nominated representatives headed by a Minister or District Collector or a non-official. It was responsible for setting up policy guidelines apart from coordination, monitoring, review, finalization of annual plans and Five Year Plans and collection of data. At the block level, the officers of different departments prepared the plan as per the guidelines received from their district heads.

This process needed further articulation to prepare the plans in consultation with the Gram Panchayats for implementing the development programmes more effectively and economically.

Planning at the village level can be very effective as it can address the problems directly and facilitate development at the grassroot level.

Emphasis on Peoples Participation

In spite of many drawbacks in launching community development programmes, the Panchayati Raj has made significant contribution to the development of the country by creating awareness among the public and by developing political leadership. The system has also helped in reducing the gap between the bureaucracy and the people. Centralisation of power and non-involvement of people in the process of development have been the major concerns ever since the introduction of Panchayati Raj. Although, it was widely acknowledged as the only hope for activating peoples participation which is the soul of a democratic system, the system had generated tension and factions. This necessitated Panchayati Raj reforms through the 73rd Constitutional Amendment in 1992, which empowered the PR institutions to shoulder the responsibility of development and decentralized planning. Till then, all the functions were carried out by the government machinery and there was no scope for participation by the villagers. This had created a dependency syndrome and enabled the government officials to dictate terms to the people (Thapliyal, 1995).

Under this constitutional amendment, 29 items of development were transferred to PRIs. These can be grouped under the following sectors: Agriculture; Forestry and Environment; Industries; Infrastructure, minimum needs; Social welfare; Poverty Alleviation and Maintenance of community assets. Considering the weak status of the Gram Panchayats to facilitate village level micro-planning for development, the District Planning Committee has been strengthened with members representing various government and non-government organisations.

To facilitate the planning at micro-level, it is proposed to strengthen the Gram Sabha (village assembly). The Gram Panchayat can use the Gram Sabha as a forum for discussion and finalization of annual plans. Such a forum can also set the priority for implementing various development programmes. Simultaneously, a suitable mechanism should be developed to sustain the interest of the villagers in Gram Sabha activities. In the absence of adequate participation, vested interests may influence the proceedings for their own benefits. Initiatives from farmers organisations, self help groups, educational institutions and other voluntary organisations to nominate their representatives on the Gram Sabha can ensure their participation in the proceedings and safeguard the interest of the common people (Hegde, 1999).

Role of Non-Government Organisations

The major factor influencing the successful implementation of rural development in India is motivation of the poor families to ensure their active participation. Development of suitable peoples organisations is also necessary to avail the benefits of various schemes, particularly by the illiterate poor. To ensure peoples involvement in the development process and to take them into confidence, they should be involved in the programme, right from the stage of planning.

Several innovative programmes implemented on a pilot scale have shown that many rational suggestions made by even the poor people can be easily implemented to produce good results. Such an approach demands flexibility in the programme. The target families should be motivated to assume the responsibility of implementing the programme, while the implementing agencies should play the role of a catalyst. In this task of integrated rural development, voluntary agencies can play an important role (Sachidananda, 1988).

The voluntary organisations or non-government organisations (NGOs) in general focus their voluntary action and service to tackle the problems of the common people or to help them face their challenges. The main characteristic of voluntary agencies is human-touch. Organisations with strong voluntarism and professionalism can implement the programme efficiently. Dedication of the volunteers and staff, their relationship with the community, flexibility in the programme, innovative approaches to solve the problems can result in greater success. Agencies having deep roots in rural areas can serve the community more effectively (Paul Choudhary, 1990).

It was only during the seventies that the government recognised the role of voluntary agencies in supplementing governments effort in rural development. Prior to this, the NGOs formed by religious institutions and enlightened public were involved in operating hospitals and educational institutions. With assistance from international donor agencies, the Ministry of Agriculture formed an independent organisation called. Freedom from Hunger Campaign to support the voluntary organisations involved in rural development. This Organisation was reorganised and renamed as Peoples Action for Development-India (PAD-I). PAD-I was merged with Council for Advancement of Rural Technology in 1986 and renamed as Council for Advancement of Peoples Action and Rural Technology (CAPART). Since then, CAPART has been providing financial assistance to voluntary agencies engaged in rural development. In the last two decades, several initiatives of the nongovernment organisations have had significant impact on the development. Widespread success of these initiatives have now encouraged many state governments to launch schemes to promote peoples participation and several centrally sponsored schemes have stipulated the development of community based organisations to plan and implement the programme.

With better opportunities for promoting self-employment through investment in agriculture and micro-enterprise, facilities were created for availing soft loans from banks and other financial institutions. The Reserve Bank of India issued guidelines to all the bankers not to insist on collateral security up to Rs.25,000 drawn by the poor for investment in development activities. As a result, over Rs.250 billion was distributed as rural credit in 1995-96, of which 50% amount was from the cooperatives and the rest from other banking institutions. Nevertheless, as the formal banking operations were not convenient for many villagers because of their rigidity, distance and high cost of operation, several innovative banking institutions have been established by the NGOs.

Peoples Initiatives for Progress

Farmers in several states have established cooperatives for processing sugarcane, oil-seeds, milk, fruits and vegetables. With professional management and application of modern technologies, these organisations have brought economic stability and eliminated exploitation by intermediary traders.

Encouragement is being given to strengthen such organisations throughout the country. Under a nationwide programme for water resource development, involvement of NGOs as facilitators and formation of water users organisations have been encouraged to prepare the microlevel plan and implement the project directly. This programme has made a significant impact on the supply of drinking water and greater awareness is being created on the need to conserve water and energy resources. There is scope for promoting such peoples organisations in other fields as well to develop necessary infrastructure required to enhance economic prosperity. Considering the need for promoting peoples initiatives and local organisations, Self Help Groups, comprising of poor families have been promoted under the Ninth Five Year Plan (1997-2002), through the Swarnajayanti Gram Swarojgar Yojana (SGSY) in 1999. SHGs consisting of 10-20 members belonging to backward socioeconomic status encourage the participants to meet regularly to collect their savings and disburse it as loan to needy members. During this process, they also discuss their problems and find suitable solutions. Finally, it is the peoples initiative which can sustain the development. The government has the will to support peoples movement and this is the only ray of hope for sustainable development of the rural poor in India.

International Community Development

Understanding Community Participation

Community life has been the basis of human existence. Most social norms, activities, interactions are a result of man's tendency to live in groups. Over the ages it has served as an agency of protection, support, administration and governance. Its history is a reflection of how important community has been to the mankind. It started as agency of protection but soon it undertook the role of defining human relationships.

Each individual while following various social and economic pursuits fulfils his or her role in the society. One can thus conclude that community is the end result of mankind's trial in achieving the greatest good of all.

The world has changed a lot in the last century. It is a world where the developing countries are trying to emerge from their colonial past, while coping with poverty, diseases, lack of infrastructure and resources. The developed countries on the other hand have to deal with a market which is quite dependent on the stability of the developing countries. Moreover, the developed countries are in search of a novel method of dealing with a society which is increasingly multiethnic and diverse. The countries today are thus, seeking a methodology which could in some ways limit role of state as an agent of reform and regulation as the existence of these problems makes it apparent that the present methods of governance are insufficient. Increasingly, it is being believed the participation at the community level i.e. local level by ordinary people is in many ways a better and more efficient method of realising the goal of good and responsible governance.

The problem with the third world especially India remains that the governance is so unitary that policies which should ensure development often fail to achieve their goals.

The reasons for this are several. The primary cause for the failure of government as the agent of change and growth is that the policies made, do not reach down to the people at lowest level, people who remain unseen but are in need of developing the most. The trickle down effect of such policies is minimal. The 73rd and 74th Amendment Act of the Constitution in India sought to implement a people oriented government at the local level.

However, the level of community participation in such a decentralised set up remains questionable. Moreover, developing countries face problems which are largely area and context specific, for instance, control of diseases such as HIV-AIDS, disaster management, natural resource management, generation of employment at the local level, management of services etc.

Community Participation: Concept

Community participation is adept in dealing with many problems that developing country of the world face today. It can be understood as a forum wherein people can participate in the decision making process and are involved in the local affairs. According to United Nations, it is defined as the creation of opportunities to enable all members of a community to actively contribute to and influence the development process and to share equitably the fruits of development. This theory of governance is in certain ways like revisiting the reasons of community life wherein the community as a whole is involved in promoting welfare. Instances of community participation infact show that when people are given the chance to participate in the decision making process, the resulting policies are often the best possible solutions to any local problem. And it be would be interesting to note that community participation is also an efficient method of recognising problems which otherwise go unnoticed at the macrolevel.

It is also desirable as it leads to better management and sustainable utilization of resources, improves access of the people to the governing body. Community participation when first heralded as the new method of promoting development in the 1960's, was seen as a method to promote sustainable and long term development.

Interestingly, most environmental covenants speak of community participation as a method of managing natural resources and promoting sustainable practices. Communal support in family life, child care and health which otherwise are informal social networks are given due recognition through such participation. Community participation thus, may seem like an equitable approach towards governance. Community participation if used rightly used can pave the road to development. It is an empowering tool whereby a community is empowered to decide for itself. Freedom of choice and access to information is essential requisites for the furtherance of a self Community participation. Empowering people leads to giving them necessary rights which they can use for their own betterment. It has been seen that an empowered community or group can flourish even when the bureaucratic set up of the country fails. In the Kecamatan Development Program of Indonesia, during the Krisis Monetar (krismon) years, the government just fell apart. Despite the political and economical uncertainty and the widespread conflict in the country this program made phenomenal gains. It spread from 2000 villages to around 34,000 villages.

Community participation is empowering people through the creation of opportunities and security which enable people to be self sufficient. It is interesting to note, empowerment goes hand in hand with the creation of a certain extent of security.

Thus, the role which the government plays in facilitating community participation is interesting to note. Most societies keep these initiatives outside the government purview and develop its own ways of bringing change and better management of services and resources.

Community Participation: International Perspective

Most societies have informal community practices. In the politically advanced countries most of these practices reflect in their forms of governance. Local governance in developed countries such as the U.K., Germany is conducted with active participation from the general public. Developing countries are now working their way towards decentralization. India in its attempt to decentralise effectively introduced new tiers of local governance in the village and urban level. Community participation was envisaged as the ideal pillar of flourishing democracy; however successful implementation of the same remains questionable. Adequate participation of women "The term empowerment has different meanings in different socio cultural and political contexts, and does not translate easily into all languages…These terms include self strength, control, self power, self reliance, own choice, life of dignity, in accordance with one's values, capacity to fight for one's rights, independence, own decision making, being free, awakening, and capability – to mention only a few." (Source: Narayan Deepa, *Empowerment and Poverty Reduction, A Sourcebook*, The World Bank, 2002) The Kecamatan Developmental Program is a national Government of Indonesia program, implemented by the Ministry of Home Affairs, Community Development Office, aims at alleviating poverty, strengthening local government and community institutions, and improving local governance. It was started in 1998 and will continue until 2009. Accessed on 05-06-06. and disadvantaged groups in village administration is still a distant dream and community participation in urban governance is only for namesake. Bolivia has a law of Popular Participation. This law was implemented in 1994 and envisaged the formation of voluntary vigilance committees called the Organizaciones Territoriales de Base (OTB). OTBs have the function of supervising municipal services. These committees also participate in public hearings, oversee government expenditures, and have standing to comment on development decisions and bring legal claims under relevant environmental and financial laws. Under this law, local communities like indigenous communities, farming communities or neighbourhood associations can petition to be recognised as an OTB. This law has institutionalised community participation in a novel way which increases accountability and enhances the involvement of community in policy making. Its impact has been far reaching geographically.

The Bolivian Law of Popular Participation is perhaps the first of it's kind which recognizes and empowers community with real administrative functions. However, in other parts of the world including India, community participation was heralded by civil society movements, community movement itself and at times with the initiative of the government. For instance, the drive to control the spread of HIV-AIDS, a campaign is being run in South Africa which includes the government, Voluntary Organisations and the community itself. The program works with certain organisations and trains community members who in turn spread awareness about the disease. This is infact an excellent example of how information can be disseminated with the help of community networks and associations.

There have been several community movements the world over. Some have demanded identity rights, some to get civil rights while others have been to find answers to their problems. An interesting example is of Alandur underground sewage scheme. This 4" Launched in February 2000, the scheme envisages the establishment of a sewage treatment plant of 24 million litres a day, on the build, operate and transfer mode, and a pumping station and laying of main and branch lines for 120 km. The executing agency, IVRCL, has been authorised to operate the plant for 14 years before handing it over to the local body." Community Participation Makes All the Difference, Nov 5, 2003. scheme was supposed to be a public-private venture, the cost of which was estimated at Rs 34 crores. However, with the change of the political regime, the scheme was bogged down with bureaucratic problems. The citizens of Alandur, a township south of Chennai, raised around Rs 11 crores. It was the initiative taken by the community and their enthusiasm which brought the project to completion. Other examples such as the widespread coöperative movements across the country and the formation of a huge number of Self Help Groups are witness to the vitality of communities.

In Nepal, to stop any further degradation of forests, the forests have been divided into National Forests and Community Forests. Community forests are managed by community forests user groups (CFUGs). There is an operational plan according which the community forests users manage and utilize the resources. This operational plan is devised by the Divisional Forest Officer, however, the matters of identification of users, participation, leadership and sharing of benefits is decided by the user groups in consultation with the Village Development Committees.

In India, to manage forest resources, a similar method called Joint Forest Management is being used. The Joint Forest Management has diversified into Community Forest Management wherein local community and community based organisations are being implemented in several states with a varied degree of success rates. Community participation though has led to a better and sustainable management of resources both in Nepal and India, there are numerous obstacles to overcome. The purpose of such "... And, it has become possible because of community involvement. Moreover, it took only about three and a half years for the benefits of the project to percolate in his area, while it took 12-15 years in Tiruchi and Coimbatore."

Ramakrishnan T., Community Participation Makes All the Difference, Nov 5, 2003. "As of 2002, there are about 12,600 CFUGs in the country, managing about one million ha of forest with involvement of one and half million people in management. This has been achieved in spite of constraints in forming of CFUG, sharing of benefits, participation, leadership and deciding the CF boundaries more so in non homogeneous communities where interests of different ethnic/caste groups clash." Maharjan Keshav, *Community Participation in Forest Resource Management in Nepal.*

"About 90 per cent of India's 64 million hectare forests is State owned; the rest is community and private forests.

This was not always the case. Until the end of the 19th Century, at least 80 per cent of India's natural resources were common property. The forest area under State control has increased progressively since British rule. Now, with its support for JFM, India is returning to the idea of community management of forests, though the State retains ownership. Thus, Indian forest management has now entered a state of transition, moving from "conventional State controlled forest management" to "decentralised community forest management" *Campaign to Save Forests*, 2001. Accessed on June 3, 2006.

projects is often manifold. Along with the sustainable management of resources, the idea is to help develop the community as well. It is the development of the resources with the aim of poverty alleviation. However, instances of women and weaker groups comprising of lower caste and poorer class getting marginalised in the development process is a problem which can not be overcome by the present day methodology. In India, the control of funds remains with the forest officers. In such a situation one can not help but wonder how much power the community has to hold the forest officers accountable.

Role of Civil Society Organisations in Community Participation

Civil society organisations in the past have led some of the most spectacular community movements towards development. Barefoot College has become one of the names to reckon with. It is an organisation based in the village of Tilonia in Rajasthan. It is a training and activity centre working on an area of 80,000 sq feet which has over the years worked with community and evolved new community oriented methods of dealing with problems of rural unemployment, lack of healthcare and sanitation, power generation and ecological care which includes programmes for water management. The organisation has so far covered a population of 1, 25,000 so far and is indeed an example of community participation. Most of the programmes are co-ordinated and carried out by the community members and such programmes often benefit the poorest in the society.

Another splendid example of empowering a community by a civil society organisation would be the case of water management in Alwar, Rajasthan. Tarun Bharat Sangh, a local NGO, facilitated this community led revival of the water sources in Alwar. Until the community got involved, Alwar faced sever environmental degradation and a huge water crisis. The construction of traditional methods of water storage called johads8 was undertaken and a part of the costs were also borne by the community.

Over the last two decades, more than 4500 water harvesting structures were built. This program initially even faced the ill directed wrath of the local government. The District "A *johad* is a semi-circular earthen check dam, designed to block the flow of streams during the monsoons and to create a small reservoir behind them, helping to recharge the ground-water to ensure sufficient water supply, even during the dry season."

Authorities declared the construction of the johads illegal and transferred the fields in the catchment area to families residing elsewhere. But now Alwar is an example of community driven growth.

It is apparent from the above examples that community is a vital, ever changing, evolving part of the state. The instances of community rising up to serve itself are many and the few recounted above tell us the ways in which it has been done so far.

The reason why the present set fails is because of its distance from the community. The people who make laws and policies often do not have the first hand knowledge of the problems and the issues facing the common man. Community must have a role in the decision making process. It not only brings the government closer to the problem but due to the control that community exercises on the governing agencies it makes the process of governance accountable and transparent.

Law on Community Participation: Is it a Pre-requisite?

In this context a specific law on community participation does seem appropriate. After the Right to Information Act 2005, a law succinctly defining the interaction of government and community would indeed empower the citizens to a level where governance would most certainly be people oriented. However, the structure and the requisites for having smooth machinery wherein both the state and citizens decide is not an easy methodology to evolve. Community participation requires certain degree of economic infrastructure in place. Major requisite is the presence of a conflict resolution agency wherein the conflicting interests of various communities can be addressed. Most of the community based programmes presently managed by the state have been plagued by the problem of lack of transparency in funds. The allocation of funds and resources to programme is out of the purview in most community based policies. Making funding transparent would not be the entire solution. While talking of community participation laws, one must give due regard to the status of administrative laws in the country. India decentralised its governance over a decade ago. This decentralization process suffers from many shortcomings but the one noteworthy problem would be the insufficient allocation of funds to the local bodies. It is necessary for the proper implementation of community participation laws that a country's access to information laws and decentralization policies are in place.

Another issue which needs to be addressed at the outset of formulating a policy on community participation is whether a uniform community participation law is possible. For a country like India where differences of caste, class, language, creed, gender define a community it is indeed difficult to imagine that a uniform community participation law is possible. Implementing a uniform law even with special reservations may not always apply to each an every issue. For instance, where disaster management is in question, it would be impossible to have community participation on caste basis. It would entirely depend on the geographic location of the area, the kind of natural or man made disaster whether or not it has occurred, the application of standards in disaster management, and perhaps special provisions for the old, sick and children. The context of every problem requires a different set of policies. However a parallel can be drawn from the legislations which have taken place after the 73rd and 74th Amendment Acts.

The states made the laws implementing the provisions of the Constitution. However, these laws were considered variable and not true to the spirit of the provisions of the Constitution. The need for a federated approach was thus felt by many wherein the Central Government could give guidelines, upon which the states could articulate suitable legislation. Perhaps, a federated approach for community participation laws would be necessary to have systemised and at the same time a law which caters to a diverse population.

Family and Child Welfare Services

India is home to almost 19% of the world's children. More than one third of the country's population, around 440 million, is below 18 years. The future and strength of the nation lies in a healthy, protected, educated and well-developed child population that will grow up to be productive citizens of the country. India must invest resources in children proportionate to their huge numbers.

Ministry of Women and Child

Development revealed that total expenditure on children in 20052006 in health, education, development and protection together amounted to merely 3.86%, rising to 4.91% in 2006-07.

The concern for children has also been expressed in various international Conventions and Standards on child protection including the UN Convention of the Rights of the Child (UNCRC) 1989, the UN Standard Minimum Rules for the Administration of Juvenile Justice (The Beijing Rules) 1985, and the UN Rules for the Protection of Juveniles.

Deprived of their Liberty 1990. The Government of India ratified the UN Convention on the Rights of the Child (UNCRC) in 1992. The Convention prescribes standards to be adhered to by all State parties in securing the best interest of the child. It emphasizes social reintegration of child victims, without resorting to judicial proceedings. The UNCRC outlines the fundamental rights of children, including the right to be protected from economic exploitation and harmful work, from all forms of sexual exploitation and abuse, and from physical or mental violence, as well as ensuring that children will not be separated from their family against their will. Major policies and legislations issued in the country to ensure children's protection and improvement in their status include the Guardian and Wards Act 1890, Factories Act 1954, Hindu Adoption and Maintenance Act 1956, Probation of Offenders Act 1958, Bombay Prevention of Begging Act 1959, Orphanages and Other Charitable Homes (Supervision and Control) Act 1960, National

Policy for Children 1974, Bonded Labour System (Abolition) Act 1976, Child Marriage and Restraint Act 1979, Immoral Traffic Prevention Act 1986, Child Labour (Prohibition and Regulation) Act 1986, National Policy on Education 1986, Prevention of Illicit Traffic in Narcotic Drugs and Psychotropic Substances Act 1987, National Policy on Child Labour 1987, Infant Milk Substitutes, Feeding Bottles and Infant Foods (Regulation of Production, Supply and Distribution) Act 1992, National Nutrition Policy 1993, Pre-natal Diagnostic Techniques (Regulation and Prevention of Misuse) Act 1994, Persons with Disabilities (Equal Protection of Rights and Full Participation) Act 2000, Juvenile Justice (Care and Protection of Children) Act 2000, National Health Policy 2002, National Charter for Children 2004 and National Plan of Action for Children in 2005.

However, these policies and legislations for children have on the whole suffered from weak implementation, owing to scant attention to issues of child protection, resulting in scarce resources, minimal infrastructure, and inadequate services to address child protection problems. 'Child Protection' is about protecting children from or against any perceived or real danger or risk to their life, their personhood and childhood. It is about reducing their vulnerability to any kind of harm and protecting them in harmful situations. It is about ensuring that no child falls out of the social security and safety net and those who do, receive necessary care, protection and support so as to bring them back into the safety net. While protection is a right of every child, some children are more vulnerable than others and need special attention.

The Government recognizes these children as 'children in difficult circumstances', characterized by their specific social, economic and geopolitical situations. In addition to providing a safe environment for these children, it is imperative to ensure that all other children also remain protected. Child protection is integrally linked to every other right of the child. Failure to ensure children's right to protection adversely affects all other rights of the child. Thus, the Millennium Development Goals (MDGs) also cannot be achieved unless child protection is an integral part of programming strategies and plans. Failure to protect children from such issues as violence in schools, child labour, harmful traditional practices, child marriage, child abuse, the absence of parental care and commercial sexual exploitation among others, means failure in fulfilling both the Constitutional and international commitments towards children.

In light of its expanded mandate, the new Ministry of Women and Child Development views Child Protection as an essential component of the country's strategy to place *'Development of the child at the centre of the 11th Plan'*. Violations of the child's right to protection, in addition to being human rights violations, are massive, under-recognized and under-reported obstacles to child survival and development. Failure to protect children has serious consequences for the physical, mental, emotional, social development of the child, with consequences in loss in productivity and the loss in human capital for the nation.

The National Plan of Action for Children 2005 articulated the rights agenda for the development of children. The NPAC 2005 is the basis for planning for children in the XI Plan in all sectors and the principles articulated in it should guide the planning and investments for children. Moreover, to achieve the Millennium Development Goals also, such a comprehensive approach to child protection is required. All budgets for child protection schemes and programmes should be in the plan category and not in the nonplan category.

The Ministry of Women and Child, therefore, endeavors to create a strong foundation for a protective environment for children. Child protection incorporates both prevention and care and recovery aspects. Children have a right to be prevented from becoming subjects of violence, abuse, neglect and exploitation, and once victimized, are entitled to services, which hasten their recovery and reduce further trauma. The Ministry will undertake a strong advocacy and implementation strategy to enhance the infrastructure for protection services, increase access to a wider range and better quality of services, and increase the investment for protection of children.

Existing Child Protection Mechanisms

The existing mechanisms for child protection in India primarily flow from the provisions under the Juvenile Justice (Care and Protection of Children) Act, 2000 and National Plan of Action for Children 2005. These comprise several programmes and schemes implemented by different ministries and departments addressing child protection issues among which are:

- A Programme for Juvenile Justice for children in need of care and protection and children in conflict with law. The Government of India provides financial assistance to the State Governments/UT Administrations for establishment and maintenance of various homes, salary of staff, food, clothing, etc. for children in need of care and protection and juveniles in conflict with law. Financial assistance is based on proposals submitted by States on a 50-50 cost sharing basis.
- An Integrated Programme for Street Children without homes and family ties. Under the scheme NGOs are supported to run 24 hours drop-in shelters and provide food, clothing, shelter, non-formal education, recreation, counselling, guidance and referral services to them. The other components of the scheme include enrolment in schools, vocational training, occupational placement, mobilizing preventive health services and reducing the incidence of drug and substance abuse, HIV/AIDS etc.
- Childline Service for children in distress, especially children in need of care and protection so as to provide them medical services, shelter, rescue from abuse, counselling and repatriation.
- Shishu Greh Scheme for care and protection of orphans/ abandoned/destitute infants or children up to 6 years and promote in-country adoption for rehabilitating them.
- Scheme for Working Children in Need of Care and Protection for children working as domestic help, at roadside dhabas, mechanic shops, etc. The scheme provides for bridge education and vocational training, medicine, food, recreation/sports equipments, etc.
- Rajiv Gandhi National Creche Scheme for the Children of Working Mothers in the age group of 0-6 years. The scheme provides for comprehensive day-care services including facilities like food, shelter, medical, recreation, etc.
- Pilot Project to Combat the Trafficking of women and Children for Commercial Sexual Exploitation in source

and destination areas for providing care and protection to trafficked and sexually abused women and children. Components of the scheme include networking with law enforcement agencies, rescue operation, temporary shelter for the victims, repatriation to hometown and legal services, etc.

Central Adoption Resource Agency (CARA)

- National Child Labour Project (NCLP) for the rehabilitation of child labour. Under the scheme, Project Societies at the district level are fully funded for opening up of special school/Rehabilitation Centres for the rehabilitation of child labour. These special schools/rehabilitation centres provide non-formal education, vocational training, supplementary nutrition, stipend etc. to children withdrawn from employment.

In early 2006 the Department of Women and Child Development became a full-fledged Ministry and the juvenile justice and adoption related matters were transferred to this new Ministry. However, Child Protection has never been a programme of any one Ministry/Department and in spite of this rationalization, child labour issues continue to be dealt with by the Labour Ministry. However, for Child Protection to be dealt with more effectively there is a need for lateral linkages by the Ministry of Women and Child Development with relevant sectors such as Railways, Industry, Trade and Commerce, Rural Development, Urban Affairs, Tourism, Banking, Legal Affairs, Home Affairs, Health and Family Welfare, and Information and Broadcasting. Some of the schemes of the Ministry of Women and Child Development under the women's welfare section address issues concerning protection of the girl child even though there is no girl child specific component and budget under these schemes. These need to be considered as child protection schemes and in the years to come they could perhaps have a clearly defined child protection component and budget.

These schemes include:

- Swadhar
- Short Stay Home
- Scheme for rescue of victims of trafficking

- Relief and rehabilitation of rape victims.

The Kishori Shakti Yojana is Another Scheme of the Ministry of Women and Child

Development that can be used to meet protection goals. While its main focus is nutrition for adolescent girls, the scheme provides platform for raising protection concerns with this age group and empowering them with information, knowledge and skills to be able to protect themselves.

The Rajiv Gandhi National Scheme for the Children of Working Mothers, implemented by the Ministry of Women and Child Development, is primarily seen as fulfilling child development goals only. However, protection needs of children aged 0-6 years are also met through crèche and day care facilities and hence it may well be taken as a child protection scheme also.

There are some schemes for the disabled persons under the Ministry of Social Justice and Empowerment. Since they do not have a child focus or specific component for children, issues of disabled children get very little attention.

Limited Resources/Budget Allocations

All the above schemes put together have an abysmally low budget.. A Child Budget exercise carried out by the Ministry of Women and Child Development revealed the persistently low level of fund allocation for child protection. The total share of child protection in the Union Budget for 2005-06 was just 0.034% and the budget estimates for the current financial year 2006-07 has remained the same.

Scarcely any allocations have been made for child protection since independence, a reflection of the low priority this sector has received in government's own planning and implementation, resulting in scant State interventions toward child protection. The share of child protection in the Union Budget has remained at 0.03 percent. However, over the years the share of child protection in the overall budget for children has seen a decline. Child protection is an overarching issue, which if not covered will affect each and every right of children. The meager financial resources invested in child protection translate into serious gaps in child protection measures and programmes.

Glaring Gaps in Services

A close examination by the newly created Ministry of Women and Child Development of existing child protection schemes has revealed major shortcomings and gaps in the infrastructure, set up and outreach services for children.

The minimal government structure that exists is rigid and a lot of time and energy goes in maintaining the structure itself rather than concentrating on programmatic outcomes. Existing programmes and schemes are marked by limitations such as:

Poor Planning and Coordination

- Lack of linkages with essential lateral services for children for example education, health, police, judiciary, services for the disabled, etc.
- No mapping has been done of the children in need of care and protection or of the services available for them at the district/city/state level;
- Lack of coordination and convergence of programmes/ services;
- Supervision, monitoring and evaluation of the juvenile justice system is weak.

Low Coverage

- Large percentage of children in need of care and protection are outside the safety net and get no support and services;
- Allotment of negligible resource to child protection and uneven utilization of allotted resources in terms of geographical spread
- Existing Schemes inadequate in outreach and funding leading to marginal coverage of destitute children
- Realising that poverty and desire for a better life is leading to a large scale migration of rural populations to urban and semi urban centres, which in turn has created a large number of vulnerable children in urban situations, demands focused strategies and interventions
- Inadequate addressal of issues like child marriage, female foeticide, street children, working children, discrimination against the girl child, etc.

- No interventions for children affected by HIV/AIDS, drug abuse, militancy, disaster (both manmade and natural), abused and exploited children and children of vulnerable groups like commercial sex workers, prisoners, migrant population, etc.

Poor Infrastructure

- Inadequate implementation of laws and legislations in terms of structures prescribed by those legislations not being in place;
- Lack of institutional infrastructure to deal with child protection;
- The CWCs and JJBs not provided with requisite facilities for their efficient functioning, resulting in delayed enquiries and disposal of cases.

Inadequate Human Resources

- Inadequate number of Child Welfare Committees (CWC) and Juvenile Justice Boards (JJB);
- Training of personnel working under the juvenile justice system and on other child protection programmes is inadequate and inequitable among States.

Serious Service Gaps

- Lack of support services to families at risk leads to more children becoming vulnerable;
- Overbearing focus on institutional support and non-institutional services negligent;
- Inter-state and Intra-state transfer of children specially for their restoration to their families have not been provided for in the existing schemes.
- Lack of standards of care (accommodation, sanitation, leisure, food, etc.) in children/observation homes due to lower funding norms and also due to lack of supervision and commitment
- Most 24-hour shelters do not provide all the basic facilities required, specially availability of shelter, food and mainstream education;
- Not all programmes address issues of drug abuse, HIV/AIDS and sexual abuse related vulnerabilities of children;

- None of the existing schemes address the needs of child beggars;
- Minimal use of non-institutional care options like adoption, foster care and sponsorship, etc. to children without home and family ties;
- Number of Shishu Grehas are inadequate leading to few adoptions;
- Lack of rehabilitation services for older children not adopted through the regular adoption process;
- Aftercare and rehabilitation programme for children above 18 years are not available in all States, and where they do exist they are run as any other institutions under the JJ Act 2000.

The Integrated Child Protection Scheme

The Integrated Child Protection Scheme concretises the Government/State responsibility for creating a system to protect children in the country.

Such a system is influenced by the nature of regulatory frameworks, structures, resources, professionals, and the relationships between them. When the child protection system functions in the best interest of the child, adequate state and voluntary institutions, services and structures are put in place, backed strongly by policies, laws and regulations. Professionals providing services for children are competent and bound by professional standards. Children's views are taken into account.

The Integrated Child Protection Scheme is based on the cardinal principles of "protection of child rights" and "best interests of the child".

The ICPS aims to promote the best interests of the child and prevent violations of child rights through appropriate punitive measure against perpetrators of abuse and crimes against children and to ensure rehabilitation for all children in need of care and protection. It aims to create a protective environment by improving regulatory frameworks, strengthening structures and professional capacities at national, state and district levels so as to cover all child protection issues and provide child friendly services at all levels.

Principles of ICPS

The following key principles underlie the ICPS approach:

(i) Child protection a shared responsibility: The responsibility for child protection is a shared responsibility of government, family, community, professionals, and civil society. It is important that each role is articulated clearly and understood by all engaged in the effort to protect children. Government has an obligation to ensure a range of services at all levels.

(ii) Reducing child vulnerability: There is a need for a focus on systematic preventive measures not just programmes and schemes to address protection failures at various levels. A strong element of prevention will be integrated into programmes, converging the provisions and services of various sectors on the vulnerable families, like livelihood support (NREGS), SHGs, PDS, health, child day care, education, to strengthen families and reduce the likelihood of child neglect, abuse and vulnerability.

(iii) Strengthen family: Children are best cared for in their own families and have a right to family care and parenting by both parents. Therefore a major thrust will be to strengthen the family capabilities to care for and protect the child by capacity building, family counselling and support services and linking to development and community support services.

(iv) Promote non-institutional care: There is a need to shift the focus of interventions from an over reliance on institutionalization of children and move towards more family and community –based alternatives for care. Institutionalization should be used as a measure of last resort after all other options have been explored.

(v) Intersectoral linkages and responsibilities: Child protection needs dedicated sectoral focus as well as strengthening protection awareness and protection response from other sectors outside the traditional protection sector including in emergencies and HIV/AIDS programming.

(vi) Create a network of services at community level: An appropriate network of essential protection services is required at all levels for supporting children and communities.

(vii) Establishing standards for care and protection: All protection services should have prescribed standards, protocols for key actions and should be monitored regularly. Institutionalisation should be for the shortest period of time with strict criteria being established for residential placement and all cases of institutionalization reviewed periodically.

(viii) Building capacities: Protection services require skilled, sensitive staff, equipped with knowledge of child rights and standards of care and protection. Capacities of all those in contact with children require strengthening on a continuing basis, including families and communities.

(ix) Providing child protection professional services at all levels: There is a need for varied special services for the many situations of child neglect, exploitation and abuse, including for shelter, care, psychological recovery, social reintegration, legal services etc. which have to be professional and child-focused.

(x) Strengthening crisis management system at all levels: First response and coordinated inter-sectoral actions for responding to crisis need to be established and institutionalized.

(xi) Reintegration with family and community: systems to be put in place for efforts to reintegrate children with their families and community and regular review of efforts instituted.

(xii) Addressing protection of children in urban poverty: Children in urban poverty are at high risk/increased vulnerability; constantly under threat of eviction; denial or exclusion from basic services; social turmoil; and the stretched capacity of the adults to function as adequate caretakers due to their poverty. This indicates the need for developing a strong social support and service system.

(xiii) Child impact monitoring: all policies, initiatives and services will be monitored for their child impact and reports made public, including for children themselves through child-friendly reports.

The Approach

In order to reach out to all children, in particular to those in difficult circumstances, the Ministry of Women and Child Development proposes to combine its existing child protection schemes under one centrally sponsored scheme titled "Integrated Child Protection Scheme (ICPS)". The proposed ICPS brings together multiple vertical schemes under one comprehensive child protection programme and integrates interventions for protecting children and preventing harm.

It does not see child protection as the exclusive responsibility of the MWCD but stresses that other sectors have vital roles to play. The Ministry looks at child protection holistically and seeks to rationalize programmes for creating a strong protective environment for children, diversify and institutionalize essential services for children, mobilize inter-sectoral response for strengthening child protection and set standards for care and services. ICPS will function as a Government – Civil Society Partnership scheme under the overarching direction and responsibility of the Central/State Governments. It will work closely with all stakeholders including government departments, the voluntary sector, community groups, academia and, most importantly, families and children to create a protective environment for children in the country. Its holistic approach to child protection services and mechanisms is reflected in stronger lateral linkages and complementary systems for vigilance, detection and response. The scheme visualizes a structure for providing services as well as monitoring and supervising the effective functioning of child protection system, involving:

- Government:. To hold primary responsibility for the development, funding and operation of the service covered under the scheme. In order to ensure effective functioning of the system, the Government shall provide flexibility by cutting down rigid structures and norms. To attract the best professional talent and strengthen public-private partnership, the scheme proposes to hire services of professionals on a contractual basis.
- Civil society organizations:
  * Voluntary sector: To provide vibrant, responsive and child friendly services for detection, counselling,

rehabilitation for all children in need as well as provide technical support; these may be financially supported by the State.

* Research and training institutions: To carryout activities related to research and capacity building of existing manpower as well as support creation of a cadre of professional manpower.
* Media and advocacy groups: To promote rights of the child and child protection issues with sensitivity and promote child's dignity and worth ° Corporate sector:

- Community groups and local leaders, youth groups, families and children: To provide protective and corrective environment for children, to act as watchdog and monitor child protection services as well as service providers, both Government and NGO functionaries.

Target Groups

Child in need of care & protection means a child who:

— is found without any home or settled place or abode and without any ostensible means of subsistence;

— resides with a person (whether a guardian of the child or not) and such person has threatened to kill or injure the child and there is a reasonable likelihood of the threat being carried out, or has killed, abused or neglected some other child or children and there is a reasonable likelihood of the child in question being killed, abused or neglected by that person;

— is a mentally or physically challenged or ill child or a child suffering from terminal diseases or incurable diseases, and/or having no one to support or look after him/her;

— has a parent or guardian and such parent or guardian is unfit or incapacitated to care for or exercise control over the child;

— does not have a parent/parents and no one is willing to take care of him/her, or whose parents have abandoned him/her or who is a missing and/or runaway child and whose parents cannot be found after reasonable inquiry

— is being or is likely to be grossly abused, tortured or exploited for the purpose of sexual abuse or illegal acts
— is found vulnerable and is likely to be inducted into drug abuse or trafficking,
— is being or is likely to be abused for unconscionable gains
— is victim of any armed conflict, civil commotion or natural calamity.

Children in conflict with the law is one who is alleged to have committed an offence. Children in contact with law is one who has come in contact with the law either as victim or as a witness or due to any other circumstance. Any other vulnerable child including, but not limited, to: Children of potentially vulnerable families and families at risk, Children of socially excluded groups like migrant families, families living in extreme poverty, lower caste families, families subjected to or affected by discrimination, minorities, children infected and/or affected by HIV/AIDS, orphans, child drug abusers, children of substance abusers, child beggars, trafficked or sexually exploited children, children of prisoners, and street and working children, would also be covered under the scheme.

Bibliography

A K Malkani : *Social Work for the Poor,* Mohit Pub, Delhi, 2008.

A K Rizwi : *Social Policy and Social Work,* Mohit Pub, Delhi, 2008.

A S Kohli : *Human Rights and Social Work, Issues, Challenges and Response,* Kanishka, Delhi, 2004.

Abha, Vijai and Prakash: *Voluntary Organisations and Social Welfare,* ABD, Delhi, 2000.

Agarwal, L.B.: *The Harijans in Rebellion,* Taraporewala, Bombay, 1934.

Ahir, D.C.: *Dr B.R. Ambedkar: Buddhist Revolution and Counter-Revolution in Ancient India,* B.R. Publishing, Delhi, 1996.

Ahmed, Akbar : *Pakistan : The Social Sciences' Perspective,* Oxford University Press, Karachi, 1990.

Akash Gulalia : *Social Work Practice : With Mobile Population Vulnerable to HIV/AIDS,* Mohit, Delhi 2008.

Anand, J. H. : *Dalit Literature is the Literature of Protest,* Delhi, ISPCK, 1995.

Ankit Prasad: *Social Welfare and Social Action : YMCA at Work,* Mittal, Delhi, 2005.

Atal, Yogesh: *The Changing Frontiers of Caste,* Delhi, National Publishing House, 1968.

B.T. Lawani and I.S. Subhedar : *Social Work Perspectives,* Om Pub, Delhi, 2006.

Bailey, F. G. : *Caste and the Economic Frontier: A Village in Highland Orissa,* Manchester, University of Manchester, 1957.

Bakshi, S. R.: *Gandhi and Hindu-Muslim Unity,* Deep & Deep Publications, New Delhi, 1987.

Baldwin, Peter: *The Politics of Social Solidarity: Class Bases of the European Welfare State, 1875–1975,* Cambridge, Cambridge University Press, 1990.

Barnes, Bob.: *Social Survey Division in the 1990s*, Population Trends, 1991.

Benjamin, Joseph: *Scheduled Castes in Indian Politics and Society*, New Delhi, Ess Ess Publications, 1989.

Berger, P. L. : *The Sacred Canopy, Elements of a Sociological Theory of Religion*, Garden City, Doubleday & Company, 1967.

Beteille, Andre.: *The Backward Classes and the New Social Order*, Oxford University Press, Delhi, 1981.

Bhagwat, Vidyut: *Dalit Women in India: Issues and Perspectives - Some Critical Reflections*, New Delhi, Gyan Publishing House, 1995.

Bhai, P. N.: *Harijan Women in Independent India,* B. R. Publishing, New Delhi, 1986.

Bhatt, Anil: *Caste, Class and Politics: An Emperical Profile of Social Stratification in Modern India*, Delhi, Manhohar Book Service, 1975.

Bose, N. K.: *The Scheduled Castes and Tribes and Their Present Conditions,* Calcutta, University of Calcutta, 1969.

Bose, Pradip Kumar: *Social Mobility and Caste Violence: A Study of the Gujarat Riots,* Delhi, Adjanta Publications, 1985.

Brijesh Mishra: *Glimpses of Social Welfare in India : Problems and Perspectives,* ABD Pub, Delhi, 2006.

Campolo, T. & Fraser, D. A. : *Sociology through the Eyes of Faith,* San Francisco, Harper & Row, Delhi, 1992.

Carsten, F. L. : *The Rise of Fascism*, London, Methuen and Co., 1967.

Chaklader, Snehamoy : *Sociolinguistics: A Guide to Language Problems in India,* New Delhi, Mittal, 1990.

Charles D Garvin; Lorraine M Gutierrez and Maeda J Galinsky: *Handbook of Social Work With Groups*, Rawat, Delhi, 2007.

Chhaya Patel: *Social Work Practice : Religio Philosophical Foundations: Essays in Honour of Professor Indira Patel*, Rawat, Delhi, 1999.

Cravens, Hamilton: *Before Head Start: The Iowa Station and America's Children,* Chapel Hill, University of North Carolina Press, 1993.

D K Lal Das and Vanila Bhaskaran : *Research Methods for Social Work* : Rawat, Delhi 2008.

D.K. Lal Das : *Practice of Social Research : Social Work* Perspective, Rawat, 2000.

David Lewis and N Ravichandran: *NGOs and Social Welfare : New Research Approaches,* Rawat, Delhi, 2008.

Debotosh Sinha : *Aspects of Industry and Occupational Social Work,* Abhijeet Pub, Delhi, 2007.

Dennis Shirley: *Community Organizing for Urban School Reform,* Austin, University of Texas Press, 1997.

Dietrich, Gabriele: *Dalit Movements and Women's Movement,* Horizons India Books, New Delhi, 1992.

Donaldson, Gordon A. : *Cultivating Leadership in Schools,* New York, College Press, 2001.

Dumont, Louis: *The Caste System and Its Implications,* London, Granada Pub. Ltd., 1970.

Edward Chambers: *Roots for Radicals,* New York, Continuum, 2003.

Elisabeth Relchert: *Social Work and Human Rights : A Foundation for Policy and Practice,* Rawat, Delhi, 2003.

Ellul, J. : *The Technological Society,* Grand Rapids, Eerdmans, 1990.

Fisher, Michael : *A Clash of Cultures: Awadh the British, and the Mughals,* New Delhi, Manohar, 1987.

Frederic G. Reamer : *Social Work Values and Ethics,* Rawat, Delhi, 2005.

Freeman, James M.: *Untouchable : An Indian Life History,* CA, Stanford University Press, 1979.

G.R. Madan : *An Eminent Scholar, Saint and Social Worker,* Radha Pub, Delhi, 2008.

Ghurye, G. S. : *Caste and Class in India,* Bombay, Popular Books, 1950.

Gibson, R. : *Critical Theory and Education,* London, Hodder & Stoughton, 1986.

Glass, Joseph W.: *The Pennsylvania Culture Region: A View From the Barn,* Ann Arbor, UMI Research Press, 1986.

Gorhe, Neelam: *Social Development and Dalit Women,* Gyan Pub. House, New Delhi, 1995.

Gorringe, H.: *Untouchable Citizens : Dalit Movements and Democratization in Tamil Nadu*, Delhi, Sage Publications, 2005.

Grunlan, Stephen A. and Milton Reimer : *Christian Perspectives on Sociology,* Grand Rapids, Mich., Zondervan, 1982.

Gurukal, Rajan: *The Formation of Caste Society in Kerala,* Rawat Publications, New Delhi, 1994.

Hajira Kumar : *Social Work, Social Development and Sustainable Development*, Regency, Delhi, 1997.

Hana Nagpaul : *Social Work in Urban India,* Rawat, Delhi, 1996.

Harry C. Boyte : *Commonwealth, A Return to Citizen Politics,* New York, The Free Press, 1989.

Heinsath, Charles : *Indian Nationalism and Hindu Social Reform*, Princeton, Princeton University Press, 1964.

Hopkins, Thomas J. : *The Hindu Religious Tradition*, Encino, California, Dickenson, 1971.

I. Sundar: *Social Work Practices in Health and Medical Profession*, Sarup Book Pub, Delhi, 2009.

I.S. Subheda : *Fieldwork Training in Social Work,* Rawat, Delhi, 2001.

Jaffrelot, Christopher: *Dr. Ambedkar and Untouchability: Fighting the Indian Caste System*, New York, Columbia University Press, 2005.

Jainendra Kumar Jha : *Social Welfare and Social Work,* Anmol, Delhi, 2002

Jogdand, P. G.: *Dalit Women in India: Issues and Perspectives,* New Delhi, Gyan Publishing House, 1995.

K. Chakraworthy: *Untouchable Social Work in India*, Sumit, Delhi, 2006.

K.D. Gangrade : *Gandhian Perspective on Global Interdepen-dence, Peace and Role of Professional Social Work*, Authorspress, Delhi, 2008.

K.K. Jacob: *Social Work Education in India*, Himanshu, Delhi, 1994.

Kamble, N. D.: *Deprived Castes and their Struggle for Equality*, Ashish Publishing House, New Delhi, 1983.

Lakshmanna, C.: *Caste Dynamics in Village India,* Nachiketa Publications, Bombay, 1973.

Lal, Shyam: *Caste and Political Mobilisation: The Bhangis,* Jaipur, Panchsheel Prakashan, 1981.

Lindburg, Donald: *Social Organization of the Kutenai.* Chicago: University of Chicago Press, 1962.

M A Khan : *Social Work and Social Policy, Concepts and Methods,* Book Enclave, Delhi, 2007.

M R Kamble : *Social Work With Children,* Aavishkar, Delhi, 2007.

M.N. Parmar and Jagdish Solanki : *Social Work Perspective on Depressed Class Population,* Anmol, Delhi, 2006.

M.S. Bedi : *Social Development and Social Work* , Himanshu, Delhi, 1994.

Mallik, Suneila: *Social Integration of the Scheduled Castes,* New Delhi, Abhinav, 1979.

Manju Gupta : *Child Abuse, A Social Work Perspective* , Mangal Deep Publications, Delhi, 2001.

Margaret Alston and Wendy Bowles : *Research for Social Workers : An Introduction to Methods,* Rawat, Delhi, 2003.

Marshall, P. & VanderVennen, R. : *Social Science in Christian Perspective,* Lanham, MD: University Press of America, 1988.

McGivney, V. : *Informal Learning in the Community, A Trigger for Change and Development,* Leicester, NIACE, 1999.

Moberg, D. : *Wholistic Christianity, An Appeal for a Dynamic Balanced Faith,* Brethren Press, 1985.

Moddie, A.D.: *The Brahmanical Culture and Modernity,* London, Asia, 1968.

Mohammad Naqi : *Social Work for Weaker Sections,* Anmol, Delhi, 2005.

Murli Desai : *Methodology of Progressive Social Work Education,* Rawat, Delhi, 2004.

Murli Desai and Siva Raju: *Gerontological Social Work in India : Some Issues and Perspectives,* B.R., Delhi, 2000.

N.C. Dobriyal : *Social Work for Older and Sick People,* Sumit Enterprises, Delhi, 2008.

Narain, A.K. & Ahir, D.C.: *Dr. Ambedkar, Buddhism and Social Change,* BR Publishing, Delhi, 1993.

Omvedt, Gail : *Reinventing Revolution: New Social Movements and the Socialist Tradition in India,* New York, Sharpe, 1993.

P Murugesan: *Social Welfare Programmes and Fertility Decline,* Abhijeet Publication, Delhi, 2009.

P.K. Bajpai : *Social Work Perspectives on Health*, Rawat, Delhi, 1998.

P.M. Parmar : *Social Work and Social Welfare in India*, Sublime, Delhi, 2002.

Pamela Trevithick: *Social Work Skills : A Practice Handbook*, Rawat, Delhi, 2009.

Patnaik, Nitayananda: *Caste and Social Change: An Anthropological Study of Three Orissa Villages*, National Institute of Community Development, Hyderabad, 1969.

Pekka Himanen: *The Information Society and the Welfare State: The Finnish Model*, Oxford UP, Oxford, 2002.

Perkins, S. & Rice, C. : *More than Equals: Racial Healing for the Sake of the Gospel*, Downers Grove, InterVarsity, 1993.

Prakash M Katare : *Social Work and Folk Culture*, Arise Pub, Delhi, 2006.

Prasanta K. Pattanaik: *Essays on Individual Decision-making and Social Welfare*, Oxford University Press, London, 2009.

Pratima Chaturvedi : *Social Work : Theories and Practices*, Book Enclave, Delhi, 2005.

Premanand Choudhary : *Child Survival, Health and Social Work Intervention*, ABD Pub, Delhi, 2008.

Profulla C Sarker : *Issues and Perspectives on Social Work and Social Development*, Serials Pub, Delhi, 2008.

R.B.S. Verma, H.S. Verma and Raj Kumar Singh: *Empowerment of the Weaker Sections in India : Interface of the Civil Society Organizations and Professional Social Work Institutions*, Serials, Delhi, 2006.

R.P. Arya : *Training for Social Work and Rural Development*, Manglam, Delhi, 2007.

Raj Bala Mathur : *Modernisation of Social Work, Planning and Administration*, Book Enclave, Delhi, 2007.

Raj Bhanti : *Field Work in Social Work Perspective*, Himanshu, Delhi, 1996.

Ramesh Chandra, *Government and Politics of India*, New York, St. Martin's Press, 1995.

Rameshwari Devi and Ravi Prakash: *Social Work : Methods, Practices and Perspectives*, Mangal Deep, Delhi, 2004.

Ranjna K. Devi : *Social Work, Philosophy, Concepts and Dimensions*, Omega, Delhi, 2009.

Rao, M. S. A.: *Social Movement and Social Transformation: A Study of Backward Class Movement*, New Delhi, Macmillian Press, 1978.

Ritter, Gerhard A.: *Social Welfare in Germany and Britain: Origins and Development*, Kim Traynor, New York, 1986.

Robert Fisher and Peter Romanofsky: *Community Organizing for Urban Social Change, A Historical Perspective*, Greenwood Press, Delhi, 1981.

Robert Fisher: *Let the People Decide, Neighborhood Organizing in America* 1984, Twayne Publishers, Delhi, 1997.

Roy Burman, B.K.: *Beyond Mandal and After Backward Classes in Perspective*, New Delhi, Mittal, 1992.

S K Sen : *Social Work Practices*, Book Enclave, Delhi, 2007.

S.K. Bhalla : *Social Work With Lawbreakers of Society*, MD Pub, Mumbai, 2008.

S.P. Ramachandran : *Social Work for Minorities*, Sumit Enterprises, Delhi, 2008.

Sandhya Joshi: *Child Survival Health and Social Work Intervention*, Concept, 1996.

Sangwan, Satpal : *Science, Technology, and Colonisation: An Indian Experience, 1757-1857*. New Delhi, Anmika Prakashan, 1991.

Sanjay Bhattacharya: *Social Work : An Integrated Approach*, Deep and Deep, Delhi, 2003.

Sarat C. Joshi : *Gandhian Social Work*, Akansha, Delhi, 2009.

Seerveld, C. : *On being human: Imaging God in the modern world*, Lanham, MD: University Press of America, 1989.

Shaikh Azhar Iqbal : *Principles and Practices of Social Work*, Sublime, Delhi, 2005.

Shaikh Azhar Iqbal: *Problems of Social Welfare and Social Work*, Sublime, Delhi, 2005.

Sherry Joseph : *Social Work Practice and Men Who Have Sex With Men*, Sage, Delhi, 2005

Shilaja Nagendra : *Social Work and Social Welfare in India*, ABD Pub, Delhi, 2005.

Silverberg, James: *Social Mobility in the Caste System in India,* Mouton Publishers, The Hague, 1968.

Simon, Robert Leopold: *Spiritual Aspects of Indian Music,* Delhi, Sundeep, 1984.

Singh, S. N.: *Reservation: Problems and Prospects,* New Delhi, Uppal Publishing House, 1987.

Skillen, James W. : *A Covenant to Keep : Meditations on the Biblical Theme of Justice,* Grand Rapids, MI: CRC Publications, Center for Public Justice, 2000.

Stephens, S. : *Children and the Politics of Culture,* Princeton, Princeton University Press, 1995.

Tejomayananda, Swami : *Hindu Culture: An Introduction,* Chinmaya Publications, Piercy, CA, 1993.

Tripathy, R. B.: *Dalits: A Sub-Human Society,* New Delhi, Ashish Publishing House, 1994.

V.V. Devasia and Ajit Kumar : *Social Work Concerns and Challenges in the 21 Century,* APH, Delhi, 2009.

Vijendra Kumar : *Problems and Perspectives on Social Work and Social Welfare,* ABD Pub, Delhi, 2002.

Whitley, O. R. : *Religious behavior: Where sociology and Religion Meet,* Engelwood Cliffs, Prentice-Hall, Inc, 1964.

Wolterstorff, N. : *Until Justice and Peace Embrace,* Grand Rapids: Eerdmans, 1983.

Wuthnow, R. : *God and Mammon in America,* New York: Free Press, 1994.

Yolton, J. W.: *John Locke: Problems and Perspectives,* Cambridge Uni. Press, 1969.

Zelliot, Eleanor: *From Untouchable to Dalit: Essays on the Ambedkar Movement,* New Delhi, Manohar, 1992.

Zimmer, Heinrich : *The Art of Indian Asia,* New York, Pantheon, 1955.

Index

□□□